NEW CONCEPT ENGLISH

FLUENCY IN ENGLISH

An Integrated Course for Advanced Students

NEW CONCEPT ENGLISH

FLUENCY IN ENGLISH

An Integrated Course for Advanced Students

L. G. ALEXANDER

LONGMAN

By the same author

Sixty Steps to Précis
Poetry and Prose Appreciation
Essay and Letter-writing
A First Book in Comprehension, Précis and Composition
The Carters of Greenwood *(Cineloops)*
Detectives from Scotland Yard *(Longman Structural Readers, Stage 1)*
Car Thieves *(Longman Structural Readers, Stage 1)*
Worth A Fortune *(Longman Structural Readers, Stage 2)*
April Fools' Day *(Longman Structural Readers, Stage 2)*
Operation Mastermind *(Longman Structural Readers, Stage 3)*
Professor Boffin's Umbrella *(Longman Structural Readers, Stage 2)*
Question and Answer: Graded Aural/Oral Exercises
For and Against
Reading and Writing English. A First Year Programme for Children
Look, Listen and Learn! Sets 1–4 An Integrated Course for Children

NEW CONCEPT ENGLISH
Uniform with this Volume:
First Things First: An Integrated Course for Beginners
Practice and Progress: An Integrated Course for Pre-Intermediate Students
Developing Skills: An Integrated Course for Intermediate Students

NEW CONCEPT ENGLISH *in two Volume edition*
First Things First Part 1–2
Practice and Progress Part 1–2

Longman Group Limited,
Longman House, Burnt Mill,
Harlow, Essex CM20 2JE, England
and Associated Companies throughout the world.

© L.G. Alexander 1967

First published 1967
Seventeenth impression 1983

ISBN 0 582 52332 X

Printed in Hong Kong by
Sheck Wah Tong Printing Press Ltd

CONTENTS

ACKNOWLEDGEMENTS

We are grateful to the following for permission to reproduce copyright material:
George Allen & Unwin Ltd for material from *Science Makes Sense* by Ritchie Calder, *Plato Today* by R. H. S. Crossman, *English Social Differences* by T. H. Pear and *Portraits from Memory* by Bertrand Russell; Associated Iliffe Press Ltd for material from 'The Past Life of the Earth' by Errol White published in Discovery (Discovery is now incorporated with *Science Journal*); The Barrie Group of Publishers (Barrie Books Ltd) for material from *Finding Fossil Man* by Robin Place; the author for material from 'Non-Auditory Effects of Noise' by D. E. Broadbent, M.A. published in *Science Survey*, 2nd Edn; Cambridge University Press for material from *Adventures of Ideas* by A. N. Whitehead; the author and Chatto & Windus Ltd for material from *Elephants* by Richard Carrington; William Collins Sons & Co. Ltd for material from *On Moral Courage* by Compton Mackenzie; the Proprietors of *The Week-End Telegraph* for material from 'The Great Escape' by Nigel Buxton published in issue 11 June 1965 and 'Are There Strangers in Space' by Anthony Michaelis published in issue 13 August 1965; David & Charles, Newton Abbot, for material from *British Canals* by Charles Hadfield, 3rd Edn. 1966; Dennis Dobson, Publishers for material from *The Pegasus Book of Inventors* by Egon Larson; the author for material from 'The Stuff of Dreams' by Dr. Christopher Evans, published in *The Listener*, 8 December 1966; Faber & Faber Ltd for material from *The Story of the French Foreign Legion* by Edgar O'Ballance, *Pieces of Mind* by C. E. M. Joad and *Our Developing World* by L. Dudley Stamp; Faber & Faber Ltd and Doubleday & Company, Inc. for material from *The Snake* by John Crompton, Copyright © 1963 by John Crompton (published in the U.S.A. under the title *Snake Lore*); the author for material from 'Virtue and a Fast Gun' by Carl Foreman, published in *The Observer*, 10 October 1965; the author's agents for material from 'Exploring the Sea-Floor' by Dr. T. F. Gaskell, published in *Science Survey*, 2nd Edn; the author's agents for material from 'Television and Education' by Grace Wyndham Goldie, published in *The Listener*, 16 April 1964; Victor Gollancz Ltd for material from *Matterhorn Man* by Walter Unsworth; Granada TV Networks Ltd for an extract from the transcript of 'The Search for Earth's Minerals' by Dr. T. F. Gaskell which was transmitted by Granada TV in their Schools programme Discovery and subsequently published by Methuen & Co. Ltd in 1961 for Granada TV Networks Ltd. Robert Hale Ltd for material from *Spies in Britain* by Bernard Newman; Hamish Hamilton Ltd and Harper & Row, Publishers for material from *Man the Unknown* by Alexis Carrel; George G. Harrap & Co. Ltd for material from *The Origin of Things* by Julius E. Lips; Heinemann Educational Books Ltd and the University of Washington Press for material from *Of Men and Galaxies* by Fred Hoyle; William Heinemann Ltd for material from 'Going out for a Walk' from *And Even Now* by Max Beerbohm; the author's agents for material from *Window in the Sea* by Ralph Nading Hill; the author for material from 'Galileo Reborn' by Michael A. Hoskin published in *The Listener*, 27 February 1964; the author for material from 'Out of the Air' by Fielden Hughes published in *The Listener*, 12 November 1964; Mrs. Laura Huxley and Chatto & Windus Ltd for material from *Themes and Variations* by Aldous Huxley; Michael Joseph Ltd for material from *A Countryman's Creed* by Sir William Beach Thomas; Le Carré Productions Ltd for material from *What Every Writer Wants* by John le Carré published in *Harper's Magazine*, November 1965; Longmans, Green & Co. Ltd and David McKay Company, Inc. for material from *The Status Seekers* by Vance Packard; Longmans, Green & Co. Ltd and St. Martin's Press, Inc. for material from *The Backward Society* by Raymond Frost; Lutterworth Press for material from *Thames Waters* by Roger Pilkington; Macgibbon & Kee Ltd for material from *The Habit of Loving* by Doris Lessing; the author for material from 'Seeing Hands' by Erik de

Mauny, published in *The Listener*, 13 August 1964; the author for material from 'The Sculptor Speaks' by Henry Moore, published originally in *The Listener*; the author for material from 'The Balloon Astronomy' by Patrick Moore, published in *The Listener*, 25 February 1965; the author's agents and Hamish Hamilton Ltd for material from *No Room in the Ark* by Alan Moorehead; Frederick Muller Ltd for material from *The Earth Beneath Us* by H. H. Swinnerton; the author for material from 'On Telling the Truth' from *Small Talk* by Sir Harold Nicholson; Odhams Books Ltd for material from *Painting as a Pastime* by Winston S. Churchill; the author for material from *Journey Through Adolescence* by Doris Odlum, published by Delisle Ltd; Oliver & Boyd Ltd for material from *Our Friends the Spiders* by T. H. Gillespie; the Estate of the late George Orwell for material from *This Sporting Spirit* by George Orwell; Penguin Books Ltd for material from *The Consumer Society and the Law* by Gordon Barrie and Aubrey L. Diamond, *Education* by W. O. Lester Smith, *The Personality of Man* by G. N. M. Tyrrell, and *Patients and Doctors* by Kenneth Walker; A. D. Peters & Co. for material from *Thoughts in the Wilderness* by J. B. Priestley; Routledge & Kegan Paul Ltd for material from *The Social Function of Science* by J. D. Bernal; Routledge & Kegan Paul Ltd and Houghton Mifflin Company for material from *Patterns of Culture* by Ruth Benedict; the author for material from *The Raising of the Vasa* by Roy Saunders published by Oldbourne Press; Thames & Hudson Ltd for material from *Learning to Live* by Beatrix Tudor-Hart; the author for material from 'The Menace of Urban Explosion' by Barbara Ward published in *The Listener*, 14 November 1963; Ward Lock & Co. Ltd for material from *Curiosities of Animal Life* by Maurice Burton; George Weidenfeld & Nicolson Ltd for material from *The Age of Automation* by Sir Leon Bagrit, and George Weidenfeld & Nicolson Ltd and The New American Library, Inc. for material from *The Process of Ageing* by Dr. Alex Comfort, Copyright © 1961, 1964 by Alex Comfort.

We have been unable to trace the copyright owner in 'The Language of Hollywood' by James T. Farrell and would welcome any information that would enable us to do so.

We are grateful to the following for permission to use the photographs throughout the book:
Aerofilms Library – Lesson 20; Barratts Photo Press – Lesson 34; BP – Lesson 16; Camera Press Limited – Lessons 2, 53; J. Allan Cash – Lessons 44B, 59; Douglas Dalton: Natural History Photo Agency – Lesson 28; Fox Photos Ltd. – Lessons 45, 47, 58; I.C.I. – Lesson 18; Keystone Press Agency – Lessons 38, 43B, 60; Malawi High Commission – Lesson 44A; Mansell Collection – Lessons 29, 36, 40; M.G.M. – Lesson 12; Novosti Press Agency – Lesson 4; PAF International – Lessons 17, 22; Paramount – Lesson 48; Paul Popper – Lessons 5, 9, 21, 24, 25, 30, 35, 43A, 51, 54, 55; Radio Times Hulton Picture Library – Lessons 1, 11, 32; L.T.C. Rolt – Lesson 50; Royal Astronomical Society – Lesson 39; Russell Preece – Lesson 15; Science Museum – Lesson 52A; Sjöhistoriska Museet – Lesson 33; Swiss National Tourist Office – Lesson 3; Syndication International – Lessons 7, 42; Thomas Photos Limited – Lesson 13; United States Information Services – Lessons 23, 27, 31, 46, 49, 56; Vu Picture Agency – Lesson 41; Warner Pathe – Lesson 10.

To the Teacher

Towards Fluency

The student who has successfully completed an Intermediate Course in English often has good reason to feel disheartened when he embarks on an Advanced Course. The reason for this is not so much that he has at his command only a fairly limited vocabulary, but that he is suddenly thrust into the world of ideas. The biggest barrier, particularly with younger students, is not language as such, but mental maturity. An advanced course necessarily presupposes a degree of mental maturity and fairly wide general knowledge which many students do not possess. In oral work, the student is expected to take part in discussions on argumentative topics covering a wide range of subjects. As far as writing is concerned, it is not enough to be able to write narrative or descriptive compositions in simple, correct English. The student must pay close attention to form and content; he must express difficult ideas and know how to handle facts and opinions. Where before his précis work consisted largely in reproducing the main sequence of events in a piece of narrative, he now has to summarize difficult passages of factual, argumentative and reflective prose. In addition to this, he frequently has to work under pressure, particularly if he is preparing for an examination. Because the syllabus is loaded, the teacher is obliged to assume that his students have, by now, grasped the fundamentals of grammar. He therefore spends little, if any, time on it, even though he knows how much his students require further practice.

The answer to these problems is again to be found in the use of carefully selected passages which can be used as multi-purpose texts to continue the student's training in the four skills, *understanding*, *speaking*, *reading* and *writing*. At this level, the texts should be selected from the work of a wide variety of authors, so that the student can become familiar with different styles of writing. The passages should be graded in terms of length, complexity and intellectual content to introduce the student gradually to the world of ideas.

About this Course

Basic Aims

1. To provide a comprehensive course for adult or secondary students who have completed an intermediate course. The course contains enough material for one or two years' work, depending on the amount of time allotted to it. The student will receive most of his training in the classroom and will be required to do some extra work in his own time.

2. To introduce the student gradually to the world of ideas and to make him familiar with a wide range of different styles of writing. The passages are graded not only from the point of view of language, but in terms of length and intellectual content as well.

3. To continue the student's training in the four skills: *understanding*, *speaking*, *reading* and *writing*—in that order. In this respect, the course sets out to do two things: to provide material which will be suitable for aural/oral practice and which can also be used to train the student systematically to write English at a difficult level. The passages will be used to develop a maturity of approach as well as to provide a stimulating basis for discussion and study.

4. To provide the student with a book which will enable him to *use* the language.

5. To provide the teacher with material which will enable him to conduct each lesson with a minimum of preparation.

6. To enable the teacher and the student to work entirely from a single volume without the need for additional 'practice books'.

7. To enable students to sit for the *English Language* and *Use of English Papers* in the Cambridge Proficiency examination if they wish to do so. This aim must be regarded as coincidental to the main purpose of continuing the students' training in the four language skills.

For Whom the Course is Intended

This course should be found suitable for:

1. Adult or secondary students who have completed *Practice and Progress* and *Developing Skills*, or who have completed *any* other intermediate course.

2. Schools and Language Institutes where 'wastage' caused by irregular attendance is a problem.

3. Advanced students who wish to study on their own.

How Much Knowledge has been Assumed?

The material in *Developing Skills*, the intermediate course which precedes this one, has been designed to 'overlap' this course. Students who have completed it will have no difficulty whatever in continuing where they left off.

Students who have learnt English from other courses and who now wish to continue their studies with this course should have a fair working knowledge of the items listed below.

Assumed Knowledge

Aural/Oral

1. The ability to understand English dealing with everyday subjects and spoken at normal speed.

2. The ability to answer questions which require short or extended answers.

3. The ability to ask questions to elicit short or extended answers.

4. The ability to use orally a large number of elementary sentence patterns.

5. The ability to reproduce orally the substance of a passage of English after having heard it several times and read it.

6. The ability to conduct a simple conversation on everyday subjects (e.g. expressing preferences; polite interchange; careers; travel; common experiences etc.)

7. The ability to give a short talk (prepared or unprepared) lasting up to four minutes on everyday subjects.

Reading

1. The ability to read a passage of English aloud. The student should have a fair grasp of the *rhythm* of the language (stress and intonation) even if he is unable to pronounce unfamiliar words correctly.

2. The ability to read silently and understand works of fiction and non-fiction of the level of Longmans' Bridge Series. The student's passive vocabulary range should be in the region of 3,000 words (*structural* and *lexical*). The student should be sufficiently familiar with a wide variety of English sentence patterns so that he can 'get the gist' of what he is reading even though he may not know the meaning of a number of individual words.

Writing

1. *Word Order*

The ability to write simple, compound and complex sentences. The ability to join simple sentences using conjunctions to form compound and complex sentences. A sound command of the *word order* in an English sentence.

2. *Comprehension*

The ability to write answers to straightforward questions on a passage of English of the level of that given in the Language Paper of the Cambridge Lower Certificate Examination.

3. *Vocabulary*

The ability to deduce the meaning of words and phrases from a context and to explain them by means of other words and phrases.

4. *Précis*

The ability to reconstruct the main sequence of events in a piece of narrative prose (e.g. describing actions or experiences). This presupposes that the student is capable of the following:

a Reading, understanding and carrying out instructions.

b Extracting specific information to write a list of *points* in note form outlining the main sequence of events in a piece of narrative prose.

c Connecting these points to form simple, compound and complex sentences and arranging them logically to write a well-constructed paragraph in a set number of words.

5. *Composition*

The ability to write a narrative or descriptive composition of about 300 words. This presupposes that the student is capable of the following:

a Making a short plan (i.e. listing a few ideas in note form).

b Connecting the ideas to write a composition of about three or four paragraphs. The composition should contain an Introduction, Development and Conclusion.

6. *Letter-writing*

The ability to write a short personal letter of about 100 words. This presupposes that the student is familiar with correct layout (Heading, Salutation, Subscription).

Command of Language

1. *Grammar (Key Structures)*

The course presupposes that the student has had a fair amount of practice in using tenses, articles and prepositions. It is clearly recognized, however, that further practice is required.

2. *Usage (Special Difficulties)*

The student should be familiar with common phrasal verbs, certain words which are often confused or misused, and a limited number of idiomatic expressions.

A Description of the Course

General Arrangement of Material

The course falls into two parts each of which is preceded by a searching test. The first part aims to teach English at the pre-advanced level: it ensures that there will be a smooth transition between intermediate and advanced levels. The second part aims to teach English at the advanced level.

Each part consists of three Units and each Unit comprises ten passages, making a total of sixty passages in all. As the course progresses, the passages become longer and more complex. Each Unit is preceded by Instructions to the Student.

The passages are multi-purpose texts. Each passage will be used to train the student in the following: aural comprehension; oral practice; reading aloud; oral composition; extended oral exercises; dictation; comprehension; vocabulary; sentence and paragraph structure; précis; composition; grammar and usage.

Instructions to the Student

The instructions which precede each Unit should be read carefully. They deal only with the difficulties presented by the central exercises in each Unit: The Sentence; The Paragraph; Précis; Composition. The successful completion of this course depends entirely on the student's ability to carry out the instructions given. Worked examples have not been provided: what the student has to do should be abundantly clear without the aid of examples. The exercises that follow each passage should be done *in the order in which they have been presented*.

Introductory Tests

The test which precedes Part 1 will enable the student to tell if he is ready for this course. The test leading to Part 2 is so designed that the student will not be expected to make too sudden a jump between one year's work and the next. It will provide a clear indication of how much the student has assimilated.

The Passages

The passages have been drawn from the work of a wide variety of modern authors and are extremely varied in style and subject-matter. Many of the passages are broadcast talks and will be suitable for oral work. The approximate length of the passages in each unit is as follows:

Unit 1: 250–300 words.
Unit 2: 250–300 words.
Unit 3: 300–350 words.
Unit 4: 350–400 words.
Unit 5: 400–500 words.
Unit 6: 550–700 words.

Oral Exercises

Oral exercises are not included in the book itself and must be supplied by the teacher. They may be along the lines suggested in the section on *How to Use this Course.*

Comprehension Questions

The questions in Part 1 are straightforward; in Part 2, they are more searching.

Vocabulary

The student will be required to explain the meaning of difficult words and phrases as they are used in each passage.

Précis and Composition

The work that will be done in précis and composition has been carefully graded and controlled by means of a series of progressive exercises which gradually become more difficult as the Course proceeds.

The treatment of these two exercises is based on the principle that précis-writing is the exact counterpart of composition, the former being largely a matter of *analysis*; the latter of *synthesis*. For instance, when setting out to write a précis, the student must be able to understand a passage, break it down into its component parts, and reconstruct the original 'plan' of the piece in note form before writing his own version. Essay writing requires the reverse procedure, for the student sets out with a subject which has to be developed first in note form and ultimately written out in continuous prose. Accordingly, the exercises will aim at training the student in these two processes and will run exactly parallel. In Part 1 many of the exercises are based directly on material contained in the passages. The student will therefore be able to correct his own work simply by referring to the passage after he has finished an exercise.

Key Structures and Special Difficulties

All the exercises on Key Structures (Essential Grammar) and Special Difficulties (Usage) are derived from each passage. No use has been made of grammatical terminology, all difficulties being presented as sentence patterns. Where explanations are necessary, this has been done by relating one pattern to another.

Practice work in the Key Structures consists largely of exercises in recall, particular attention being paid to the use of verbs, prepositions, articles and the position of adverbs. The student will again be able to correct a great deal of his own work by referring to the passage after he has completed an exercise.

The exercises on Special Difficulties deal entirely with problems concerning usage: vocabulary, phrasal verbs and idiomatic expressions. Many of these are deliberately repetitive, the aim being to eliminate common recurring errors.

How to Use this Course

Allocation of Time

Ideally, two classroom lessons of approximately 50 minutes each should be spent
on each text. The first lesson should be devoted to Guided and Free Conversation; the second to Composition and Language Study. This means that there is
enough material in this book for 120 lessons. However, you may choose to spend
only *one* classroom lesson on each text—in which case, every lesson may be
devoted to Guided and Free Conversation and a selection of written exercises
may be set as homework. Your first task is to decide how much time you have in
your programme in relation to the material available in the course.

The suggestions given below outline the basic steps in each lesson. You may
decide to follow them closely, adapt them to suit your style of teaching, or reject
them altogether—BUT PLEASE READ THEM FIRST!

Lesson 1: Guided and Free Conversation

Books Required:

> *Fluency in English* (for teachers and students)
> *Recorded Drills Tapescript* (for teachers only)

The Stages of the Lesson

1 Aural/Oral Presentation:	about 15 minutes
2 Question and Answer Practice:	about 10 minutes
3 Pattern Drill:	about 5 minutes
4 Oral Reconstruction (Optional):	about 10–20 minutes
5 Talking Points:	about 10–20 minutes

Let's see what each step involves:

1 Aural/Oral Presentation:
  a Listening (Books shut)
  b Intensive Reading (Books open)
  c Listening (Books shut)
  d Reading Aloud (Books open)

a Listening (Books shut). Read the passage once. The students should *listen* and
try to understand as much as they can.

b Intensive Reading (Books open). Read the text in small units (e.g. a sentence at
a time, or less) making sure the students *really* understand it. Rather than give
direct explanations, try to get as much information as possible from the students.
(Think of it as 'a corkscrew operation'!) Explanations should be given entirely in
English, but don't carry direct-method teaching to absurd lengths. If your students fail to understand in spite of all your efforts, translate briefly and move on.
Remember, if you don't translate a particular difficulty, then someone in the
class will!

c Listening (Books shut). Read the passage once more.
d Reading Aloud (Books open). Ask a few individual students to read small portions of the text.

2 Question and Answer Practice

Question and answer practice should be based mainly on the text. However, you may frequently vary this with questions which relate to the student's own experience. If you find it difficult to ask questions spontaneously, prepare yourself in advance. Questions should be asked individually round the class—preferably at speed. Two exercises are suggested:
  a Mixed Questions
  b Asking Questions in Pairs

a Mixed Questions. General comprehension questions may be asked. Here, for instance, are a number of questions which relate to Text 1.

Teacher: Where did people first learn to write?
        How long ago?
        Was it 5000 years ago?   etc.

b Asking Questions in Pairs. Train the student to ask a question using an auxiliary verb and then to ask *precisely the same question again* preceding it with a question word.

Teacher: Ask me if people first learned to write 5000 years ago.
Student: Did people first learn to write 5000 years ago?
Teacher: How long ago . . . (Always provide the question word.)
Student: How long ago did people first learn to write?

3 Pattern Drill

The publication entitled 'Fluency in English, Recorded Drills: Tapescript' contains situational drills based on language points in the texts. Here, for instance, is part of the drill which relates to Text 1:

Teacher: Do you think the artist used photographs?
Student: He may have used photographs. It's hard to tell.
Teacher: Then perhaps he painted it in his own studio?
Student: He may have painted it in his own studio. It's hard to tell.   etc.

The students may be trained to answer in chorus or groups, or the drill may be conducted rapidly round the class with individual students responding. A brief grammatical explanation may be given before the drill is conducted. If a language-laboratory is available, this will be adequate preparation for further practice. However, it must be stressed that a laboratory is by no means indispensable: it is quite possible to do all the drilling live in the classroom. Alternatively, teachers who have tape-recorders may choose to play the drills in the class.

4 Oral Reconstruction

This is an optional exercise and may be omitted when the text provides ample material for general discussion (see point 5 below). Write a few brief notes ('key words') on the blackboard summarising a portion of the text (say a paragraph). Now invite individual students to reconstruct the text by referring to the notes. Here, for instance, are some notes which relate to the first paragraph in Text 1:

1 Read—5000—Near East—people—write.
2 Some parts world—people—now—write.
3 Can preserve history—sagas—legends—generation.

4 Useful—migrations—people long ago—none could write.

5 Anthropologists wondered—ancestors Polynesia—came from.

6 Sagas—Indonesia—2000 years ago.

5 Talking Points

Where a text immediately suggests a subject or subjects for general discussion, the students should be invited to participate. Here, for instance, are a few talking points suggested by Text 1.

a Exchange information about local history and pre-history.

b Exchange information about the migration of peoples in ancient and modern times.

c Exchange information about a famous journey to establish the migration of peoples: e.g. Kontiki, Ra, etc.

(Note that not all discussions need necessarily be arguments or debates.)

Lesson 2: Composition and Language Study

All the printed exercises are intended for writing. As has already been indicated, this entire lesson may be omitted and a selection of written exercises may, instead, be set as homework. If this approach is adopted, then the Précis and Composition exercises should always be set. Needless to say, more satisfactory results will be obtained where a complete classroom lesson can be devoted to written exercises. These should be tackled in the order in which they are given. While the students are writing, you may go round the class helping individuals. Exercises not completed in class time, may be set as homework. The written exercises become more demanding and time-consuming as the student progresses through the course. However, it is not necessary to complete every single exercise.

Dictations

Depending on the amount of time available, dictations should be given frequently. A few sentences taken from a passage the students have already studied may be dictated. The students may correct their own work by comparing their version with the passage.

Additional Reading Material

If the student is not working for an examination and is not studying prescribed books, the following scheme is recommended:

Part 1: Works of fiction and non-fiction from Longman Abridged and Heritage Series.

Part 2: Unsimplified and unabridged works of fiction and non-fiction, plays, newspaper and magazine articles (particularly from *The Listener*, published by the B.B.C.)

Additional Oral Practice

If additional oral practice is required, it may be obtained from *For and Against* published by Longman Group Limited.

Additional Written Practice

If additional practice in writing is required, it may be obtained from the following:

Précis: Sixty Steps to Précis (Longman) Part 2, Passages 31–60.

Composition: Essay and Letter Writing (Longman) Part 2, Chapters 6–9.

IF YOU CAN DO THIS TEST GO ON TO PART 1

Read the following passage carefully, then do the exercises below:

The boy put on his goggles, fitted them tight, tested the vacuum. His hands were shaking. Then he chose the biggest stone he could carry and slipped over the edge of the rock until half of him was in the cool, enclosing water and half in the hot sun. He looked up once at the empty sky, filled his lungs once, twice, and
5 then sank fast to the bottom with the stone. He let it go and began to count. He took the edges of the hole in his hands and drew himself into it, wriggling his shoulders in sideways as he remembered he must, kicking himself along with his feet.

Soon he was clear inside. He was in a small rock-bound hole filled with
10 yellowish-grey water. The water was pushing him up against the roof. The roof was sharp and pained his back. He pulled himself along with his hands—fast, fast—and used his legs as levers. His head knocked against something; a sharp pain dizzied him. Fifty, fifty-one, fifty-two . . . He was without light, and the water seemed to press upon him with the weight of rock. Seventy-one, seventy-
15 two . . . There was no strain on his lungs. He felt like an inflated balloon, his lungs were so light and easy, but his head was pulsing.

He was being continually pressed against the sharp roof, which felt slimy as well as sharp. Again he thought of octopuses, and wondered if the tunnel might be filled with weed that could tangle him. He gave himself a panicky, convulsive
20 kick forward, ducked his head, and swam. His feet and hands moved freely, as if in open water. The hole must have widened out. He thought he must be swimming fast, and he was frightened of banging his head if the tunnel narrowed.

A hundred, a hundred and one . . . The water paled. Victory filled him. His lungs were beginning to hurt. A few more strokes and he would be out. He was
25 counting wildly; he said a hundred and fifteen, and then, a long time later, a hundred and fifteen again. The water was a clear jewel-green all around him. Then he saw, above his head, a crack running up through the rock. Sunlight was falling through it, showing the clean dark rock of the tunnel, a single mussel shell, and darkness ahead.

30 He was at the end of what he could do. He looked up at the crack as if it were filled with air and not water, as if he could put his mouth to it to draw in air. A hundred and fifteen, he heard himself say inside his head—but he had said that long ago. He must go on into the blackness ahead, or he would drown. His head was swelling, his lungs cracking. A hundred and fifteen, a hundred and fifteen
35 pounded through his head, and he feebly clutched at rocks in the dark, pulling himself forward, leaving the brief space of sunlit water behind. He felt he was dying. He was no longer quite conscious. He struggled on in the darkness be-tween lapses into unconsciousness. An immense, swelling pain filled his head, and then the darkness cracked with an explosion of green light. His hands, grop-
40 ing forward, met nothing, and his feet, kicking back, propelled him out into the open sea.

DORIS LESSING *Through the Tunnel* from *The Habit of Loving*

Comprehension

Give short answers to these questions in your own words as far as possible. Use one complete sentence for each answer.

a Why was the boy able to get to the sea-bed quickly?

b Why did the boy find it difficult to swim after he was inside the tunnel?

c Why did the boy get into a panic as he swam through the tunnel?

Vocabulary

Explain the meaning of the following words and phrases as they are used in the passage: goggles (l. 1); filled his lungs (l. 4); wriggling (l. 6); as levers (l. 12); dizzied (l. 13); inflated (l. 15); slimy (l. 17).

Précis

In not more than 80 words write an account of the boy's experiences under the sea as described in lines 23–41 ('A hundred . . . the open sea.') Use your own words as far as possible. Do not include anything that is not in the last two paragraphs.

Composition

Write a composition of about 300 words on one of the following subjects:

a The most frightening experience I have ever had.

b A holiday by the sea.

c Dangerous sports.

Part 1

Unit 1

INSTRUCTIONS TO THE STUDENT

Content

This Unit consists of ten passages followed by exercises on Comprehension, Vocabulary, the Sentence, Key Structures and Special Difficulties.

Aim

To provide practice in the writing of complex sentences.

How to Work

1. Read each passage carefully two or three times.
2. Answer the questions in the order in which they are given.

The Sentence

All the exercises given under this heading are based directly on the passage. You may correct your own answers to some of the questions by referring to the passage immediately after you have completed the exercises. The following types of exercise have been given:

1. Joining simple statements to make complex statements.
2. Supplying conjunctions (joining words) to make complex statements.
3. Completing sentences taken from the passage in any way you wish.
4. Writing sentences related to the subject-matter of the passage.

I

We can read of things that happened 5,000 years ago in the Near East, where people first learned to write. But there are some parts of the world where even now people cannot write. The only way that they can preserve their history is to recount it as sagas—legends handed down from one generation of story-tellers to another. These legends are useful because they can tell us something about migrations of people who lived long ago, but none could write down what they did. Anthropologists wondered where the remote ancestors of the Polynesian peoples now living in the Pacific Islands came from. The sagas of these people explain that some of them came from Indonesia about 2,000 years ago.

But the first people who were like ourselves lived so long ago that even their sagas, if they had any, are forgotten. So archaeologists have neither history nor legends to help them to find out where the first 'modern men' came from.

Fortunately, however, ancient men made tools of stone, especially flint, because this is easier to shape than other kinds. They may also have used wood and skins, but these have rotted away. Stone does not decay, and so the tools of long ago have remained when even the bones of the men who made them have disappeared without trace.

ROBIN PLACE *Finding Fossil Man*

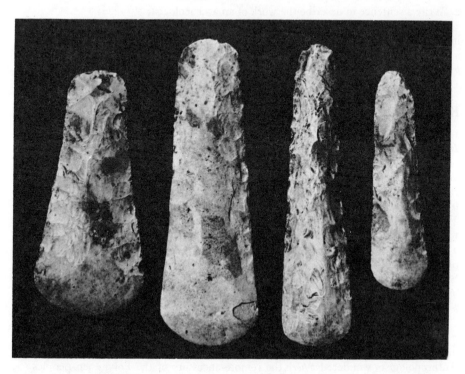

Polished axeheads found at Seamers Moor in Yorkshire

Comprehension

Give short answers to these questions in your own words as far as possible. Use one complete sentence for each answer.

a How can anthropologists learn about the history of ancient peoples who have not left written records?

b Why did ancient men prefer to use flint for making tools?

Vocabulary

Give another word or phrase to replace these words as they are used in the passage: preserve (l. 3); recount (l. 4); migrations (l. 6); anthropologists (l. 7); remote (l. 7); decay (l. 15); without trace (l. 17).

The Sentence

1. Combine the following statements to make complete sentences. Add conjunctions and relative pronouns of your own and omit the words or phrases in italics. Do not refer to the passage until you have finished the exercise:

a These legends are useful. They can tell us something about migrations of people. *These people* lived long ago. None could write down what they did. (ll. 5–7)

b The first people who were like ourselves lived long ago. Even their sagas, if they had any, are forgotten. (ll. 10–11)

c Archaeologists have *no* history to help them to find out where the first 'modern men' came from. *Archaeologists have no* legends *to help them to find out where the first modern men came from.* (ll. 11–12)

d Fortunately, however, ancient men made tools of stone, especially flint. This is easier to shape than other kinds. (ll. 13–14)

e They may also have used wood and skins. These have rotted away. (ll. 14–15)

2. Write a sentence to describe the work of an archaeologist.

3. Write three short sentences on the history of early man using the following words in each sentence:

a Written records.

b Sagas.

c Stone tools.

Key Structures

1. Compare these two sentences:

Instead of saying: The only way that they can preserve their history is to recount it as sagas—*legends which have been handed down* from one generation of story-tellers to another.

We can say: The only way that they can preserve their history is to recount it as sagas—*legends handed down* from one generation of story-tellers to another. (ll. 3–5)

Write sentences using the following phrases:

tools made of stone; legends recorded; remains found.

2. Note the use of *tell* in this sentence: They can *tell us* something about migrations of people. (ll. 5–6)

Supply the correct form of *say* or *tell* in these sentences:

a What did he *say* to you?

b He *told* everybody that he had been ill.

c Did you *say* that you have written a novel?

d I can't *tell* you about it now.

3. Note the use of *where . . . from* in this sentence:

Anthropologists wondered *where* the remote ancestors of the Polynesian peoples . . . came *from.* (ll. 7–8)

Write two sentences using the same construction with the verbs *get* and *buy*.

4. Compare these two sentences:

Instead of saying: So archaeologists have neither history nor legends to *help them to find* out where the first 'modern men' came from. (ll. 11–12)

We can say: So archaeologists have neither history nor legends to *help them find out* where the first 'modern men' came from.

Write two sentences using these expressions: help me to lift; helped me make.

5. Supply the word *the* where necessary in this paragraph. Do not refer to the passage until you have finished the exercise:

Fortunately, however, . . . ancient men made . . . tools of . . . stone, especially . . . flint, because this is easier to shape than . . . other kinds. They may also have used . . . wood and . . . skins, but these have rotted away. . . . stone does not decay, and so . . . tools of long ago have remained when even . . . bones of . . . men who made them have disappeared without trace. (ll. 13–17)

6. Compare these two sentences:

Instead of saying: It is possible that they used wood and skins, but these have rotted away.

We can say: They may have used wood and skins, but these have rotted away. (ll. 14–15)

Write these sentences again using the construction with *may have*.

a It is possible that your mother called when you were out.

b It is possible that you left your umbrella in the waiting-room.

c It is possible that he changed his mind.

Special Difficulties

1. Write sentences to bring out the difference between the following pairs of words: parts (l. 2), places; history (l. 3), story; wondered (l. 7), wandered; like (l. 10), as; find out (l. 12), find; ancient (l. 13), old; tools (l. 13), instruments; stone (l. 13), rock; skin (l. 15), leather.

2. Study the use of *happen* in these sentences:

We can read of things that *happened* 5,000 years ago. (l. 1)

He *happened* to be an archaeologist.

It *happened* that he knew the answer.

Complete the following sentences:

a Do you happen . . .

b It so happens that . . .

c Can you tell me what . . .

2

Why, you may wonder, should spiders be our friends? Because they destroy so many insects, and insects include some of the greatest enemies of the human race. Insects would make it impossible for us to live in the world; they would devour all our crops and kill our flocks and herds, if it were not for the protection we get from insect-eating animals. We owe a lot to the birds and beasts who eat insects but all of them put together kill only a fraction of the number destroyed by spiders. Moreover, unlike some of the other insect eaters, spiders never do the least harm to us or our belongings.

Spiders are not insects, as many people think, nor even nearly related to them. One can tell the difference almost at a glance for a spider always has eight legs and an insect never more than six.

How many spiders are engaged in this work on our behalf? One authority on spiders made a census of the spiders in a grass field in the south of England, and he estimated that there were more than 2,250,000 in one acre; that is something like 6,000,000 spiders of different kinds on a football pitch. Spiders are busy for at least half the year in killing insects. It is impossible to make more than the wildest guess at how many they kill, but they are hungry creatures, not content with only three meals a day. It has been estimated that the weight of all the insects destroyed by spiders in Britain in one year would be greater than the total weight of all the human beings in the country.

T. H. GILLESPIE *Spare that Spider* from *The Listener*

A spider destroys a grasshopper

Comprehension

Give short answers to these questions in your own words as far as possible. Use one complete sentence for each answer.

a Why have we reason to be grateful to insect-eating animals?
b How can we tell the difference between a spider and an insect?
c What do you understand by the statement 'One authority on spiders made a census of the spiders in a grass field.'? (ll. 12–13)

Vocabulary

Give another word or phrase to replace these words as they are used in the passage: destroy (l. 1); devour (l. 4); fraction (l. 6); belongings (l. 8); estimated (l. 14).

The Sentence

1. Combine the following sentences to make one complex statement out of each group. Make any changes you think necessary, but do not alter the sense of the original. Do not refer to the passage until you have finished the exercise:
a Moreover, spiders are unlike some of the other insect eaters. They never do the least harm to us or our belongings. (ll. 7–8)
b Spiders are not insects. They are not even nearly related to them. Many people think they are. (l. 9)
c One can tell the difference almost at a glance. A spider has eight legs. An insect never has more than six. (ll. 10–11)
d How many do they kill? It is impossible to make more than the wildest guess at this. They are hungry creatures. They are not content with only three meals a day. (ll. 16–18)
2. Complete the following sentences in any way you wish. Then compare what you have written with the sentences in the passage:
a Why, you may wonder, should spiders be our friends? Because . . . (l. 1)
b We owe a lot to birds and beasts who . . . (l. 5)
c One authority on spiders . . . (ll. 12–13)
d It has been estimated that . . . (l. 18)
3. Write three sentences saying why you like or dislike spiders.

Key Structures

1. Compare these two sentences:
Instead of saying: I wonder why spiders are our friends?
We can say: Why . . . should spiders be our friends? (l. 1)
Write these sentences again using the construction with *should* in place of the phrases in italics:
a I *wonder why he is* so disappointed.
b I *wonder why you are* so unwilling to change your mind.
c I *wonder why there are* so many traffic accidents.
2. Note the form of the verb *be* in this sentence: They would devour all our crops . . . if it *were* not for the protection we get from insect-eating animals. (ll. 3–5)
Supply the correct form of *be* in these sentences:
a I certainly wouldn't buy that car if I (be) in your position.
b Do you think you would buy it if it (be) cheaper?
c If I (be) made such an offer I would certainly accept it.
3. Supply *a*, *an*, and *the* where necessary in the spaces below. Do not refer to the passage until you have finished the exercise:
. . . spiders are not . . . insects, as . . . many people think, nor even nearly related to

9

them. One can tell . . . difference almost at . . . glance for . . . spider always has eight legs and . . . insect never more than six.

How many spiders are engaged in this work on our behalf? One authority on . . . spiders made . . . census of . . . spiders in . . . grass field in . . . south of . . . England, and he estimated that there were more than 2,250,000 in . . . acre; that is something like 6,000,000 spiders of different kinds on . . . football pitch. (ll. 9–15)

Special Difficulties

1. Write sentences to bring out the difference between the following pairs of words: all . . . together (l. 6), altogether; other (l. 7), else; least (l. 8), last; harm (l. 8), hurt; glance (l. 10), glimpse; work (l. 12), job; estimated (l. 14), calculated.

2. Which verbs could be used in place of *get* in these sentences:

a They would devour all our crops and kill our flocks and herds, if it were not for the protection we *get* from insect-eating animals. (ll. 3–5)

b I *got* this hat at the shop on the corner.

c Will you *get* that book for me please? It's on the shelf. *bring*

d I *got* a letter from my brother yesterday. *receive*

e I'm sorry, I didn't *get* that remark. *hear*

f I didn't laugh because I didn't *get* the joke. *understand*

3. Note the use of *tell* in this sentence:

One can *tell the difference* almost at a glance. (l. 10)

Supply the correct form of *say* or *tell* in these sentences:

a Will you please *tell* me the time?

b I'm not very good at *telling* stories.

c You must *say* your prayers and go to bed.

d Please *say* nothing more about it.

e I can *tell* you something about it.

f We *said* goodbye and left.

g I want you to *tell* the truth.

4. Note the use of *make* in this sentence:

One authority on spiders *made a census*. (ll. 12–13)

Supply the correct form of *make* or *do* in the following sentences:

a I *made* a number of proposals, none of which was accepted.

b I'll *do* the washing up.

c Will you help me to *do* this crossword puzzle?

d You've *made* quite a few mistakes.

e I've *made* an appointment for you for next week.

f They *made* an announcement about it on the radio.

g I'll *do* my best to help you.

5. Write sentences using the following phrases with *at*: at a glance (l. 10); at least (l. 16); at any rate; at a loss; at sight; at a time.

do → perform

make → create
a   compose
cake   fashion
              produce

10

3

Modern alpinists try to climb mountains by a route which will give them good sport, and the more difficult it is, the more highly it is regarded. In the pioneering days, however, this was not the case at all. The early climbers were looking for the easiest way to the top because the summit was the prize they sought, especi-
5 ally if it had never been attained before. It is true that during their explorations they often faced difficulties and dangers of the most perilous nature, equipped in a manner which would make a modern climber shudder at the thought, but they did not go out of their way to court such excitement. They had a single aim, a solitary goal—the top!

10   It is hard for us to realize nowadays how difficult it was for the pioneers. Except for one or two places such as Zermatt and Chamonix, which had rapidly become popular, Alpine villages tended to be impoverished settlements cut off from civilization by the high mountains. Such inns as there were were generally dirty and flea-ridden; the food simply local cheese accompanied by bread often
15 twelve months old, all washed down with coarse wine. Often a valley boasted no inn at all, and climbers found shelter wherever they could—sometimes with the local priest (who was usually as poor as his parishioners), sometimes with shepherds or cheese-makers. Invariably the background was the same: dirt and poverty, and very uncomfortable. For men accustomed to eating seven-course
20 dinners and sleeping between fine linen sheets at home, the change to the Alps must have been very hard indeed.

WALTER UNSWORTH *Matterhorn Man*

Bergdorf, a mountain village
in Switzerland

11

Comprehension

Give short answers to these questions in your own words as far as possible. Use one complete sentence for each answer.

a In what way does the attitude of the modern climber towards mountains differ from that of the pioneer?

b Name three factors which made most Alpine villages inhospitable places.

Vocabulary

Give another word or phrase to replace these words as they are used in the passage: route (l. 1); regarded (l. 2); summit (l. 4); sought (l. 4); faced (l. 6); perilous (l. 6); shudder (l. 7); court (l. 8); solitary (l. 9); coarse (l. 15); boasted (l. 15); invariably (l. 18).

The Sentence

1. Combine the following statements to make complete sentences. Add conjunctions of your own and omit the words or phrases in italics. Do not refer to the passage until you have finished the exercise:

a It is true that during their explorations they often faced difficulties. *They often faced* dangers of the most perilous nature. *They were* equipped in a manner which would make a modern climber shudder at the thought. They did not go out of their way to court such excitement. (ll. 5–8)

b One or two places such as Zermatt and Chamonix had rapidly become popular. Alpine villages tended to be impoverished settlements. *They were* cut off from civilization by high mountains. (ll. 10–13)

c Often a valley boasted no inn at all. Climbers found shelter wherever they could. *They* sometimes *found shelter* with the local priest. (*He* was usually as poor as his parishioners.) *They* sometimes *found shelter* with shepherds or cheese-makers. (ll. 15–18)

2. Write three sentences saying why you like or dislike mountaineering.

Key Structures

1. Study the form of these sentences:

The more difficult it is, *the more highly* it is regarded. (l. 2)

The quicker you work, *the sooner* you will finish.

Write sentences using the following words:

a The more . . . the less . . .

b The more . . . the worse . . .

c The sooner . . . the better . . .

2. Give the correct form of the verbs in brackets in the paragraph below. Do not refer to the passage until you have finished the exercise:

Modern alpinists try to climb mountains by a route which will give them good sport, and the more difficult it is, the more highly it is regarded. In the pioneering days, however, this (be) not the case at all. The early climbers (look) for the easiest way to the top because the summit (be) the prize they (seek), especially if it (never attain) before. It is true that during their explorations they often (face) difficulties and dangers of the most perilous nature, equipped in a manner which (make) a modern climber shudder at the thought, but they (not go) out of their way to court such excitement. They (have) a single aim, a solitary goal—the top! (ll. 1–9)

3. Note the position of the word *often* in these sentences:

They *often* faced difficulties and dangers. (l. 6)

The food (was) simply local cheese accompanied by bread (which was) *often* twelve months old. (ll. 14–15)

Often a valley boasted no inn at all. (ll. 15–16)

In the following sentences, the word *often* can be placed in two or more different positions. Indicate the correct positions in each sentence:

a I am in such a hurry, I don't have time for breakfast.

b We buy things we don't really need.

c He is sent abroad by his firm.

4. Compare these two sentences:

It is hard for us to realize . . . how difficult it was. (l. 10)

It is hard to realize how difficult it was.

Complete the following sentences:

a It was impossible for them . . .

b It is difficult . . .

c It is easy for you . . .

5. Note the use of *such* in these two sentences:

They did not go out of their way to court *such* excitement. (l. 8)

Such inns as there were were generally dirty. (ll. 13–14)

Write sentences using the following phrases:

such requests; such freedom; such difficulty; such films.

6. Note the form of the verb in italics:

For men accustomed to *eating* seven-course dinners . . . (ll. 19–20)

Complete the following using a verb after each phrase:

a I am used to . . .

b Do you object to my . . .

c I am looking forward to . . .

Special Difficulties

1. Write sentences to bring out the difference between the following pairs of words:
case (l. 3), situation; especially (ll. 4–5), specially; realize (l. 10), understand; except for (ll. 10–11), except; coarse (l. 15), course; home (l. 20), house.

2. Explain the meaning of the phrases in italics:

a They did not go *out of their way* to court such excitement. (l. 8)

b Please ask him to get *out of the way*; I can't get past.

c We bought a beautiful *out-of-the-way* cottage, miles from anywhere.

d Please move that table. Can't you see it's *in the way*?

e I'll call in and see you *on my way* home from work.

f We must do this exercise *in the way* we have been taught.

4

In the Soviet Union several cases have been reported recently of people who can read and detect colours with their fingers, and even see through solid doors and walls. One case concerns an eleven-year-old schoolgirl, Vera Petrova, who has normal vision but who can also perceive things with different parts of her
5 skin, and through solid walls. This ability was first noticed by her father. One day she came into his office and happened to put her hands on the door of a locked safe. Suddenly she asked her father why he kept so many old newspapers locked away there, and even described the way they were done up in bundles.

Vera's curious talent was brought to the notice of a scientific research institute
10 in the town of Ulyanovsk, near where she lives, and in April she was given a series of tests by a special commission of the Ministry of Health of the Russian Federal Republic. During these tests she was able to read a newspaper through an opaque screen and, stranger still, by moving her elbow over a child's game of Lotto she was able to describe the figures and colours printed on it; and, in an-
15 other instance, wearing stockings and slippers, to make out with her foot the outlines and colours of a picture hidden under a carpet. Other experiments showed that her knees and shoulders had a similar sensitivity. During all these tests Vera was blindfold; and, indeed, except when blindfold she lacked the ability to perceive things with her skin. It was also found that although she
20 could perceive things with her fingers this ability ceased the moment her hands were wet.

ERIC DE MAUNY *Seeing Hands* from *The Listener*

Another Russian girl, Rosa Kuleshova,
reads blindfold

Comprehension

Give short answers to these questions in your own words as far as possible. Use one complete sentence for each answer.

a How did Vera's father accidentally discover that his daughter possessed unusual powers of perception?

b Under what conditions was Vera incapable of perceiving objects with her skin?

c Under what conditions did Vera lose the ability to perceive objects with her fingers?

Vocabulary

Give another word or phrase to replace these words as they are used in the passage: several (l. 1); detect (l. 2); vision (l. 4); perceive (l. 4); curious (l. 9); series (l. 11); outlines (l. 16); a similar (l. 17); ceased (l. 20).

The Sentence

1. Supply the missing words in the following sentences. Do not refer to the passage until you have finished the exercise:

a In the Soviet Union several cases have been reported recently of people ... can read ... detect colours with their fingers, ... even see through solid doors and walls. One case concerns an eleven-year-old schoolgirl, Vera Petrova, ... has normal vision ... ... can also perceive things with different parts of her skin, ... through solid walls. (ll. 1–5)

b It was also found that ... she could perceive things with her fingers this ability ceased ... ... her hands were wet. (ll. 19–21)

2. Complete these sentences in any way you wish. Then compare what you have written with the sentences in the passage:

a One day she came into his office and ... (ll. 5–6)

b Suddenly she asked her father why ... (l. 7)

c Vera's curious talent was ... (l. 9)

d During these tests she ... (l. 12)

e It was also found that ... (l. 19)

3. Write three sentences describing Vera's unusual abilities.

Key Structures

1. Supply the correct form of the verbs in brackets. Do not refer to the passage until you have finished the exercise:

a In the Soviet Union several cases (report) recently of people who can read and detect colours with their fingers. (ll. 1–2)

b This ability first (notice) by her father. (l. 5)

c Vera's curious talent (bring) to the notice of a scientific research institute in the town of Ulyanovsk, near where she lives, and in April she (give) a series of tests by a special commission of the Ministry of Health of the Russian Federal Republic. (ll. 9–12)

d It also (find) that although she (can) perceive things with her fingers, this ability (cease) the moment her hands (be) wet. (ll. 19–21)

2. Compare the word order in these two sentences:

Why did he keep so many old newspapers locked away there?

She asked her father *why he kept* so many old newspapers locked away there. (ll. 7–8)

Write these sentences again, beginning each one with the words *I asked him* ...

a When did he buy that car?

b Where did he find that book?

c Why did he send a telegram?

d How did he know I was here?

e Which one did he like best?

3. Note the form of the verb in italics in this sentence:

By *moving* her elbow over a child's game of Lotto she was able to describe the figures and colours printed on it. (ll. 13–14)

Supply the correct form of the verbs in brackets:

a He can walk for miles without (get) tired.

b On (arrive) at the station, I went and bought a ticket.

c While (try) to climb over that wall, he fell down and broke his leg.

d You will never succeed in (persuade) me to come with you.

4. Compare these two sentences:

Instead of saying: She *was able to describe* the colours and figures printed on it. (l. 14)

We can say: She *succeeded in describing* the colours and figures printed on it.

Supply *could* or *was able to* in the following sentences:

1. I . . . easily swim across this river if I wanted to.

2. He . . . run a mile in five minutes when he was younger.

3. Amundsen . . . reach the South Pole before Scott.

4. I rang up several times before I . . . contact him.

5. I . . . get these tickets because I was willing to stand in the queue for several hours.

Special Difficulties

1. Write sentences to bring out the difference between the following pairs of words: normal (l. 4), ordinary; skin (l. 5), complexion; noticed (l. 5), remarked; office (l. 6), study; game (l. 13), toy; lacked (l. 18), needed; wet (l. 21), damp.

2. Explain the expressions in italics:

a Newspapers . . . were *done up* in bundles. (ll. 7–8)

b It's too late to save him now. He's *done for*.

c She'll never go back to her husband. She's *done with* him for good.

d This room looks lovely now that we've *done it up*.

e I wouldn't trust him if I were you. He once *did me out of* a lot of money.

3. Explain the word *figure* in these sentences:

a By moving her elbow over a child's game of Lotto she was able to describe the *figures* and colours printed on it. (ll. 13–14)

b I could make out the *figure* of a man on the bridge.

c She has such a beautiful *figure*, I'm not surprised she won the beauty contest.

4. Explain the expressions with *make* in these sentences:

a She was able . . . to *make out* with her foot the outlines and colours of a picture. (ll. 14–16)

b The thief *made off* with quite a lot of money.

c He's a strange fellow. I just can't *make him out*.

d Before he died he *made over* all his money to his wife.

e Are you any good at *making up* stories for children?

5

The gorilla is something of a paradox in the African scene. One thinks one knows him very well. For a hundred years or more he has been killed, captured, and imprisoned in zoos. His bones have been mounted in natural history museums everywhere, and he has always exerted a strong fascination upon scientists and romantics alike. He is the stereotyped monster of the horror films and the adventure books, and an obvious (though not perhaps strictly scientific) link with our ancestral past.

Yet the fact is we know very little about gorillas. No really satisfactory photograph has ever been taken of one in a wild state, no zoologist, however intrepid, has been able to keep the animal under close and constant observation in the dark jungles in which he lives. Carl Akeley, the American naturalist, led two expeditions in the nineteen-twenties, and now lies buried among the animals he loved so well. But even he was unable to discover how long the gorilla lives, or how or why it dies, nor was he able to define the exact social pattern of the family groups, or indicate the final extent of their intelligence. All this and many other things remain almost as much a mystery as they were when the French explorer Du Chaillu first described the animal to the civilized world a century ago. The Abominable Snowman who haunts the imagination of climbers in the Himalayas is hardly more elusive.

ALAN MOOREHEAD *No Room in the Ark*

A family of gorillas

Comprehension

Give short answers to these questions in your own words as far as possible. Use one complete sentence for each answer.

a Why, according to the author, is the gorilla something of a paradox in the African scene?

b Name three basic facts about the gorilla which Carl Akeley, the American naturalist, failed to find out.

Vocabulary

Give another word or phrase to replace these words as they are used in the passage: captured (l. 2); mounted (l. 3); stereotyped (l. 5); link (l. 6); intrepid (l. 9); constant (l. 10); indicate (l. 15); extent (l. 15); elusive (l. 19).

The Sentence

1. Combine the following sentences to make *two* complex statements out of each group. Make any changes you think necessary, but do not alter the sense of the original. Do not refer to the passage until you have finished the exercise:

a For a hundred years or more he has been killed. He has been captured. He has been imprisoned in zoos. His bones have been mounted in natural history museums everywhere. He has always exerted a strong fascination upon scientists. He has exerted a strong fascination upon romantics, too. (ll. 2–5)

b Carl Akeley was an American naturalist. He led two expeditions in the nineteen-twenties. He now lies buried among the animals he loved so well. But even he was unable to discover how long the gorilla lives. He was unable to discover how or why it dies. He was not able to define the exact social pattern of the family groups. He was unable to indicate the final extent of their intelligence. (ll. 11–15)

2. Complete these sentences in any way you wish. Then compare what you have written with the sentences in the passage:

a Yet the fact is . . . (l. 8)

b No really satisfactory . . . (l. 8)

c All this and many other things . . . (ll. 15–16)

3. Write a short sentence on each of the following:

a Horror films.

b Our ancestral past.

c The Abominable Snowman.

Key Structures

1. Note the use of *for* and *since* in these sentences:

For a hundred years or more he has been killed, captured, and imprisoned in zoos. (ll. 2–3)

International exhibitions have been held regularly ever *since* the first one in 1851.

Supply *for* or *since* in the following sentences:

a He has been missing . . . three years. He set out to find the Abominable Snowman and has not been heard of . . .

b I have been waiting for you . . . two o'clock. I've been here . . . nearly two hours.

c I haven't seen my parents . . . last Christmas.

d The kettle has been boiling . . . several minutes.

2. Supply the correct form of the verbs in brackets. Do not refer to the passage until you have finished the exercise:

No really satisfactory photograph ever (take) of one in a wild state, no zoologist, however intrepid, (be) able to keep the animal under close and constant observation in the

18

dark jungles in which he (live). Carl Akeley, the American naturalist, (lead) two expeditions in the nineteen-twenties, and now (lie) buried among the animals he (love) so well. (ll. 8–13)

3. Compare these two sentences:

Instead of saying: . . . in the dark jungles *in which he lives.* (ll. 10–11)

We can say: . . . in the dark jungles *he lives in.*

Write these sentences again omitting the words *whom* and *which* and changing the position of the words in italics:

a The person *from* whom I got this information is an expert on the subject.

b The incident *to* which you referred occurred several years ago.

c Biochemistry is a subject *about* which I know very little.

4. Note the phrase in italics in this sentence:

All this and many other things remain almost *as much a mystery as* they were when the French explorer Du Chaillu first described the animal to the civilized world a century ago. (ll. 15–18)

Complete the following sentences:

a There were as many people present . . .

b It was as much a surprise to me . . .

c We have received as many Christmas cards . . .

Special Difficulties

1. Write sentences to bring out the difference between the following pairs of words: captured (l. 2), arrested; natural (l. 3), physical; alike (l. 5), the same; past (l. 7), passed; among (l. 12), between; discover (l. 13), invent.

2. Explain the word *all* in these sentences:

a *All* this remains a mystery. (Cp. ll. 15–16)

b Many students were late and we weren't able to begin the lesson until they had *all* come.

c *All* was quiet.

d *All* were quiet.

3. Study the pattern in italics:

Du Chaillu first *described the animal to* the civilized world. (l. 17)

Complete the following sentences:

a As I could not understand the problem, he explained . . .

b As I did not know anyone present, he introduced . . .

c He proposed a toast . . .

d He presented a book . . .

4. Explain the meaning of *haunt* in these sentences:

a The Abominable Snowman *haunts* the imagination of climbers (l. 18)

b That old castle is said to be *haunted.*

c The penguins spend the summer months at their breeding *haunts.*

d He often comes here. It is one of his *haunts.*

6

People are always talking about 'the problem of youth'. If there is one—which I take leave to doubt—then it is older people who create it, not the young themselves. Let us get down to fundamentals and agree that the young are after all human beings—people just like their elders. There is only one difference be-
5 tween an old man and a young one: the young man has a glorious future before him and the old one has a splendid future behind him: and maybe that is where the rub is.

When I was a teenager, I felt that I was just young and uncertain—that I was a new boy in a huge school, and I would have been very pleased to be regarded
10 as something so interesting as a problem. For one thing, being a problem gives you a certain identity, and that is one of the things the young are busily engaged in seeking.

I find young people exciting. They have an air of freedom, and they have not a dreary commitment to mean ambitions or love of comfort. They are not anxious
15 social climbers, and they have no devotion to material things. All this seems to me to link them with life, and the origins of things. It's as if they were in some sense cosmic beings in violent and lovely contrast with us suburban creatures. All that is in my mind when I meet a young person. He may be conceited, ill-mannered, presumptuous or fatuous, but I do not turn for protection to dreary
20 clichés about respect for elders—as if mere age were a reason for respect. I accept that we are equals, and I will argue with him, as an equal, if I think he is wrong.

FIELDEN HUGHES from *Out of the Air, The Listener*

Mods and Rockers in the streets of Hastings in 1964

Comprehension

Give short answers to these questions in your own words as far as possible. Use one complete sentence for each answer.

a What, according to the writer, is the one difference between an old man and a young one?

b Why would the writer have been pleased to have been regarded as a problem when he was young?

c Name three qualities in young people which the author particularly admires.

Vocabulary

Give another word or phrase to replace these words as they are used in the passage: create (l. 2); teenager (l. 8); devotion (l. 15); link (l. 16); origins (l. 16); dreary (l. 19).

The Sentence

1. Complete the following sentences in any way you wish. Then compare what you have written with the sentences in the passage:

a There is only one difference between an old man and a young one: . . . (ll. 4–5)

b When I was a teenager, I . . . (l. 8)

c I find young people exciting. They . . . (l. 13)

2. Combine the following statements to make complete sentences. Add conjunctions of your own and omit the words in italics. Do not refer to the passage until you have finished the exercise.

a If there is one, I take leave to doubt *it*. It is older people who create it. *It is* not the young themselves. (ll. 1–3)

b They are not anxious social climbers. They have no devotion to material things. (ll. 14–15)

3. Write three statements which an adult might make to criticize adolescents.

4. Write three statements which an adolescent might make to criticize adults.

Key Structures

1. Compare these two sentences:

People *are always talking* about 'the problem of youth'. (l. 1)

Whenever I meet him, he *always talks* about his personal problems.

The first sentence describes something that happens *all the time*; the second sentence describes something that happens *frequently*.

Write similar pairs of sentences using the following verbs:

change; make; tell; ask.

2. Compare these two sentences:

It is older people who create it, not *the young* themselves. (ll. 2–3)

There is only one difference between an old man and a young one: . . . (ll. 4–5)

Write similar pairs of sentences using the following words:

the rich, a rich man; the sick, a sick man; the blind, a blind man; the dead, a dead man.

3. Compare these two sentences:

Instead of saying: I would have been very pleased *if anyone regarded me* as a problem.

We can say: I would have been very pleased *to be regarded* as a problem. (ll. 9–10)

Write these sentences again using this construction with *to be* in place of the phrases in italics:

a You would not like *it if you were accused* of theft.

b I was astonished *when they told me* that all the tickets had been sold out.

c I expect *they will inform me* about it tomorrow.

4. Compare these two sentences:

Instead of saying: To be a problem gives you a certain identity.

We can say: Being a problem gives you a certain identity. (ll. 10–11)

Rewrite these sentences changing the form of the verbs in italics:

a It is not very pleasant *to have* to write so many letters.

b *To expect* others to help you and then not *to help* them in return is hardly commendable.

c It is very enjoyable *to teach* young children.

5. Note the construction in italics:

That is one of the things the young are busily engaged *in seeking.* (ll. 11–12)

Write sentences using the same construction with the following verbs: delight; interest; persist; believe.

6. Compare these two sentences:

Instead of saying: They *have no* devotion to material things. (l. 15)

We can say: They *haven't any* devotion to material things.

Write these sentences again using *not . . . any* in place of *no.*

a He doesn't know. There's no point in asking him.

b You'll pass your driving test if you make no mistakes.

c I have no faith in him.

Special Difficulties

1. Write sentences to bring out the difference between the following pairs of words: older (l. 2), elder; agree (l. 3), accept (l. 21); between (ll. 4–5), among; pleased (l. 9), begged; regarded (l. 9), looked at; interesting (l. 10), interested; exciting (l. 13), excited; reason (l. 20), cause.

2. Note this phrase with *get*:

Let us *get down to* fundamentals. (l. 3)

Explain these expressions with *get*:

a The children are very quiet. I wonder what they're *getting up to*.

b I can't see how we can *get round* this difficulty.

c I've been abroad three times this year. I *get about* quite a bit.

d Hasn't she *got over* her illness yet?

e Don't think you'll *get off* so lightly if you're caught.

f It's your turn to do the washing up and it's no use your trying to *get out of* it.

3. Note the phrase in italics:

He may be . . . *ill-mannered*. (ll. 18–19)

Write sentences using the following expressions:

ill-advised; ill-protected; ill-tempered; ill-fated; ill-used; ill-bred; ill-natured.

7

I am always amazed when I hear people saying that sport creates goodwill between the nations, and that if only the common peoples of the world could meet one another at football or cricket, they would have no inclination to meet on the battlefield. Even if one didn't know from concrete examples (the 1936 Olympic Games, for instance) that international sporting contests lead to orgies of hatred, one could deduce it from general principles.

Nearly all the sports practised nowadays are competitive. You play to win, and the game has little meaning unless you do your utmost to win. On the village green, where you pick up sides and no feeling of local patriotism is involved, it is possible to play simply for the fun and exercise: but as soon as the question of prestige arises, as soon as you feel that you and some larger unit will be disgraced if you lose, the most savage combative instincts are aroused. Anyone who has played even in a school football match knows this. At the international level sport is frankly mimic warfare. But the significant thing is not the behaviour of the players but the attitude of the spectators: and, behind the spectators, of the nations who work themselves into furies over these absurd contests, and seriously believe—at any rate for short periods—that running, jumping and kicking a ball are tests of national virtue.

GEORGE ORWELL *The Sporting Spirit*

Policemen chase a fan at the 1966 Football Association Cup final at Wembley

Comprehension

Give short answers to these questions in your own words as far as possible. Use one complete sentence for each answer.
a Why, according to the author, do international sporting contests lead to orgies of hatred?
b What, according to the author, do spectators believe when they watch international sporting contests?

Vocabulary

1. Give another word or phrase to replace these words as they are used in the passage: amazed (l. 1); goodwill (l. 1); inclination (l. 3); deduce (l. 6); utmost (l. 8); prestige (l. 11); disgraced (ll. 11–12); significant (l. 14).
2. Explain the following phrases as they have been used in the passage: pick up sides (l. 9); local patriotism (l. 9); the most savage combative instincts are aroused (l. 12); frankly mimic warfare (l. 14); absurd contests (l. 16).

The Sentence

1. Supply the missing words in the following paragraph. Do not refer to the passage until you have finished the exercise:
You play to win, ... the game has little meaning ... you do your utmost to win. On the village green, ... you pick up sides ... no feeling of local patriotism is involved, it is possible to play simply for the fun and exercise; but ... the question of local prestige arises, ... you feel that you and some larger unit will be disgraced ... you lose, the most savage combative instincts are aroused. Anyone ... has played even in a school football match knows this. (ll. 7–13)
2. Combine the following sentences to make one complete statement. Make any changes you think necessary, but do not change the sense of the original. Refer to the passage when you have finished the exercise:
The significant thing is not the behaviour of the players. It is the attitude of the spectators. Behind the spectators, it is the attitude of the nations. They work themselves up into furies over these absurd contests. Running, jumping and kicking a ball are tests of national virtue. They seriously believe this—at any rate for short periods. (ll. 14–17)
3. Complete the following sentences in any way you wish. Then compare what you have written with the sentences in the passage:
a I am always amazed when ... (l. 1)
b Nearly all the sports practised ... (l. 7)
4. State in a single sentence what you think the author believes about competitive sports.

Key Structures

1. Study the form of the verbs after *if* in these sentences:
If only the common peoples of the world *could meet* one another at football or cricket, they *would have* no inclination to meet on the battlefield. (ll. 2–4)
If one didn't know from concrete examples ... that international sporting contests lead to orgies of hatred, one *could deduce* it from general principles. (ll. 4–6)
Some larger unit *will be disgraced if you lose*. (ll. 11–12)
Complete the following in any way you wish:
a If you play a game to win ...
b If only we could afford to ...
c You could learn to play golf if you ...
d You won't find it difficult if you ...

2. Note carefully the form of the verbs after the phrase *as soon as* in this sentence:
As soon as the question of prestige *arises*, *as soon as* you *feel* that you and some larger unit will be disgraced . . . the most savage combative instincts *are aroused*. (ll. 10–12)
Supply the correct form of the verbs in brackets in these sentences:
a If he (make) any trouble, he will be asked to leave the meeting.
b You will feel much better when you (stop) smoking.
c As soon as he (arrive) in New York, he will send me a telegram.
d You can wait here until the rain (stop).
e When you (move) to your new house you will be far more comfortable than you are now.
3. Supply the missing words in the following paragraph. Do not refer to the passage until you have finished the exercise:
Anyone who has played even . . . a school football match knows this. . . . the international level sport is frankly mimic warfare. But the significant thing is not the behaviour . . . the players but the attitude . . . the spectators: and, . . . the spectators, . . . the nations who work themselves . . . furies . . . these absurd contests. (ll. 12–16)

Special Difficulties

1. Write sentences to bring out the difference between the following pairs of words: hear (l. 1), listen; even (l. 4), still; lead (l. 5), guide; principle (l. 6), principal; practise (l. 7), practice; win (l. 8), beat; lose (l. 12), loose; arise (l. 11), arouse (l. 12); level (l. 13), flat.
2. Explain the meaning of the word *peoples* in this sentence:
If only the common *peoples* of the world could meet . . . (l. 2)
Write two sentences using the words *people* and *peoples*.
3. Compare these two expressions:
Instead of saying: The Olympic Games that were held in 1936 . . .
We can say: The 1936 Olympic Games . . . (ll. 4–5)
What can we say in place of the phrases in italics:
a I shall catch the *train that leaves at four o'clock.*
b I have a copy of the *edition that was published in 1937.*
c The *Education Act of 1944* aimed at providing equal opportunities for every child in the country.
d The *revolution of 1917* had important consequences.
4. Compare these two sentences:
One could deduce it from general principles. (l. 6)
You play to win, and the game has little meaning unless *you* do your utmost to win. (ll. 7–8)
Write two sentences using the words *one* and *you* in the ways shown above.
5. Explain the words and phrases in italics:
a It is possible to play simply *for the fun* and exercise. (ll. 9–10)
b There was a lot of *fun* and laughter at the party.
c He didn't mean any harm; it was all *in good fun.*
d He's upset because everyone *made fun of* him.

8

Parents have to do much less for their children today than they used to do, and home has become much less of a workshop. Clothes can be bought ready made, washing can go to the laundry, food can be bought cooked, canned or preserved, bread is baked and delivered by the baker, milk arrives on the doorstep, meals
5 can be had at the restaurant, the works' canteen, and the school dining-room.

It is unusual now for father to pursue his trade or other employment at home, and his children rarely, if ever, see him at his place of work. Boys are therefore seldom trained to follow their father's occupation, and in many towns they have a fairly wide choice of employment and so do girls. The young wage-earner often
10 earns good money, and soon acquires a feeling of economic independence. In textile areas it has long been customary for mothers to go out to work, but this practice has become so widespread that the working mother is now a not unusual factor in a child's home life, the number of married women in employment having more than doubled in the last twenty-five years. With mother earning
15 and his older children drawing substantial wages father is seldom the dominant figure that he still was at the beginning of the century. When mother works economic advantages accrue, but children lose something of great value if mother's employment prevents her from being home to greet them when they return from school.

W. O. LESTER SMITH *Education*

A family photograph taken in 1877

Comprehension

Give short answers to these questions in your own words as far as possible. Use one complete sentence for each answer.

a Give three reasons why parents have to do much less for their children today.

b Why are boys seldom trained to follow their father's occupation?

c Why is father rarely the dominant figure in the modern home?

Vocabulary

Give another word or phrase to replace these words as they are used in the passage: pursue (l. 6); employment (l. 6); acquires (l. 10); textile areas (l. 11); customary (l. 11); widespread (l. 12); substantial (l. 15); dominant (l. 15); accrue (l. 17).

The Sentence

1. Combine these pairs of sentences in four different ways using the following conjunctions: *as*, *because*, *so*, and *and*. Then compare your answers with the sentences in the passage:

a Parents have to do much less for their children today than they used to do. Home has become much less of a workshop. (ll. 1–2)

b It is unusual now for father to pursue his trade or other employment at home. His children rarely, if ever, see him at his place of work. (ll. 6–7)

c The young wage-earner often earns good money. He soon acquires a feeling of economic independence. (ll. 9–10)

2. Combine the following sentences to make one complex statement out of each group. Make any changes you think necessary but do not alter the sense of the original. Refer to the passage when you have finished the exercise:

a Boys are therefore seldom trained to follow their father's occupation. In many towns they have a fairly wide choice of employment. Girls have a wide choice, too. (ll. 7–9)

b In textile areas it has long been customary for mothers to go out to work. This practice has become widespread. The working mother is now a not unusual factor in a child's home life. The number of married women in employment has more than doubled in the last twenty-five years. (ll. 10–14)

3. Write three sentences in your own words explaining why a family may suffer when mother goes out to work.

Key Structures

1. Compare these two sentences:

Parents have to do *much less* for their children today. (l. 1)

Far fewer people are prepared to work long hours today.

Complete these sentences by adding *much less* or *far fewer*:

a There is . . . demand for this model than there used to be.

b Now that we have installed calculating machines in the office, . . . time is wasted.

c Now that the new regulations have come into force, there are . . . accidents on the roads.

d This year the universities received . . . applications from students intending to study science than they did last year.

2. Compare these two sentences:

Parents have to do much less for their children today than they *used to do*. (l. 1)

When we first came to Australia we did not like the hot weather, but we *are used to* it now.

Supply *used to* or the correct form of *to be used to* in these sentences:

a I don't mind the cold weather. I . . . it.

b He . . . collect stamps when he was a boy.

c At one time, I . . . drive nearly a hundred miles a day.

d I . . . driving long distances.

3. Supply the correct form of the verbs in brackets. Do not refer to the passage until you have finished the exercise:

Clothes (can buy) ready made, washing can go to the laundry, food (can buy) cooked, canned or preserved, bread (bake) and (deliver) by the baker, milk (arrive) on the door-step, meals (can have) at the restaurant. (ll. 2–5)

4. Put the words in brackets in their correct positions in these sentences. In some cases more than one position is possible. Do not refer to the passage until you have finished the exercise:

a It is unusual for father to pursue his trade or other employment at home. (now) (l. 6)

b Children see him at his place of work. (rarely) (l. 7)

c Boys are therefore trained to follow their father's occupation. (seldom) (ll. 7–8)

d The young wage-earner earns good money, and acquires a feeling of economic independence. (often, soon) (ll. 9–10)

e In textile areas it has been customary for mothers to go out to work. (long) (ll. 10–11)

f Father is the dominant figure that he was at the beginning of the century. (seldom, still) (ll. 15–16)

5. Note the phrase in italics in this sentence:

It is unusual now for father to pursue his trade . . . *at home*. (l. 6)

Write sentences using the following phrases:

at school; at the school; in hospital; in the hospital; to market; to the market; in prison; in the prison.

Special Difficulties

1. Write sentences to bring out the difference between the following pairs of words: home (l. 2), house; clothes (l. 2), cloths; bake (l. 4), roast; follow (l. 8), watch; earn (l. 10), win; last (l. 14), latest; still (l. 16), yet; prevent (l. 18), avoid; greet (l. 18), salute.

2. Compare these two phrases:

Instead of saying: The dining-room of the school.

We can say: The school dining-room. (l. 5)

How can the following phrases be expressed differently:

the key of the front door; the clock tower of the church; the cinema in the village; hotels in London; the gate of the garden; a spokesman of the Ministry of Education.

3. Note the use of *fairly* in this sentence:

They have a *fairly* wide choice of employment. (ll. 8–9)

Write three sentences using each of the following words:

fairly, rather, enough.

9

Not all sounds made by animals serve as language, and we have only to turn to that extraordinary discovery of echo-location in bats to see a case in which the voice plays a strictly utilitarian rôle.

To get a full appreciation of what this means we must turn first to some recent
5 human inventions. Everyone knows that if he shouts in the vicinity of a wall or a mountainside, an echo will come back. The further off this solid obstruction, the longer time will elapse for the return of the echo. A sound made by tapping on the hull of a ship will be reflected from the sea bottom, and by measuring the time interval between the taps and the receipt of the echoes the depth of the
10 sea at that point can be calculated. So was born the echo-sounding apparatus, now in general use in ships. Every solid object will reflect a sound, varying according to the size and nature of the object. A shoal of fish will do this. So it is a comparatively simple step from locating the sea bottom to locating a shoal of fish. With experience, and with improved apparatus, it is now possible not only
15 to locate a shoal but to tell if it is herring, cod, or other well-known fish, by the pattern of its echo.

A few years ago it was found that certain bats emit squeaks and by receiving the echoes they could locate and steer clear of obstacles—or locate flying insects on which they feed. This echo-location in bats is often compared with radar, the
20 principle of which is similar.

MAURICE BURTON *Curiosities of Animal Life*

A bat, who loves eating bananas, here flies round one

Comprehension

Give short answers to these questions in your own words as far as possible. Use one complete sentence for each answer.

a How is the echo-location principle applied to measure the depth of the sea?
b Why do the sounds reflected by solid objects vary?
c What use do bats make of the principle of echo-location?

Vocabulary

Give another word or phrase to replace these words as they are used in the passage: strictly utilitarian (l. 3); vicinity (l. 5); elapse (l. 7); tapping (l. 7); apparatus (l. 10); shoal (l. 12); comparatively (l. 13); emit (l. 17); steer clear (l. 18).

The Sentence

1. Combine the following sentences to make one complex statement out of each group. Make any changes you think necessary but do not alter the sense of the original. Refer to the passage when you have finished the exercise:

a Not all sounds made by animals serve as language. We have only to turn to that extraordinary discovery of echo-location in bats. We can see a case in which the voice plays a strictly utilitarian rôle. (ll. 1-3)
b A sound can be made by tapping on the hull of a ship. It will be reflected from the sea bottom. We can measure the time interval between the taps and the receipt of the echoes. The depth of the sea at that point can be calculated. (ll. 7-10)
c Every solid object will reflect a sound. This varies according to the size and nature of the object. (ll. 11-12)
d With experience, and with improved apparatus, it is now possible to locate a shoal. It is possible to tell if it is herring, cod, or other well-known fish, by the pattern of its echo. (ll. 14-16)
e A few years ago it was found that certain bats emit squeaks. They received the echoes. They could locate obstacles. They could steer clear of obstacles. They could locate flying insects on which they feed. (ll. 17-19)

2. Without referring to the passage write three sentences indicating three different uses of the principle of echo-location.

Key Structures

1. Compare these two sentences:
Instead of saying: If we wish to get a full appreciation of what this means we must turn first to some recent human inventions.
We can say: To get a full appreciation of what this means we must turn first to some recent human inventions. (ll. 4-5)
Complete the following sentences:
a To understand . . .
b To enjoy . . .
c To succeed . . .

2. Supply *a*, *an*, or *the* where necessary in the following paragraph. Do not refer to the passage until you have finished the exercise:
Everyone knows that if he shouts in . . . vicinity of . . . wall or . . . mountainside, . . . echo will come back. . . . further off this solid obstruction, . . . longer time will elapse for . . . return of . . . echo. . . . sound made by tapping on . . . hull of . . . ship will be reflected from . . . sea bottom, and by measuring . . . time interval between . . . taps and . . . receipt of . . . echoes . . . depth of . . . sea at that point can be calculated. So

was born . . . echo-sounding apparatus, now in . . . general use in . . . ships. Every solid object will reflect . . . sound, varying according to . . . size and . . . nature of . . . object. . . . shoal of . . . fish will do this. So it is . . . comparatively simple step from locating . . . sea bottom to locating . . . shoal of . . . fish. (ll. 5–14)

3. Study the form of the verbs in italics in these sentences:

A sound made by *tapping* on the hull of a ship will be reflected from the sea bottom, and by *measuring* the time interval between the taps and the receipt of the echoes the depth of the sea at that point can be calculated. (ll. 7–10)

It was found that certain bats emit squeaks and by *receiving* the echoes they could locate . . . obstacles. (ll. 17–18)

Write three sentences in the same way using *by* followed by the *-ing* form of a verb.

4. Note that the verb *compared* is followed by *with* in this sentence: Echo-location in bats is . . . *compared with* radar. (l. 19)

Supply *with*, *for*, or *to* in the following sentences:

a I have been corresponding . . . him for many years.

b He was arrested and charged . . . murder.

c How much do you charge . . . this service?

d I can't provide you . . . all the things you need.

e We have provided . . . every emergency.

f Did you apply . . . that job?

g If you want a loan you should apply . . . the bank.

h He's much too quick for me. I just can't compete . . . him.

Special Difficulties

1. Write sentences to bring out the difference between the following pairs of words: sound (l. 1), echo (l. 6); discovery (l. 2), invention (l. 5); appreciation (l. 4), estimation; obstruction (l. 6), obstacle (l. 18); steer (l. 18), drive.

2. Supply the missing words in these sentences:

a Not all the sounds made . . . animals serve as language. (l. 1)

b This camera was made . . . Japan.

c Glass is made . . . sand and lime.

d This watch is made . . . gold.

3. Explain the word *experience* in these sentences:

a With *experience* . . . it is now not only possible to locate a shoal but to tell if it is herring, cod, or other well-known fish. (ll. 14–15)

b He is a very *experienced* surgeon.

c It was one of the strangest *experiences* I have ever had.

4. What does the phrase *to tell if* mean in this sentence:

It is now possible . . . *to tell if* it is herring, cod, or other well-known fish. (ll. 14–15)

Write two sentences using *to tell if*.

5. Note the spelling of *echoes* (l. 18). Write the plural of the following words: potato, piano, tomato, negro, solo.

In our new society there is a growing dislike of original, creative men. The manipulated do not understand them; the manipulators fear them. The tidy committee men regard them with horror, knowing that no pigeonholes can be found for them. We could do with a few original, creative men in our political life—if
5 only to create some enthusiasm, release some energy—but where are they? We are asked to choose between various shades of the negative. The engine is falling to pieces while the joint owners of the car argue whether the footbrake or the handbrake should be applied. Notice how the cold, colourless men, without ideas and with no other passion but a craving for success, get on in this society,
10 capturing one plum after another and taking the juice and taste out of them. Sometimes you might think the machines we worship make all the chief appointments, promoting the human beings who seem closest to them. Between midnight and dawn, when sleep will not come and all the old wounds begin to ache, I often have a nightmare višion of a future world in which there are billions of
15 people, all numbered and registered, with not a gleam of genius anywhere, not an original mind, a rich personality, on the whole packed globe. The twin ideals of our time, organization and quantity, will have won for ever.

J. B. PRIESTLEY *Thoughts in the Wilderness*

A scene from the film of George Orwell's horrifying novel, *1984*

Comprehension

Give short answers to these questions in your own words as far as possible. Use one complete sentence for each answer.

a What do you think the author means by the sentence 'We are asked to choose between various shades of the negative.'? (ll. 5–6)

b What do you understand by the metaphor 'the engine is falling to pieces'? (ll. 6–7)

c What do you understand by this metaphor: 'capturing one plum after another and taking the juice and taste out of them'? (l. 10)

Vocabulary

Give another word or phrase to replace these words as they are used in the passage: the manipulators (ll. 1–2); pigeonholes (l. 3); do with (l. 4); enthusiasm (l. 5); release (l. 5); craving (l. 9); get on (l. 9); worship (l. 11); ache (l. 13); gleam (l. 15); packed (l. 16).

The Sentence

1. Combine the following sentences to make one complex statement out of each group. Make any changes you think necessary but do not alter the sense of the original. Refer to the passage when you have finished the exercise:

a The tidy committee men regard them with horror. They know that no pigeonholes can be found for them. (ll. 2–4)

b The engine is falling to pieces. The joint owners of the car argue. Should the footbrake or the handbrake be applied? (ll. 6–8)

c Notice how the cold, colourless men get on in this society. They have no ideas. They have no other passion but a craving for success. They capture one plum after another. They take the juice and taste out of them. (ll. 8–10)

d Sometimes you might think the machines we worship make all the chief appointments. They promote the human beings who seem closest to them. (ll. 11–12)

e Between midnight and dawn sleep will not come. All the old wounds begin to ache. I often have a nightmare vision of a future world. There are billions of people in it. They are all numbered and registered. There is not a gleam of genius anywhere. There is not an original mind, a rich personality, on the whole packed globe. (ll. 12–16)

2. Without referring to the passage, explain in a sentence what it is the author is angry about.

Key Structures

1. Write these sentences again changing the position of the words or phrases in italics. In some cases more than one position is possible. Do not refer to the passage until you have finished the exercise:

a There is *in our new society* a growing dislike of original, creative men. (l. 1)

b *While* the engine is falling to pieces the joint owners of the car argue whether the footbrake or the handbrake should be applied. (ll. 6–8)

c You might *sometimes* think the machines we worship make all the chief appointments. (ll. 11–12)

d *When* between midnight and dawn, sleep will not come and all the old wounds begin to ache, *often* I have a nightmare vision of a future world. (ll. 12–14)

2. Compare these two sentences:

We could do with *a few* original, creative men. (l. 4)

There are *few* original, creative men in our society.

Write two sentences to bring out the difference in meaning between *a few* and *few*.

3. Supply the missing words in the following sentences. Do not refer to the passage until you have finished the exercise:

a The tidy committee men regard them . . . horror, knowing that no pigeonholes can be found . . . them. (ll. 2–4)

b We could do . . . a few original creative men . . . our political life. (l. 4)

c Notice how the cold, colourless men, . . . ideas and . . . no other passion but a craving . . . success, get . . . . . . this society, capturing one plum . . . another and taking the juice and taste . . . . . . them. (ll. 8–10)

d I often have a nightmare vision . . . a future world . . . which there are billions . . . people, all numbered and registered, . . . not a gleam . . . genius anywhere, not an original mind, a rich personality, . . . the whole packed globe. (ll. 14–16)

Special Difficulties

1. Write sentences to bring out the difference between the following pairs of words: tidy (l. 2), neat; regard (l. 3), look at; shade (l. 6), shadow; engine (l. 6), machine (l. 11); worship (l. 11), warship.

2. Compare the use of *but* in these two sentences:

We could do with a few original, creative men . . . *but* where are they? (ll. 4–5)

Notice how the cold, colourless men, without ideas and with no other passion *but* a craving for success, get on in this society. (ll. 8–9)

Complete the following sentences:

a I did not enjoy the film, but . . .

b You can blame no one but . . .

c There was nothing but . . .

d I would like to stay longer but . . .

e Who but . . .

3. Explain the meaning of *apply* in these sentences:

a The handbrake should be *applied*. (ll. 7–8)

b I don't think these new regulations *apply* to us.

c I am going to *apply* for a new job.

d You should wait twenty-four hours after *applying* the first coat of paint.

e You'll finish the job quickly if you *apply* yourself to the task.

4. Write sentences using the following phrases:

one after another (l. 10); one another; each other; from one to another; another one.

5. Note the use of *whole* (in preference to a phrase with *all*) here: *the whole* packed globe. (l. 16)

Write sentences using the following phrases: the whole country; the whole book; the whole time.

Unit 2

INSTRUCTIONS TO THE STUDENT

Content

This Unit consists of ten passages followed by exercises on Comprehension, Vocabulary, the Paragraph, Key Structures and Special Difficulties.

Aim

To provide practice in paragraph construction.

How to Work

1. Read each passage carefully two or three times.
2. Answer the questions in the order in which they are given.

The Paragraph

All the exercises given under this heading are based directly on the passage. You may correct your own answers to some of the questions by referring to the passage immediately after you have completed the exercises. The following types of exercise have been given:

1. Selecting a suitable title for the passage.
2. Selecting a statement which best expresses the main idea of a paragraph.
3. Expressing the main idea of a paragraph in a sentence.
4. Rearranging sentences taken from the passage so as to make up a complete paragraph.

II

Alfred the Great acted as his own spy, visiting Danish camps disguised as a minstrel. In those days wandering minstrels were welcome everywhere. They were not fighting men, and their harp was their passport. Alfred had learned many of their ballads in his youth, and could vary his programme with acrobatic
5 tricks and simple conjuring.

While Alfred's little army slowly began to gather at Athelney, the king himself set out to penetrate the camp of Guthrum, the commander of the Danish invaders. These had settled down for the winter at Chippenham: thither Alfred went. He noticed at once that discipline was slack: the Danes had the self-
10 confidence of conquerors, and their security precautions were casual. They lived well, on the proceeds of raids on neighbouring regions. There they collected women as well as food and drink, and a life of ease had made them soft.

Alfred stayed in the camp a week before he returned to Athelney. The force there assembled was trivial compared with the Danish horde. But Alfred had
15 deduced that the Danes were no longer fit for prolonged battle: and that their commissariat had no organization, but depended on irregular raids.

So, faced with the Danish advance, Alfred did not risk open battle but harried the enemy. He was constantly on the move, drawing the Danes after him. His patrols halted the raiding parties: hunger assailed the Danish army. Now Alfred
20 began a long series of skirmishes—and within a month the Danes had surrendered. The episode could reasonably serve as a unique epic of royal espionage!

BERNARD NEWMAN *Spies in Britain*

Alfred, disguised as a harpist, in the camp of the Danes

Comprehension

Give short answers to these questions in your own words as far as possible. Use one complete sentence for each answer.

a Give two reasons why it was easy for Alfred the Great to penetrate the Danish camp.
b Explain briefly how Alfred defeated the Danes.

Vocabulary

Explain the meaning of the following words and phrases as they are used in the passage: disguised (l. 1); thither (l. 8); slack (l. 9); security precautions (l. 10); proceeds (l. 11); trivial (l. 14); harried (l. 17); assailed (l. 19); skirmishes (l. 20); unique (l. 21).

The Paragraph

1. Suggest a suitable title for this passage.
2. Which of the following statements are correct:
a In Alfred's time it was easy for a minstrel to gain access to an enemy camp.
b Guthrum was the place where the Danish invaders had their camp.
c Alfred defeated the Danes because he had a large army.
d During the English attack, the Danes found it difficult to obtain food.
3. The following sentences have been taken from the second paragraph (ll. 6–12). Arrange them in their correct order. Do not refer to the passage until you have finished the exercise:
a He noticed at once that discipline was slack: the Danes had the self-confidence of conquerors, and their security precautions were casual.
b These had settled down for the winter at Chippenham: thither Alfred went.
c There they collected women as well as food and drink, and a life of ease had made them soft.
d While Alfred's little army slowly began to gather at Athelney, the king himself set out to penetrate the camp of Guthrum, the commander of the Danish invaders.
e They lived well, on the proceeds of raids on neighbouring regions.

Key Structures

1. Note how we can use *a lot of* in place of *many* (*of*) and *much* (*of*):
Instead of saying: Alfred had learned *many of* their ballads in his youth. (ll. 3–4)
We can say: Alfred had learned *a lot of* their ballads in his youth.
Write these sentences again using *much* (*of*) or *many* (*of*) in place of *a lot of*:
a There were *a lot of* people present at the reception.
b I haven't got *a lot of* books.
c I haven't brought *a lot of* luggage with me.
d *A lot of* the machinery in this factory is out of date.
e *A lot of* the shops in this area close on Wednesday afternoon.
2. Put the words in brackets in their correct position in these sentences. Do not refer to the passage until you have finished the exercise:
a He noticed that discipline was slack. (at once) (l. 9)
b They lived on the proceeds of raids on neighbouring regions. (well) (ll. 10–11)
c But Alfred had deduced that the Danes were fit for prolonged battle. (no longer) (ll. 14–15)
3. Note how *as well as* can be used to mean *in addition to*:
There they collected women *as well as* food and drink. (ll. 11–12)
Write two sentences using *as well as* in the same way.

4. Compare these two sentences:

Instead of saying: Their commissariat had *no* organization. (ll. 15–16)

We can say: Their commissariat hadn't *any* organization.

Supply suitable compounds with *no* or *any* in the following:

a . . . called while you were out.

b Did you go . . . last night?

c Haven't you got . . . to do?

d He said he knew . . . about it.

e I don't know . . . by that name.

5. Give the correct form of the verbs in brackets. Do not refer to the passage until you have finished the exercise:

So, faced with the Danish advance, Alfred not (risk) open battle but (harry) the enemy. He (be) constantly on the move, (draw) the Danes after him. His patrols (halt) the raiding parties: hunger (assail) the Danish army. Now Alfred (begin) a long series of skirmishes—and within a month the Danes (surrender). (ll. 17–21)

Special Difficulties

1. Write sentences to bring out the difference between the following pairs of words: wandering (l. 2), wondering; learned (l. 3), taught; noticed (l. 9), remarked; conquerors (l. 10), winners; force (l. 13), strength.

2. Explain the meaning of the verbs and expressions in italics:

a These had *settled down* for the winter at Chippenham. (l. 8)

b Have you *settled* your account yet?

c They *settled* in Australia before the war.

d It's time we *settled* this question.

e He *settled* all his property on his wife.

3. Note this compound with *self*:

The Danes had the *self-confidence* of conquerors. (ll. 9–10)

Write sentences using the following:

self-assurance; self-denial; self-governing; self-centred.

4. Explain the words and expressions in italics:

a The Danes were no longer *fit for* prolonged battle. (l. 15)

b Does that coat *fit* you?

c I can't *fit* all these clothes *into* this suitcase.

d He may win the race today. He's extremely *fit* and in good form.

e He wrote that book in a sudden *fit* of energy.

f It's a good idea, but it doesn't *fit in with* our plans.

12

What characterizes almost all Hollywood pictures is their inner emptiness. This is compensated for by an outer impressiveness. Such impressiveness usually takes the form of a truly grandiose realism. Nothing is spared to make the setting, the costumes, all of the surface details correct. These efforts help to mask the
5 essential emptiness of the characterization, and the absurdities and trivialities of the plots. The houses look like houses; the streets look like streets; the people look and talk like people; but they are empty of humanity, credibility, and motivation. Needless to say, the disgraceful censorship code is an important factor in predetermining the content of these pictures. But the code does not disturb
10 the profits, nor the entertainment value of the films; it merely helps to prevent them from being credible. It isn't too heavy a burden for the industry to bear. In addition to the impressiveness of the settings, there is a use of the camera which at times seems magical. But of what human import is all this skill, all this effort, all this energy in the production of effects, when the story, the representa-
15 tion of life is hollow, stupid, banal, childish?

JAMES T. FARRELL *The Language of Hollywood*

rom *Quo Vadis*

Comprehension

Give short answers to these questions in your own words as far as possible. Use one complete sentence for each answer.

a Why, according to the author, do Hollywood films seem extremely realistic?

b What does the author find wrong with the way people are portrayed in Hollywood films?

c What effect does the censorship code have on Hollywood films?

Vocabulary

Explain the meaning of the following words and phrases as they are used in the passage: characterizes (l. 1); compensated for (l. 2); grandiose (l. 3); nothing is spared (l. 3); essential (l. 5); trivialities (l. 5); motivation (ll. 7–8); predetermining (l. 9); credible (l. 11); burden (l. 11).

The Paragraph

1. Suggest a suitable title for the passage.

2. Which of the following statements best expresses the main idea of the passage:

a Hollywood films are impressive.

b Though Hollywood films seem to be very impressive, in actual fact they have very little to say.

c The representation of life in Hollywood films is hollow, stupid, banal, childish.

3. The following sentences have been taken from lines 1–8. Arrange them in their correct order. Do not refer to the passage until you have finished the exercise:

a What characterizes almost all Hollywood pictures is their inner emptiness.

b The houses look like houses; the streets look like streets; the people look and talk like people; but they are empty of humanity, credibility, and motivation.

c Nothing is spared to make the setting, the costumes, all of the surface details correct.

d Such impressiveness usually takes the form of a truly grandiose realism.

e This is compensated for by an outer impressiveness.

f These efforts help to mask the essential emptiness of the characterization, and the absurdities and trivialities of the plots.

Key Structures

1. Compare these two sentences:

Instead of saying: The thing that characterizes almost all Hollywood pictures is their inner emptiness.

We can say: What characterizes almost all Hollywood pictures is their inner emptiness. (l. 1)

Complete the following sentences in any way you wish:

a What I think happened . . .

b What he believes . . .

c What you must try to do . . .

2. Supply the missing words in these sentences. Do not refer to the passage until you have finished the exercise:

a This is compensated . . . by an outer impressiveness. (ll. 1–2)

b Such impressiveness usually takes the form . . . a truly grandiose realism. (ll. 2–3)

c They are empty . . . humanity, credibility, and motivation (ll. 7–8)

d It merely helps to prevent them . . . being credible. (ll. 10–11)

e . . . addition . . . the impressiveness . . . the settings, there is a use . . . the camera which . . . times seems magical. (ll. 12–13)

3. Note the use of *look* in this sentence:
The houses look like houses; the streets look like streets; the people look and talk like people. (ll. 6–7)
Write sentences using the following expressions:
taste like; feel like; smell like; seem like.
4. Supply *a(n)* or *the* where necessary in the following:
Needless to say, . . . disgraceful censorship code is . . . important factor in predetermining . . . content of these pictures. But . . . code does not disturb . . . profits, nor . . . entertainment value of . . . films; it merely helps to prevent them from being credible. It isn't too heavy . . . burden for . . . industry to bear. In addition to . . . impressiveness of . . . settings, there is . . . use of . . . camera which at times seems magical. (ll. 8–13)
5. Study this sentence pattern:
It isn't *too heavy* a burden *for* the industry to bear. (l. 11)
Write sentences using the same pattern with the following words: difficult; hot; easy.

Special Difficulties

1. Write sentences to bring out the difference between the following pairs of words: emptiness (l. 1), vacancy; costume (l. 4), suit; effort (l. 4), trial; entertainment (l. 10), amusement; credible (l. 11), credulous; effects (l. 14), affects.
2. Note the use of *inner* and *outer* in these phrases:
inner emptiness (l. 1); outer impressiveness (l. 2).
Write sentences using the following expressions:
inner room; inner tube; outer world; outer shell.
3. The words in italics have been used figuratively in the following sentences. Write sentences using these words in such a way as to bring out their literal meaning:
a Nothing is spared to make the setting, the costumes, all of the *surface* details correct. (ll. 3–4)
b These efforts help to *mask* the essential emptiness of the characterization. (ll. 4–5)
c It isn't too heavy a *burden* for the industry to bear. (l. 11)
d The representation of life is *hollow*. (ll. 14–15)
4. Supply the correct suffix (*-ism*, *-ment*, *-ness*, *-ship*, *-ation*, *-ity*) to the following words: empty; impressive; real; absurd; trivial; human; credible; motive; censor; entertain.
5. Explain the meaning of *plot* in these sentences:
a These efforts help to mask the . . . trivialities of the *plots*. (ll. 4–6)
b We *plotted* our course on the map.
c They are *plotting* to bring about the downfall of the government.
d Now that I've got this *plot*, I'll be able to build a house when I can afford it.

13

Oxford has been ruined by the motor industry. The peace which Oxford once knew, and which a great university city should always have, has been swept ruthlessly away; and no benefactions and research endowments can make up for the change in character which the city has suffered. At six in the morning the old
5 courts shake to the roar of buses taking the next shift to Cowley and Pressed Steel; great lorries with a double deck cargo of cars for export lumber past Magdalen and the University Church. Loads of motor-engines are hurried hither and thither and the streets are thronged with a population which has no interest in learning and knows no studies beyond servo-systems and distributors,
10 compression ratios and camshafts.

Theoretically the marriage of an old seat of learning and tradition with a new and wealthy industry might be expected to produce some interesting children. It might have been thought that the culture of the university would radiate out and transform the lives of the workers. That this has not happened may be the
15 fault of the university, for at both Oxford and Cambridge the colleges tend to live in an era which is certainly not of the twentieth century, and upon a planet which bears little resemblance to the war-torn Earth. Wherever the fault may lie the fact remains that it is the theatre at Oxford and not at Cambridge which is on the verge of extinction, and the only fruit of the combination of industry
20 and the rarefied atmosphere of learning is the dust in the streets, and a pathetic sense of being lost which hangs over some of the colleges.

ROGER PILKINGTON *Thames Waters*

The High at Oxford

Comprehension

Give short answers to these questions in your own words as far as possible. Use one complete sentence for each answer.

a Why has Oxford changed in character?

b Why, according to the author, has Oxford university had no effect on the workers of the motor industry?

Vocabulary

Explain the meaning of the following words and phrases as they are used in the passage: ruined (l. 1); research endowments (l. 3); thronged (l. 8); transform (l. 14); tend (l. 15); bears little resemblance (l. 17); on the verge of extinction (l. 19); rarefied (l. 20).

The Paragraph

1. Suggest a suitable title for the passage.

2. Which of the following statements do you think the author would agree with? Give reasons for your choice:

a Oxford has changed for the worse.

b The marriage of the old seat of learning and tradition with the new and wealthy industry has produced some interesting children.

c Oxford and Cambridge belong more to the past than to the present.

3. The following statements are taken from lines 11–17. Arrange them in their correct order. Do not refer to the passage until you have finished the exercise:

a That this has not happened may be the fault of the university, for at both Oxford and Cambridge the colleges tend to live in an era which is certainly not of the twentieth century, and upon a planet which bears little resemblance to the war-torn Earth.

b It might have been thought that the culture of the university would radiate out and transform the lives of the workers.

c Theoretically the marriage of an old seat of learning and tradition with a new and wealthy industry might be expected to produce some interesting children.

Key Structures

1. Supply *a* or *the* where necessary in the following paragraph. Do not refer to the passage until you have finished the exercise:

... Oxford has been ruined by ... motor industry. ... peace which ... Oxford once knew, and which ... great university city should always have, has been ruthlessly swept away; and no benefactions and ... research endowments can make up for ... change in ... character which ... city has suffered. At six in ... morning ... old courts shake to ... roar of ... buses taking ... next shift to ... Cowley and Pressed Steel; ... great lorries with ... double deck cargo of ... cars for export lumber past ... Magdalen and ... University Church. (ll. 1–7)

2. Supply the missing words where necessary in the following sentences. Do not refer to the passage until you have finished the exercise:

a The peace ... Oxford once knew, and ... a great university city should always have, has been swept ruthlessly away; and no benefactions and research endowments can make up for the change in character ... the city has suffered. (ll. 1–4)

b The streets are thronged with a population ... has no interest in learning. (ll. 8–9)

c The colleges tend to live in an era ... is certainly not of the twentieth century and upon a planet ... bears little resemblance to the war-torn Earth. (ll. 15–17)

d Wherever the fault may lie the fact remains ... it is the theatre at Oxford and not at

Cambridge . . . is on the verge of extinction, and the only fruit of the combination of industry and the rarefied atmosphere of learning is the dust in the streets, and a pathetic sense of being lost . . . hangs over some of the colleges. (ll. 17–21)

Special Difficulties

1. Write sentences to bring out the difference between the following pairs of words: ruined (l. 1), destroyed; past (l. 6), passed; interesting (l. 12), interested; fault (l. 15), blame; lie (l. 18), lay.
2. Explain the following words as they are used in the passage: suffered (l. 4); roar (l. 5); marriage (l. 11); seat (l. 11); children (l. 12); radiate (l. 13); fruit (l. 19).
3. Explain the expressions in italics:
a No benefactions and research endowments can *make up for* the change in character which the city has suffered. (ll. 3–4)
b My wife and I quarrelled last night and we haven't *made it up* yet.
c He's a peculiar person. I simply can't *make him out*.
4. Explain the meaning of *court* in these sentences:
a At six in the morning the old *courts* shake to the roar of buses. (ll. 4–5)
b The magistrate cleared the *court*.
c It was a struggle between the *court* and the peasants.
d I think he's *courting* the girl next door.
e To do that would be to *court* disaster.
5. In which of these sentences would it be possible to use *for* in place of *because*:
a That this has not happened may be the fault of the university, *because* at both Oxford and Cambridge the colleges tend to live in an era which is certainly not of the twentieth century. (ll. 14–16)
b *Because* he was tired he went to bed.

people are oppressed by the fear of death. In the young there is a justi-
ication for this feeling. Young men who have reason to fear that they will be
killed in battle may justifiably feel bitter in the thought that they have been
cheated of the best things that life has to offer. But in an old man who has known
5 human joys and sorrows, and has achieved whatever work it was in him to do,
the fear of death is somewhat abject and ignoble. The best way to overcome it—
so at least it seems to me—is to make your interests gradually wider and more
impersonal, until bit by bit the walls of the ego recede, and your life becomes increasingly merged in the universal life. An individual human existence should
10 be like a river—small at first, narrowly contained within its banks, and rushing
passionately past boulders and over waterfalls. Gradually the river grows wider,
the banks recede, the waters flow more quietly, and in the end, without any
visible break, they become merged in the sea, and painlessly lose their individual
being. The man who, in old age, can see his life in this way, will not suffer from
15 the fear of death, since the things he cares for will continue. And if, with the
decay of vitality, weariness increases, the thought of rest will be not unwelcome.
I should wish to die while still at work, knowing that others will carry on what
I can no longer do, and content in the thought that what was possible has been
done.

BERTRAND RUSSELL *How to Grow Old* from *Portraits from Memory*

Bertrand Russell speaking at a protest meeting in Trafalgar Square

Comprehension

Give short answers to these questions in your own words as far as possible. Use one complete sentence for each answer.
a Why, according to the author, is it justifiable for a young man to fear death?
b How does the author regard the fear of death in old people?
c What, in the opinion of the author, is the best way for an old person to overcome the fear of death?

Vocabulary

Explain the meaning of the following words and phrases as they are used in the passage: oppressed (l. 1); justification (ll. 1–2); cheated (l. 4); recede (l. 8); merged (l. 9); decay of vitality (l. 16); weariness (l. 16).

The Paragraph

1. Which of these statements best expresses the main idea of the passage? Give reasons for your answer:
a Old people fear death.
b While it is justifiable for a young man to fear death, it is not so in an old man who has known human joys and sorrows and has accomplished whatever work it was in him to do.
c It is justifiable for young people to fear death.
d An old man will not fear death if he knows that there are others who will carry on what he can no longer do.
2. The following sentences have been taken from lines 9–19. Arrange them in their correct order. Do not refer to the passage until you have finished the exercise:
a I should wish to die while still at work, knowing that others will carry on what I can no longer do, and content in the thought that what was possible has been done.
b The man who, in old age, can see his life in this way, will not suffer from the fear of death, since the things he cares for will continue.
c An individual human existence should be like a river—small at first, narrowly contained within its banks, and rushing passionately past boulders and over waterfalls.
d Gradually the river grows wider, the banks recede, the waters flow more quietly, and in the end, without any visible break, they become merged in the sea, and painlessly lose their individual being.
e And if, with the decay of vitality, weariness increases, the thought of rest will be not unwelcome.

Key Structures

1. Supply the correct form of the verbs in brackets in the following paragraph. Do not refer to the passage until you have finished the exercise:
Some old people (oppress) by the fear of death. In the young there is a justification for this feeling. Young men who have reason to fear that they (kill) in battle may justifiably feel bitter in the thought that they (cheat) of the best things that life has to offer. But in an old man who (know) human joys and sorrows, and (achieve) whatever work it was in him to do, the fear of death (be) somewhat abject and ignoble. (ll. 1–6)
2. Note the form of the verbs used after *until* in this sentence:
Make your interests gradually wider and more impersonal, until bit by bit the walls of the ego *recede*, and your life *becomes* increasingly merged in the universal life. (ll. 7–9)
Supply the correct form of the verbs in brackets in the following sentences:
a I don't think he will be very pleased when he (find) out the truth.

47

b He will send a telegram as soon as he (arrive) in Zurich.

c We should wait until the weather (change) before we go on holiday.

3. Study these sentences:

Instead of saying: An individual human existence *should* be like a river . . . (ll. 9–10)

We can say: An individual human existence *ought to* be like a river . . .

Now compare the following sentence with the two given above:

I can't leave now: I *must* finish my work first.

Supply *should* (*ought to*) or *must* in these sentences:

a I really . . . finish this letter, but I think it can wait until tomorrow.

b I have no alternative: I *must* do what I am told to do.

c By rights, you *should* pay a fine on this book as it is long overdue, but it doesn't matter.

d I *must* be at work on time every morning or I'll lose my job.

4. Supply the missing words in the following sentences. Do not refer to the passage until you have finished the exercise:

Gradually the river grows wider, the banks recede, the waters flow more quietly and . . . the end, without any visible break, they become merged . . . the sea and painlessly lose their individual being. The man who, . . . old age, can see his life . . . this way, will not suffer . . . the fear . . . death, since the things he cares . . . will continue. (ll. 11–15)

5. Give the correct form of the verb in brackets. Do not refer to the passage until you have completed the exercise:

And if, with the decay of vitality, weariness (increase), the thought of rest will be not unwelcome. (ll. 15–16)

Special Difficulties

1. Write two sentences to bring out the difference between the verbs *flow* (l. 12) and *fly* (l. 12).

2. Note that the word *water* is rarely used in the plural: 'the waters flow more quietly' (l. 12). Write a sentence using *water* in the plural.

3. Explain the meaning of *since* in these sentences:

a He will not suffer from the fear of death, *since* the things he cares for will continue. (ll. 14–15)

b I have not seen him *since* last year.

4. Note the use of *no longer* and *any longer* in these sentences:

Others will carry on what I can *no longer* do. (ll. 17–18)

Others will carry on what I cannot do *any longer*.

Write two sentences using *no longer* and *any longer*.

15

When anyone opens a current account at a bank, he is lending the bank money, repayment of which he may demand at any time, either in cash or by drawing a cheque in favour of another person. Primarily, the banker-customer relationship is that of debtor and creditor—who is which depending on whether the cus-
5 tomer's account is in credit or is overdrawn. But, in addition to that basically simple concept, the bank and its customer owe a large number of obligations to one another. Many of these obligations can give rise to problems and complications but a bank customer, unlike, say, a buyer of goods, cannot complain that the law is loaded against him.
10 The bank must obey its customer's instructions, and not those of anyone else. When, for example, a customer first opens an account, he instructs the bank to debit his account only in respect of cheques drawn by himself. He gives the bank specimens of his signature, and there is a very firm rule that the bank has no right or authority to pay out a customer's money on a cheque on which its cus-
15 tomer's signature has been forged. It makes no difference that the forgery may have been a very skilful one: the bank must recognize its customer's signature. For this reason there is no risk to the customer in the modern practice, adopted by some banks, of printing the customer's name on his cheques. If this facilitates forgery it is the bank which will lose, not the customer.

GORDON BARRIE and AUBREY L. DIAMOND *The Consumer Society and the Law*

A country bank at Alfriston in Sussex

Comprehension

Give short answers to these questions in your own words as far as possible. Use one complete sentence for each answer.

a What is meant by the statement that 'the banker–customer relationship is that of debtor and creditor'? (ll. 3–4)

b Quote a sentence from the second paragraph which illustrates this statement: 'a bank customer ... cannot complain that the law is loaded against him.' (ll. 8–9)

c Why does a customer give the bank specimens of his signature when he first opens an account?

Vocabulary

Explain the meaning of the following words and phrases as they are used in the passage: cash (l. 2); primarily (l. 3); debtor (l. 4); creditor (l. 4); in credit (l. 5); concept (l. 6); give rise to (l. 7); specimens (l. 13); forged (l. 15); facilitates (l. 18).

The Paragraph

1. Write a sentence in your own words expressing what you consider to be the main idea in the first paragraph of the passage.

2. Which of these sentences best expresses the main idea in the second paragraph? Give reasons for your choice:

a The bank must obey its customer's instructions, and not those of anyone else.

b The bank must honour a cheque even when the signature on it has been forged.

c The bank must always recognize its customer's signature.

3. The following sentences have been taken from the second paragraph (lines 10–19). Arrange them in their correct order. Do not refer to the passage until you have finished the exercise:

a The bank must obey its customer's instructions, and not those of anyone else.

b For this reason there is no risk to the customer in the modern practice, adopted by some banks, of printing the customer's name on his cheques.

c It makes no difference that the forgery may have been a very skilful one: the bank must recognize its customer's signature.

d If this facilitates forgery it is the bank which will lose, not the customer.

e He gives the bank specimens of his signature, and there is a very firm rule that the bank has no right or authority to pay out a customer's money on a cheque on which its customer's signature has been forged.

f When, for example, a customer first opens an account, he instructs the bank to debit his account only in respect of cheques drawn by himself.

Key Structures

1. Note the way these two sentences have been combined:

When anyone opens a current account at a bank, he is lending the bank money. He may demand repayment of *it* at any time.

When anyone opens a current account at a bank, he is lending the bank money, repayment of *which* he may demand at any time. (ll. 1–2)

Combine the following sentences using *which*:

a The bank has no right or authority to pay out a customer's money on a cheque. Its customer's signature on it has been forged. (ll. 13–15)

b The source is very reliable. I obtained this information from it.

c We have certain principles. We should act on them.

2. Compare these two sentences:
Instead of saying: The banker-customer relationship is *a relationship of* debtor and creditor.
We can say: The banker-customer relationship is *that of* debtor and creditor. (ll. 3–4)
Rewrite these sentences using *that of*:
a I am not referring to our policy but to the policy of our opponents.
b The only system I know which will help you to remember what you have heard at a lecture is the system of keeping notes.
3. Compare these two sentences:
Instead of saying: He instructs the bank to debit his account only in respect of cheques *which have been drawn* by himself.
We can say: He instructs the bank to debit his account only in respect of cheques *drawn* by himself. (ll. 11–12)
Rewrite these sentences in the same way:
a The exhibition consists entirely of pictures which have been painted by young children.
b The report on education which has been prepared by a government committee will soon be published.
c According to the regulations, income which has been earned overseas will not be taxed.

Special Difficulties

1. Write sentences to bring out the difference between the following pairs of words: current (l. 1), currant; lend (l. 1), borrow; in favour of (l. 3), for the sake of; whether (l. 4), weather; loaded (l. 9), laden; else (l. 10), other; specimen (l. 13), example; customer (l. 14), client; cheque (l. 14), check; practice (l. 17), practise; adopted (l. 17), adapted; print (l. 18), type.
2. Explain the meaning of the word *account* in these sentences:
a When anyone opens a current *account* at a bank, he is lending the bank money. (l. 1)
b I can't settle my *account* until next month.
c How do you *account* for his change of attitude?
d He gave an interesting *account* of his travels in China.
e Please don't go to all this trouble on my *account*.
f Trains were delayed on *account* of the bad weather.
3. Note how *say* has been used in the sense of *for example* in this sentence:
A bank customer, unlike, *say*, a buyer of goods, cannot complain that the law is loaded against him. (ll. 8–9)
Write two sentences using *say* in this way.
4. Note that the verb *obey* is not followed by a preposition:
The bank must *obey* its customer's instructions. (l. 10)
Write sentences using the following verbs: enter, discuss, reach, and leave.
5. Write sentences using the following words and phrases:
in addition to (l. 5); a large number of (l. 6); unlike (l. 8); in respect of (l. 12); for this reason (l. 17).

16

The deepest holes of all are made for oil, and they go down to as much as 25,000 feet. But we do not need to send men down to get the oil out, as we must with other mineral deposits. The holes are only borings, less than a foot in diameter. My particular experience is largely in oil, and the search for oil has done more to
5 improve deep drilling than any other mining activity. When it has been decided where we are going to drill, we put up at the surface an oil derrick. It has to be tall because it is like a giant block and tackle, and we have to lower into the ground and haul out of the ground great lengths of drill pipe which are rotated by an engine at the top and are fitted with a cutting bit at the bottom.
10 The geologist needs to know what rocks the drill has reached, so every so often a sample is obtained with a coring bit. It cuts a clean cylinder of rock, from which can be seen the strata the drill has been cutting through. Once we get down to the oil, it usually flows to the surface because great pressure, either from gas or water, is pushing it. This pressure must be under control, and we control it by
15 means of the mud which we circulate down the drill pipe. We endeavour to avoid the old, romantic idea of a gusher, which wastes oil and gas. We want it to stay down the hole until we can lead it off in a controlled manner.

T. F. GASKELL *The Search for the Earth's Minerals* from *Discovery*

An oilrig drilling in the Abu Dhabi offshore
oilfields in the Persian Gulf

Comprehension

a In a single sentence explain the purpose of an oil derrick.

b Explain in a sentence how oilmen prevent oil from gushing to the surface.

Vocabulary

Explain the meaning of the following words and phrases as they are used in the passage:
in diameter (l. 3); drilling (l. 5); haul (l. 8); rotated (l. 8); every so often (l. 10); strata
(l. 12); endeavour (l. 15).

The Paragraph

1. Which of these phrases would best serve as a title for the passage? Give reasons for
your choice: Geology Today; Drilling for Oil; Mining Methods; Mineral Deposits.
2. Which of these statements do you think the author would agree with? Give reasons
for your choice:
a The search for oil has led to an improvement in drilling techniques.
b When drilling for oil, it is difficult to obtain samples of the rocks the drill has been
cutting through.
c Once oil has been found, it is impossible to prevent it from gushing to the surface.
3. The following sentences have been taken from the first paragraph (lines 1–9).
Arrange them in their correct order. Do not refer to the passage until you have finished
the exercise:
a My particular experience is largely in oil, and the search for oil has done more to
improve deep drilling than any other mining activity.
b When it has been decided where we are going to drill, we put up at the surface an
oil derrick.
c The deepest holes of all are made for oil, and they go down to as much as 25,000 feet.
d The holes are only borings, less than a foot in diameter.
e But we do not need to send men down to get the oil out, as we must with other
mineral deposits.
f It has to be tall because it is like a giant block and tackle, and we have to lower into
the ground and haul out of the ground great lengths of drill pipe which are rotated
by an engine at the top and are fitted with a cutting bit at the bottom.

Key Structures

1. Supply the correct form of the missing verbs (*must*, *need* or *have to*) in these sentences. Do not refer to the passage until you have finished the exercise:
a We do not . . . to send men down to get the oil out as we . . . with other mineral
deposits. (ll. 2–3)
b It . . . be tall because it is like a giant block and tackle and we . . . lower into the
ground and haul out of the ground great lengths of drill pipe. (ll. 6–8)
c The geologist . . . to know what rocks the drill has reached. (l. 10)
d This pressure . . . be under control and we control it by means of the mud which we
circulate down the drill pipe. (ll. 14–15)
2. Supply *a* or *the* where necessary in the following. Do not refer to the passage until
you have finished the exercise:
. . . deepest holes of all are made for . . . oil, and they go down to as much as 25,000
feet. But we do not need to send . . . men down to get . . . oil out, as we must with . . .
other mineral deposits. . . . holes are only borings, less than . . . foot in . . . diameter.
. . . my particular experience is largely in . . . oil, and . . . search for . . . oil has done
more to improve . . . deep drilling than any other mining activity. (ll. 1–5)

3. Supply (*be*) *going to* or *will* in these sentences:

a When it has been decided where we . . . drill, we put up at the surface an oil derrick. (ll. 5–6)

b Ask Mary. I'm sure she . . . be able to help you.

c He . . . be far more co-operative if you speak to him nicely.

d If ever you want any information, we . . . always be glad to help you.

e He's changed his mind again. He . . . make out another will.

4. Note the order of the words in italics:

The geologist needs to know *what rocks the drill has reached.* (l. 10)

Complete the following sentences:

a Tell me where . . .

b I don't know why . . .

c Ask him how . . .

d Did he tell you when . . .

5. Note the word order in this sentence:

We want *it* to stay down the hole. (ll. 16–17)

Write sentences using the same pattern with the following verbs: allow, ask, teach, cause, warn and advise.

Special Difficulties

1. Write sentences to bring out the difference between the following pairs of words: hole (l. 1), whole; oil (l. 1), petrol; engine (l. 9), machine; fit (l. 9), suit; clean (l. 11), clear; control (l. 14), check; waste (l. 16), waist.

2. Supply verbs which could be used in place of the expressions in italics:

a When it has been decided where we are going to drill, we *put up* at the surface an oil derrick. (ll. 5–6)

b It took them several hours to *put out* the fire.

c I won't *put up with* this sort of thing any longer.

d Because of the bad weather, the match has been *put off* until next week.

3. Explain the meaning of the words or phrases in italics:

a *Once* we get down to the oil, it usually flows to the surface. (ll. 12–13)

b I'm ashamed to say I've only been to the Louvre *once*.

c *Once upon a time* there was a poor woodcutter who lived in a forest.

d I see him *once in a while*.

e I'll come *at once*.

f *All at once* there was a loud explosion.

4. Write sentences using the following expressions:

under control (l. 14); out of control; beyond control.

5. Note the use of *off* in this sentence: We want it to stay down the hole until we can *lead it off* in a controlled manner. (ll. 16–17)

Write sentences using the following verbs: drive off; cool off; hurry off; switch off; wear off.

17

The fact that we are not sure what 'intelligence' is, nor what is passed on, does not prevent us from finding it a very useful working concept, and placing a certain amount of reliance on tests which 'measure' it.

In an intelligence test we take a sample of an individual's ability to solve
5 puzzles and problems of various kinds, and if we have taken a representative sample it will allow us to predict successfully the level of performance he will reach in a wide variety of occupations.

This became of particular importance when, as a result of the 1944 Education Act, secondary schooling for all became law, and grammar schools, with the ex-
10 ception of a small number of independent foundation schools, became available to the whole population. Since the number of grammar schools in the country could accommodate at most approximately 25 per cent of the total child population of eleven-plus, some kind of selection had to be made. Narrowly academic examinations and tests were felt, quite rightly, to be heavily weighted in favour
15 of children who had had the advantage of highly-academic primary schools and academically biased homes. Intelligence tests were devised to counteract this narrow specialization, by introducing problems which were not based on specifically scholastically-acquired knowledge. The intelligence test is an attempt to assess the general ability of any child to think, reason, judge, analyse and syn-
20 thesize by presenting him with situations, both verbal and practical, which are within his range of competence and understanding.

BEATRIX TUDOR-HART *Learning to Live*

A child playing with an educational toy

Comprehension

Give short answers to these questions in your own words as far as possible. Use one complete sentence for each answer.

a Name one way in which intelligence tests can prove useful.

b Why are narrowly academic examinations unfair?

c How can intelligence tests be used to counteract narrow academic specialization?

Vocabulary

Explain the meaning of the following words and phrases as they are used in the passage: concept (l. 2); reliance (l. 3); occupations (l. 7); particular (l. 8); approximately (l. 12); heavily weighted (l. 14); scholastically-acquired knowledge (l. 18); assess (l. 19); competence (l. 21).

The Paragraph

1. Which of these phrases best indicates what the passage is about? Give reasons for your choice: secondary schooling; intelligence tests; selection for grammar schools.

2. Which of these statements best expresses the main idea of the passage? Give reasons for your choice:

a We can place a certain amount of reliance on intelligence tests.

b An intelligence test is an attempt to assess the general ability of any child to think, reason, judge, analyse and synthesize by presenting him with situations, both verbal and practical, which are within his range of competence and understanding.

c Intelligence tests were devised to counteract narrow academic specialization.

3. The following sentences have been taken from the third paragraph (lines 8–16). Arrange them in their correct order. Do not refer to the passage until you have finished the exercise:

Since the number of grammar schools in the country could accommodate at most approximately 25 per cent of the total child population of eleven-plus, some kind of selection had to be made. Narrowly academic examinations and tests were felt, quite rightly, to be heavily weighted in favour of children who had had the advantage of highly academic primary schools and academically biased homes. This became of particular importance when, as a result of the 1944 Education Act, secondary schooling for all became law, and grammar schools, with the exception of a small number of independent foundation schools, became available to the whole population.

Key Structures

1. Which of the following verbs are normally followed by *of* and which by *from*: prevent (l. 2); emerge, escape, boast, convince, despair, hinder, differ, consist, assure, accuse, protect, complain, get rid.

2. Note the form of the verbs in italics in this sentence:

If we *have taken* a representative sample it *will allow* us to predict successfully the level of performance he will reach in a wide variety of occupations. (ll. 5–7)

Write sentences using the same pattern with these words: when, after, as soon as, before.

3. Compare these two sentences:

Instead of saying: the level of *performance which he* will reach.

We can say: the level of *performance he* will reach. (ll. 6–7)

Add a suitable clause after the words in italics in these sentences. Omit *who* or *which* where possible:

a *Buildings* . . . should be pulled down.

b He is the best *swimmer* . . .

c The *review* . . . praises the book highly.
d The *people* . . . were asked to report to the police.
e *Accidents* . . . should be prevented.
4. Study this sentence pattern:
Examinations and tests were *felt* . . . *to be* heavily *weighted* . . . (l. 14)
Write sentences using the same pattern with the following verbs: *think* and *believe*.
5. Note the form of the verbs in italics in this sentence:
Narrowly academic examinations and tests *were felt*, quite rightly, to be heavily weighted in favour of children who *had had* the advantage of highly academic primary schools. (ll. 13–15)
Supply the correct form of the verbs in brackets in these sentences:
a He (apply) for the job even though he (have) no previous experience.
b After the man (hang), the police (realize) they (convict) the wrong person.
c The boy (insist) that he (spend) the day at school even though it (be) obvious to his parents that he (play) truant.

Special Difficulties

1. Write sentences to bring out the difference between the following pairs of words: fact (l. 1), event; passed (l. 1), past; prevent (l. 2), avoid; very (l. 2), too; measure (l. 3), count; result (l. 8), effect; attempt (l. 18), trial; judge (l. 19), criticize.
2. Explain the meaning of the verbs in italics:
a The fact that we are not sure what 'intelligence' is, nor what is *passed on*, does not prevent us from finding it a very useful working concept. (ll. 1–2)
b He *passed away* quietly at four o'clock this morning.
c When he told me what had happened, I got such a shock I nearly *passed out*.
d Would you *pass round* the cakes please Susan?
e This is the counterfeit painting which he tried to *pass off* as an original Vermeer.
3. Write sentences using the following phrases:
a certain amount of (ll. 2–3); of various kinds (l. 5); the level of performance (l. 6); as a result of (l. 8); with the exception of (ll. 9–10); some kind of (l. 13).
4. Explain the words in italics:
a *Narrowly* academic examinations . . . were felt . . . to be heavily weighted in favour of children who had had the advantage of highly-academic primary schools. (ll. 13–15)
b He *narrowly* escaped being captured.
c You should not take such a *narrow* view of the situation.
d He is a very *narrow-minded* person.

18

Two factors weigh heavily against the effectiveness of scientific research in industry. One is the general atmosphere of secrecy in which it is carried out, the other the lack of freedom of the individual research worker. In so far as any inquiry is a secret one, it naturally limits all those engaged in carrying it out
5 from effective contact with their fellow scientists either in other countries or in universities, or even, often enough, in other departments of the same firm. The degree of secrecy naturally varies considerably. Some of the bigger firms are engaged in researches which are of such general and fundamental nature that it is a positive advantage to them not to keep them secret. Yet a great many processes
10 depending on such research are sought for with complete secrecy until the stage at which patents can be taken out. Even more processes are never patented at all but kept as secret processes. This applies particularly to chemical industries, where chance discoveries play a much larger part than they do in physical and mechanical industries. Sometimes the secrecy goes to such an extent that the
15 whole nature of the research cannot be mentioned. Many firms, for instance, have great difficulty in obtaining technical or scientific books from libraries because they are unwilling to have their names entered as having taken out such and such a book for fear the agents of other firms should be able to trace the kind of research they are likely to be undertaking.

J. D. BERNAL *The Social Function of Science*

A scientist working at the 'Arcton' Laboratories in Cheshire

Comprehension

Give short answers to these questions in your own words as far as possible. Use one complete sentence for each answer.

a Which two factors weigh heavily against the effectiveness of scientific research in industry?

b Why are some processes in chemical industries never patented at all?

c Why are some firms reluctant to borrow books from libraries?

Vocabulary

Explain the meaning of the following words and phrases as they are used in the passage: weigh heavily against (l. 1); lack (l. 3); effective contact (l. 5); fundamental (l. 8); processes (l. 9); applies (l. 12); trace (l. 18); likely (l. 19).

The Paragraph

1. Which of these statements best expresses the main idea of the passage? Give reasons for your choice:

a The effectiveness of scientific research in industry is hampered by the general atmosphere of secrecy which surrounds it and by the lack of freedom of the individual research worker.

b Scientific research in industry is not very effective because big firms wish to keep so many processes secret.

c Many scientific processes in industry are kept secret until they can be patented.

2. The following sentences have been taken from lines 6–14. Arrange them in their correct order. Do not refer to the passage until you have finished the exercise:

a The degree of secrecy naturally varies considerably.

b This applies particularly to chemical industries, where chance discoveries play a much larger part than they do in physical and mechanical industries.

c Some of the bigger firms are engaged in researches which are of such general and fundamental nature that it is a positive advantage to them not to keep them secret.

d Even more processes are never patented at all but kept as secret processes.

e Yet a great many processes depending on such research are sought for with complete secrecy until the stage at which patents can be taken out.

Key Structures

1. Change the form of the verbs in each of these sentences. Omit the words in italics. Do not refer to the passage until you have completed the exercise:

a One is the general atmosphere of secrecy in which *they* carry it out. (l. 2)

b *They* seek for a great many processes with complete secrecy until the stage at which *they* can take out patents. (ll. 9–11)

c Even more processes *they* never patent at all but keep as secret processes. (ll. 11–12)

d Sometimes the secrecy goes to such an extent that *they* cannot mention the whole nature of the research. (ll. 14–15)

2. Give the correct form of the verbs in brackets in the following sentences. Do not refer to the passage until you have completed the exercise:

a In so far as any inquiry is a secret one, it naturally limits all those engaged in (carry) it out. (ll. 3–4)

b Many firms, for instance, have great difficulty in (obtain) technical or scientific books from libraries. (ll. 15–16)

3. Complete the following sentences using a verb after the words in italics:

a He was engaged *in* . . .

b He was prevented *from* . . .

c He insisted *on* . . .

d If you persist *in* . . .

4. Note the position of *not* in this sentence:

It is a positive advantage to them *not* to keep them secret. (ll. 8–9)

Supply *not* in each of the following sentences:

a He told me to mention it to you.

b Please tell him to call in the morning.

c Didn't I beg you to write to him?

5. What is the difference between these two sentences:

They are unwilling *to enter their names* as having taken out such and such a book.

They are unwilling *to have their names entered* as having taken out such and such a book. (ll. 17–18)

Write these sentences again using the correct form of *have* with the verbs in italics:

a We are going to *decorate* this room soon.

b I *repaired* this watch last year.

c Will you *install* the television in this room?

6. Note that in the following sentence we may use the word *lest* in place of *for fear*:

Many firms . . . are unwilling to have their names entered as having taken out such and such a book *lest* (or *for fear*) the agents of other firms should be able to trace the kind of research they are likely to be undertaking. (ll. 15–19)

Write two sentences using *lest* and *for fear*.

Special Difficulties

1. Note the use of *fellow* in this phrase: 'with their *fellow scientists*' (l. 5). Write three sentences using *fellow* with the following words: men; students; workers.

2. Write sentences using the following phrases:

in so far as (l. 3); often enough (l. 6); to such an extent (l. 14); the whole nature of (ll. 14–15).

3. Explain the expressions in italics in the following sentences:

a In so far as any inquiry is a secret one, it naturally limits all those engaged in *carrying it out*. (ll. 3–4)

b I think we can *carry on* without your help.

c The audience was completely *carried away by* the wonderful performance of the soloist.

d The government failed to *carry through* the new bill on housing in the House of Commons last night.

4. What do you understand by the phrase in italics:

They are unwilling to have their names entered as having taken out *such and such* a book. (ll. 17–18)

Write a sentence using the phrase *such and such*.

19

A gentleman is, rather than does. He is interested in nothing in a professional way. He is allowed to cultivate hobbies, even eccentricities, but must not practise a vocation. He must know how to ride and shoot and cast a fly. He should have relatives in the army and navy and at least one connection in the diplo-
5 matic service. But there are weaknesses in the English gentleman's ability to rule us today. He usually knows nothing of political economy and less about how foreign countries are governed. He does not respect learning and prefers 'sport'. The problem set for society is not the virtues of the type so much as its adequacy for its function, and here grave difficulties arise. He refuses to consider suf-
10 ficiently the wants of the customer, who must buy, not the thing he desires but the thing the English gentleman wants to sell. He attends inadequately to techno-logical development. Disbelieving in the necessity of large-scale production in the modern world, he is passionately devoted to excessive secrecy, both in finance and method of production. He has an incurable and widespread nepotism in
15 appointment, discounting ability and relying upon a mystic entity called 'character,' which means, in a gentleman's mouth, the qualities he traditionally possesses himself. His lack of imagination and the narrowness of his social loyal-ties have ranged against him one of the fundamental estates of the realm. He is incapable of that imaginative realism which admits that this is a new world to
20 which he must adjust himself and his institutions, that every privilege he formerly took as of right he can now attain only by offering proof that it is directly relevant to social welfare.

T. H. PEAR *English Social Differences*

Lord Curzon, Viceroy of India, invests the Maharajah of Cochin
with the Star of India in 1903

Comprehension

a Quote three statements which show that a gentleman (in the author's definition of the word) is interested in nothing in a professional way.
b Why is a 'gentleman' passionately devoted to excessive secrecy in finance and method of production?

Vocabulary

Explain the meaning of the following words and phrases as they are used in the passage: practise a vocation (ll. 2–3); connection (l. 4); function (l. 9); nepotism in appointment (ll. 14–15); entity (l. 15); directly relevant to social welfare (ll. 21–22).

The Paragraph

1. Which of the following statements do you think the author would agree with? Give reasons for your choice:
a A man should only be allowed to enjoy privileges when he proves he is worthy of them.
b An English gentleman's attitude to such things as government and industry is amateur in the extreme.
c The only person fit to wield power and authority is the gentleman.
2. In this passage, the author implies that people in power should possess certain qualities. Name five such qualities. You may refer to the passage if you wish to do so.

Key Structures

1. Supply the missing words in the following sentences. Do not refer to the passage until you have finished the exercise:
a He is interested . . . nothing . . . a professional way. (ll. 1–2)
b He should have relatives . . . the army and navy. (ll. 3–4)
c He usually knows nothing . . . political economy and less . . . how foreign countries are governed. (ll. 6–7)
d The problem set . . . society is not the virtues . . . the type so much as its adequacy . . . its function. (ll. 8–9)
e He attends inadequately . . . technological development. (ll. 11–12)
f Disbelieving . . . the necessity . . . large-scale production . . . the modern world, he is passionately devoted . . . excessive secrecy, both . . . finance and method . . . production. He has an incurable and widespread nepotism . . . appointment, discounting ability and relying . . . a mystic entity called 'character'. (ll. 12–16)
g His lack . . . imagination and the narrowness . . . his social loyalties have ranged . . . him one . . . the fundamental estates . . . the realm. He is incapable . . . that imaginative realism which admits that this is a new world . . . which he must adjust himself and his institutions. (ll. 17–20)
2. Note this use of *how* after the verb *know*: 'He must know *how* to ride . . .' (l. 3)
Write sentences using the same pattern with the following verbs: teach and learn.
3. Compare these two sentences:
Instead of saying: It is desirable for him to have relatives in the army and navy.
We can say: He should have relatives in the army and navy. (ll. 3–4)
Write three sentences using *should* in this way.
4. Study this sentence:
The problem set for society is *not* the virtues of the type *so much as* its adequacy for its function. (ll. 8–9)
Write two sentences using the pattern *not . . . so much as*.

62

5. Note the form of the verb in italics in this sentence:
Disbelieving in the necessity of large-scale production in the modern world, he is passionately devoted to excessive secrecy . . . (ll. 12–13)
Complete the following sentences:
a Realizing . . . I . . .
b Leaving . . . he . . .
c Finding . . . they . . .

Special Difficulties

1. Write sentences to bring out the difference between the following pairs of words: allowed (l. 2), aloud; even (l. 2), still; vocation (l. 3), vacation; refuse (l. 9), deny; attend (l. 11), follow; admit (l. 19), agree; formerly (l. 20), formally.
2. Explain the meaning of the word *service* in these sentences:
a He should have relatives in the diplomatic *service*. (ll. 3–5)
b Their after-sales *service* is excellent.
c I have just completed my National *Service*.
d He asked to see the manager and complained of the poor *service*.
e We have a very good railway *service* in our part of the world.
3. Supply full stops and commas where necessary in the following paragraph. Do not refer to the passage until you have finished the exercise:
He refuses to consider sufficiently the wants of the customer who must buy not the thing he desires but the thing the English gentleman wants to sell he attends inadequately to technological development disbelieving in the necessity of large-scale production in the modern world he is passionately devoted to excessive secrecy both in finance and method of production he has an incurable and widespread nepotism in appointment discounting ability and relying upon a mystic entity called 'character' which means in a gentleman's mouth the qualities he traditionally possesses himself. (ll. 9–17)
4. The opposites of the following words are to be found in the passage. What are they? amateur; forbidden; inability; adequately; believing; curable; capable; irrelevant.

20

In the organization of industrial life the influence of the factory upon the physiological and mental state of the workers has been completely neglected. Modern
industry is based on the conception of the maximum production at lowest cost,
in order that an individual or a group of individuals may earn as much money as
5   possible. It has expanded without any idea of the true nature of the human beings
who run the machines, and without giving any consideration to the effects produced on the individuals and on their descendants by the artificial mode of existence imposed by the factory. The great cities have been built with no regard for
us. The shape and dimensions of the skyscrapers depend entirely on the neces-
10   sity of obtaining the maximum income per square foot of ground, and of offering
to the tenants offices and apartments that please them. This caused the construction of gigantic buildings where too large masses of human beings are crowded
together. Civilized men like such a way of living. While they enjoy the comfort
and banal luxury of their dwelling, they do not realize that they are deprived of
15   the necessities of life. The modern city consists of monstrous edifices and of
dark, narrow streets full of petrol fumes, coal dust, and toxic gases, torn by the
noise of the taxi-cabs, lorries and buses, and thronged ceaselessly by great
crowds. Obviously, it has not been planned for the good of its inhabitants.

ALEXIS CARREL *Man, the Unknown*

An aerial view of Pittsburgh, Pennsylvania

Comprehension

Give short answers to these questions in your own words as far as possible. Use one complete sentence for each answer.
a In what way is a modern factory similar to a large city?
b What, according to the author, led to the building of huge skyscrapers?
c What do those who enjoy living in cities fail to realize?

Vocabulary

Explain the meaning of the following words and phrases as they are used in the passage: physiological (ll. 1–2); neglected (l. 2); expanded (l. 5); artificial mode of existence (ll. 7–8); regard (l. 8); the maximum income (l. 10); construction (ll. 11–12); banal (l. 14); monstrous edifices (l. 15); toxic (l. 16); thronged ceaselessly by great crowds (ll. 17–18).

The Paragraph

1. Which of these statements best expresses the author's main argument? Give reasons for your choice:
a Modern cities have not been planned for the good of their inhabitants.
b Man is obsessed by the desire for profit.
c Great cities, like modern factories, impose on us an artificial way of life.
2. The following sentences are taken from lines 1–8. Arrange them in their correct order. Do not refer to the passage until you have finished the exercise:
Modern industry is based on the conception of the maximum production at lowest cost, in order that an individual or a group of individuals may earn as much money as possible. In the organization of industrial life the influence of the factory upon the physiological and mental state of the workers has been completely neglected. It has expanded without any idea of the true nature of the human beings who run the machines, and without giving any consideration to the effects produced on the individuals and on their descendants by the artificial mode of existence imposed by the factory.

Key Structures

1. Give the correct form of the verbs in brackets. Do not refer to the passage until you have finished the exercise:
In the organization of industrial life the influence of the factory upon the physiological and mental state of the workers completely (neglect). Modern industry (base) on the conception of the maximum production at lowest cost, in order that an individual or a group of individuals may earn as much money as possible. It (expand) without any idea of the true nature of the human beings who (run) the machines, and without (give) any consideration to the effect produced on the individuals and on their descendants by the artificial mode of existence imposed by the factory. The great cities (build) with no regard for us. (ll. 1–9)
2. Study the pattern in italics in this sentence:
Modern industry is based on the conception of the maximum production at lowest cost, *in order that an individual or a group of individuals may* (or *might*) earn as much money as possible. (ll. 2–5)
Complete the following sentences:
a He is attending English classes in order that . . .
b She works very hard in order that . . .
c The Prime Minister has gone abroad in order that . . .

3. Note the phrase in italics: '. . . in order that an individual or a group of individuals may earn *as much money as possible*. (ll. 4–5)
Write sentences using the following phrases:
as many as possible; as far as possible; as few as possible; as little as possible.
4. Write sentences using the following expressions:
influence upon (l. 1); based on (l. 3); the true nature of (l. 5); mode of (l. 7); regard for (l. 8); depend on (l. 9); the necessity of (ll. 9–10); deprived of (l. 14); consist of (l. 15); full of (l. 16).
5. Compare these two sentences:
Instead of saying: Although they enjoy the comfort and banal luxury of their dwelling, they do not realize that they are deprived of the necessities of life.
We can say: While they enjoy the comfort and banal luxury of their dwelling, they do not realize that they are deprived of the necessities of life. (ll. 13–15)
Complete the following sentences:
a While we are less concerned . . .
b While modern cities have grown in size . . .
c While factory conditions have improved . . .

Special Difficulties

1. Write sentences to bring out the difference between the following pairs of words:
physiological (ll. 1–2), psychological; neglect (l. 2), ignore; modern (l. 2), contemporary; earn (l. 4), win; please (l. 11), beg; petrol (l. 16), benzine; inhabitants (l. 18), residents.
2. Note this use of *per* in the sense of *for each*:
'. . . the necessity of obtaining the maximum income *per* square foot of ground . . .'
(ll. 9–10)
Write sentences using the following expressions:
per mile; per hour; per person; per yard; per cent.
3. Explain the meaning of the verb *crowd* in these sentences:
a Large masses of human beings are *crowded* together. (ll. 12–13)
b When it began to rain, everyone *crowded* into the building.
c He *crowded* a lot of information into the last chapter.
4. What is the plural of the following words:
necessity; mass; bus; gas; lorry; taxi-cab; city.

Unit 3

INSTRUCTIONS TO THE STUDENT

Content

This Unit consists of ten passages followed by exercises on Comprehension, Vocabulary, the Paragraph, Key Structures and Special Difficulties.

Aim

To provide more advanced practice in paragraph construction.

How to Work

1. Read each passage carefully two or three times.
2. Answer the questions in the order in which they are given.

The Paragraph

All the exercises under this heading are based on the passage. The following types of exercise have been given:

1. Writing a list of points in note form to answer a question on the main ideas contained in part of the passage.
2. Enabling you to reconstruct in your own words a paragraph taken from the passage by providing you with the main ideas in note form.
3. Writing a short paragraph of your own on a subject which is in some way related to the passage.

21

In the early days of the settlement of Australia, enterprising settlers unwisely introduced the European rabbit. This rabbit had no natural enemies in the Antipodes, so that it multiplied with that promiscuous abandon characteristic of rabbits. It overran a whole continent. It caused devastation by burrowing and by devouring the herbage which might have maintained millions of sheep and cattle. Scientists discovered that this particular variety of rabbit (and apparently no other animal) was susceptible to a fatal virus disease, *myxomatosis*. By infecting animals and letting them loose in the burrows, local epidemics of this disease could be created. Later it was found that there was a type of mosquito which acted as the carrier of this disease and passed it on to the rabbits. So while the rest of the world was trying to get rid of mosquitoes, Australia was encouraging this one. It effectively spread the disease all over the continent and drastically reduced the rabbit population. It later became apparent that rabbits were developing a degree of resistance to this disease, so that the rabbit population was unlikely to be completely exterminated. There were hopes, however, that the problem of the rabbit would become manageable.

Ironically, Europe, which had bequeathed the rabbit as a pest to Australia, acquired this man-made disease as a pestilence. A French physician decided to get rid of the wild rabbits on his own estate and introduced *myxomatosis*. It did not, however, remain within the confines of his estate. It spread through France, where wild rabbits are not generally regarded as a pest but as a sport and a useful food supply, and it spread to Britain where wild rabbits are regarded as a pest

Rabbits drinking at a water-hole in Australia

but where domesticated rabbits, equally susceptible to the disease, are the basis of a profitable fur industry. The question became one of whether Man could con-
25 trol the disease he had invented.

RITCHIE CALDER Science Makes Sense

Comprehension

Answer these questions:
a Why is the rabbit regarded as a serious pest in Australia?
b Why did it prove impossible to exterminate rabbits completely in Australia?
c How was *myxomatosis* introduced to Europe?

Vocabulary

Explain the meaning of the following words and phrases as they are used in the passage: enterprising (l. 1); devastation (l. 4); burrowing (l. 4); devouring the herbage (l. 5); susceptible (l. 7); fatal (l. 7); epidemics (l. 8); drastically reduced (ll. 12–13); completely exterminated (l. 15); bequeathed (l. 17); the confines of his estate (l. 20); domesticated (l. 23).

The Paragraph

1. Drawing your information from the first paragraph (lines 1–16) write a list of points in note form to answer the following question: How did the rabbit overrun the continent of Australia, and what steps were taken to exterminate it?
2. Read the second paragraph again. (Lines 17–25). Then, using the list of points given below, reconstruct the paragraph in your own words as far as possible. Do not refer to the passage until you have finished the exercise.
a Australia acquired rabbit from Europe: a pest.
b Europe acquired from Australia *myxomatosis*: a pestilence.
c French physician introduced it—estate.
d It spread.
e France: rabbit not a pest; sport; food supply.
f Britain: rabbit: a pest; tame rabbits: fur industry.
g Could man control this artificial disease?
3. Write a paragraph of about 200 words on one of the following subjects:
a Pest control.
b The balance of nature.

Key Structures

1. Put the words in brackets in their correct position in these sentences. In many cases, more than one position is possible. Do not refer to the passage until you have finished the exercise:
a In the early days of the settlement of Australia, enterprising settlers introduced the European rabbit. (unwisely) (ll. 1–2)
b It was found that there was a type of mosquito which acted as the carrier of this disease and passed it on to the rabbits. (later) (ll. 9–10)
c It spread the disease all over the continent and reduced the rabbit population. (effectively, drastically) (ll. 12–13)
d It became apparent that rabbits were developing a degree of resistance to the disease, so that the rabbit population was unlikely to be exterminated. (later, completely) (ll. 13–15)

70

e Europe, which had bequeathed the rabbit as a pest to Australia, acquired this man-made disease as a pestilence. (ironically) (ll. 17–18)

2. Compare these two uses of *so that*:

a This rabbit had no natural enemies in the Antipodes, *so that* it multiplied with that promiscuous abandon characteristic of rabbits. (ll. 2–4)

b I went to Switzerland last winter *so that* I could do some skiing.

Write two sentences using *so that* in the ways shown above.

3. Note the form of the verbs in italics in this sentence:

So while the rest of the world *was trying* to get rid of mosquitoes, Australia *was encouraging* this one. (ll. 10–12)

Complete the following sentences:

a While Tom was doing his homework, his sister . . .

b While my wife was seeing to the evening meal, I . . .

4. Supply the missing words in this sentence. Do not refer to the passage until you have finished the exercise:

It spread through France, . . . wild rabbits are not generally regarded as a pest but as a sport and a useful food supply, and it spread to Britain . . . wild rabbits are regarded as a pest but . . . domesticated rabbits, equally susceptible to the disease, are the basis of a profitable fur industry. (ll. 20–24)

Special Difficulties

1. Write sentences to bring out the difference between the following pairs of words: discovered (l. 6), invented (l. 25); fatal (l. 7), fateful; disease (l. 7), decease; loose (l. 8), lose; apparent (l. 13), obvious; degree (l. 14), rank; acquired (l. 18), obtained; domesticated (l. 23), domestic; basis (l. 23), base.

2. Note the use of *early* in this phrase: in the *early* days (l. 1). Write sentences using the following phrases:

in the early hours; in the early years; at an early age.

3. Write sentences to illustrate the use of the following verbs: overrun (l. 4); overtake; overdo; overlook.

4. Compare the use of *spread* in these two sentences:

a It (the mosquito) effectively *spread* the disease all over the continent. (l. 12)

b It (the disease) *spread* through France. (l. 20)

Write two sentences to illustrate these uses of *spread*.

5. Note the spelling of this word: *manageable* (l. 16). Add *able* to the following words retaining or dropping the *e* where necessary: move; love; peace; knowledge; change; service; believe.

6. Note the use of *own* in this phrase: on his *own* estate. Write sentences using the following phrases: my own; on my own; of my own.

22

There has long been a superstition among mariners that porpoises will save drowning men by pushing them to the surface, or protect them from sharks by surrounding them in defensive formation. Marine Studio biologists have pointed out that, however intelligent they may be, it is probably a mistake to credit dol-
5   phins with any motive of life-saving. On the occasions when they have pushed to shore an unconscious human being they have much more likely done it out of curiosity or for sport, as in riding the bow waves of a ship. In 1928 some porpoises were photographed working like beavers to push ashore a waterlogged mattress. If, as has been reported, they have protected humans from sharks, it may have
10 been because curiosity attracted them and because the scent of a possible meal attracted the sharks. Porpoises and sharks are natural enemies. It is possible that upon such an occasion a battle ensued, with the sharks being driven away or killed.

Whether it be bird, fish or beast, the porpoise is intrigued with anything that
15 is alive. They are constantly after the turtles, the Ferdinands of marine life, who peacefully submit to all sorts of indignities. One young calf especially enjoyed raising a turtle to the surface with his snout and then shoving him across the tank like an aquaplane. Almost any day a young porpoise may be seen trying to turn a 300-pound sea turtle over by sticking his snout under the edge of his
20 shell and pushing up for dear life. This is not easy, and may require two porpoises working together. In another game, as the turtle swims across the oceanarium, the first porpoise swoops down from above and butts his shell with his belly.

Dolphins jumping at Marineland in California

This knocks the turtle down several feet. He no sooner recovers his equilibrium
than the next porpoise comes along and hits him another crack. Eventually the
25 turtle has been butted all the way down to the floor of the tank. He is now satisfied merely to try to stand up, but as soon as he does so a porpoise knocks him
flat. The turtle at last gives up by pulling his feet under his shell and the game
is over.

RALPH NADING HILL *Window in the Sea*

Comprehension

Answer these questions:
a Name one outstanding quality which porpoises possess.
b Why do you think that the author refers to turtles as 'the Ferdinands of marine
life'? (l. 15)

Vocabulary

Explain the meaning of the following words and phrases as they are used in the passage:
superstition (l. 1); in defensive formation (l. 3); motive (l. 5); waterlogged (l. 8);
ensued (l. 12); intrigued (l. 14); constantly (l. 15); shoving (l. 17); sticking his snout
(l. 19); butts (l. 22); recovers his equilibrium (l. 23).

The Paragraph

1. Drawing your information from the second paragraph (lines 14–28) write a list of
points in note form to answer the following question: How does the author prove that
the porpoise is intrigued with anything alive?
2. Read the first paragraph again. (Lines 1–13). Then, using the list of points given
below, reconstruct the paragraph in your own words as far as possible. Do not refer to
the passage until you have finished the exercise:
a Superstition among mariners.
b Porpoises will save drowning men or protect them—sharks.
c Marine Studio biologists: probably not true.
d Done out of curiosity or for sport.
e E.g. pushing a mattress to the shore.
f Saving men from sharks: porpoises and sharks: natural enemies.
3. Write a paragraph of about 200 words on one of the following subjects:
a Dolphins.
b Intelligence in animals.

Key Structures

1. Supply the correct form of the verbs in brackets in the following paragraph. Do not
refer to the passage until you have finished the exercise:
There has long been a superstition among mariners that porpoises (save) drowning
men by (push) them to the surface, or (protect) them from sharks by (surround) them
in defensive formation. Marine Studio biologists (point) out that, however intelligent
they may be, it (be) probably a mistake to credit dolphins with any motive of life-
saving. On the occasions when they (push) to shore an unconscious human being they
much more likely (do) it out of curiosity or for sport, as in (ride) the bow waves of a
ship. In 1928 some porpoises (photograph) (work) like beavers to push ashore a waterlogged mattress. If, as (report), they (protect) humans from sharks, it may have been

because curiosity (attract) them and because the scent of a possible meal (attract) the sharks. Porpoises and sharks (be) natural enemies. It (be) possible that upon such an occasion as battle (ensue) with the sharks (drive) away or (kill). (ll. 1–13)

2. Note the form of the verb used after *enjoyed* in this sentence: One young calf especially enjoyed *raising* a turtle to the surface . . . (ll. 16–17)

Complete the following sentences using the construction given above:

a I can't remember . . .

b You should avoid . . .

c Will you stop . . .

d Fancy . . .

e I can't imagine him . . .

f Pardon my . . .

3. Study the following sentence:

He *no sooner* recovers his equilibrium *than* the next porpoise comes along and hits him another crack. (ll. 23–24)

Write a sentence using the phrase *no sooner . . . than*.

Special Difficulties

1. Write sentences to bring out the difference between the following pairs of words: drown (l. 2), choke; unconscious (l. 6), insensitive; curiosity (l. 7), strangeness; indignity (l. 16), disrespect; raise (l. 17), rise; game (l. 21), play; eventually (l. 24), finally.

2. Explain the meaning of the words in italics:

a They have much more *likely* done it out of curiosity or for sport. (ll. 6–7)

b It's rather *unlikely* that he will come now.

c That's a *likely* story, I must say.

d He's a *likely* person. I'm sure he'll help you.

3. Note the verb in italics:

A battle ensued with the sharks being *driven away* or killed. (ll. 12–13)

Write sentences using the following expressions idiomatically: drive off; drive out; drive back; drive up.

4. Explain the verbs in italics:

a They *are* constantly *after* the turtles. (l. 15)

b The game *is over*. (ll. 27–28)

c You can't see him now. *He's out*.

d When will he *be back*?

e Our team will not be playing next week. The match *is off*.

f The fire *is out*.

g *What's on* at the Regal today?

5. Explain the meaning of the verb in italics:

The turtle at last *gives up* by pulling his feet under his shell. (l. 27)

Write sentences using the following expressions:

give oneself up; give off; give back.

23

It is fairly clear that the sleeping period must have some function, and because there is so much of it the function would seem to be important. Speculations about its nature have been going on for literally thousands of years, and one odd finding that makes the problem puzzling is that it looks very much as if sleeping
5 is not simply a matter of giving the body a rest. 'Rest', in terms of muscle relaxation and so on, can be achieved by a brief period lying, or even sitting down. The body's tissues are self-repairing and self-restoring to a degree, and function best when more or less continuously active. In fact a basic amount of movement occurs during sleep which is specifically concerned with preventing muscle inactivity.
10   If it is not a question of resting the body, then perhaps it is the brain that needs resting? This might be a plausible hypothesis were it not for two factors. First the electroencephalograph (which is simply a device for recording the electrical activity of the brain by attaching electrodes to the scalp) shows that while there is a change in the pattern of activity during sleep, there is no evidence that the
15 total amount of activity is any less. The second factor is more interesting and more fundamental. In 1960 an American psychiatrist named William Dement published experiments dealing with the recording of eye-movements during sleep. He showed that the average individual's sleep cycle is punctuated with peculiar bursts of eye-movements, some drifting and slow, others jerky and rapid.
20 People woken during these periods of eye-movements generally reported that they had been dreaming. When woken at other times they reported no dreams. If one group of people were disturbed from their eye-movement sleep for several

An encephalograph in use

nights on end, and another group were disturbed for an equal period of time but
when they were not exhibiting eye-movements, the first group began to show
25 some personality disorders while the others seemed more or less unaffected. The
implications of all this were that it was not the disturbance of sleep that mattered,
but the disturbance of dreaming.

CHRISTOPHER EVANS *The Stuff of Dreams* from *The Listener*

Comprehension

Answer these questions:
a How does the author disprove the idea that we sleep in order to rest our muscles?
b What is the relationship between eye-movements during sleep and dreaming?

Vocabulary

Explain the meaning of the following words and phrases as they are used in the passage:
function (l. 2); speculations (l. 2); specifically (l. 9); plausible hypothesis (l. 11);
evidence (l. 14); fundamental (l. 16); punctuated (l. 18); jerky and rapid (l. 19); implications (l. 26).

The Paragraph

1. Drawing your information from the second paragraph (lines 10–27) write a list of
points in note form to answer the following question: What appears to be the main
function of the sleeping period?
2. Read the first paragraph again. (Lines 1–9). Then, using the list of points given
below, reconstruct the paragraph in your own words as far as possible. Do not refer to
the passage until you have finished the exercise:
a We sleep a great deal: sleep must have a function.
b Problem has puzzled mankind thousands of years.
c Purpose of sleep is not to give the body a rest.
d We do not have to sleep to relax the muscles: this can be done by lying or sitting down
for short periods.
e Body tissues function best when muscles are active.
f Movement occurs during sleep to prevent muscle inactivity.
3. Write a paragraph of about 200 words on one of the following subjects:
a Briefly describe a dream you had and attempt to interpret it.
b Sleep.

Key Structures

1. Supply the missing words in the following sentences. Do not refer to the passage
until you have finished the exercise:
a Speculations . . . its nature have been going on . . . literally thousands . . . years.
(ll. 2–3)
b In fact a basic amount . . . movement occurs . . . sleep which is specifically concerned
. . . preventing muscle inactivity. (ll. 8–9)
c . . . 1960 an American psychiatrist named William Dement published experiments
dealing . . . the recording . . . eye-movements . . . sleep. (ll. 16–18)
d One group . . . people were disturbed . . . their eye-movement sleep . . . several
nights . . . end, and another group were disturbed . . . an equal period . . . time. (ll.
22–23)

2. Note the use of *for* in this sentence:
Speculations about its nature have been going on *for* literally thousands of years. (ll. 2–3)
Supply *for* or *since* in the following sentences:
a He has been going to work regularly . . . he recovered from his illness.
b They have been working overtime . . . several months.
c The election results have been coming in steadily . . . midnight.
d She's been working on her novel . . . the beginning of the year.
3. Study this sentence:
Perhaps it is the brain that needs resting. (ll. 10–11)
Write similar sentences using the verbs *want* or *need* with the following words: cleaning; mending; decorating.
4. Compare these two sentences:
Instead of saying : This might be a plausible hypothesis *were it not* for two factors. (l. 11)
We can say : This might be a plausible hypothesis *if it were* not for two factors.
Rewrite the following sentences using *if*:
a Were it possible, I would leave tomorrow.
b I would take action at once were it not too late.
c Were this allegation true, he would be arrested.

Special Difficulties

1. Write sentences to bring out the difference between the following pairs of words: fairly (l. 1), enough; puzzling (l. 4), confusing; a rest (l. 5), the rest; continuously (l. 8), continually; device (l. 12), devise; factor (l. 15), fact; interesting (l. 15), interested.
2. Explain the meaning of the verbs in italics in these sentences:
a William Dement published experiments *dealing with* the recording of eye-movements. (ll. 16–17)
b We have been *dealing with* the same firm for a number of years.
c He's an extremely difficult child. His father is the only person who knows how to *deal with* him.
3. Explain the meaning of the phrases in italics in these sentences:
a One group of people were disturbed from their eye-movement sleep for several nights *on end*. (ll. 22–23)
b It wasn't an accident. That window was broken *on purpose*.
c *On the whole*, business has been very good this year.
d The doctor's very tired. He's been *on duty* for fourteen hours.
e How many soldiers are *on leave?*
f You mustn't open the door *on any account* when I'm out.
g It's getting late. I must be *on my way*.

24

Walking for walking's sake may be as highly laudable and exemplary a thing as it is held to be by those who practise it. My objection to it is that it stops the brain. Many a man has professed to me that his brain never works so well as when he is swinging along the high road or over hill and dale. This boast is not
5 confirmed by my memory of anybody who on a Sunday morning has forced me to partake of his adventure. Experience teaches me that whatever a fellow-guest may have of power to instruct or to amuse when he is sitting in a chair, or standing on a hearth-rug, quickly leaves him when he takes one out for a walk. The ideas that come so thick and fast to him in any room, where are they now? where
10 that encyclopaedic knowledge which he bore so lightly? where the kindling fancy that played like summer lightning over *any* topic that was started? The man's face that was so mobile is set now; gone is the light from his fine eyes. He says that A (our host) is a thoroughly good fellow. Fifty yards further on, he adds that A is one of the best fellows he has ever met. We tramp another furlong or so,
15 and he says that Mrs A is a charming woman. Presently he adds that she is one of the most charming women he has ever known. We pass an inn. He reads vapidly aloud to me: 'The King's Arms. Licensed to sell Ales and Spirits.' I foresee that during the rest of the walk he will read aloud any inscription that occurs. We pass a milestone. He points at it with his stick, and says 'Uxminster.
20 11 Miles.' We turn a sharp corner at the foot of the hill. He points at the wall, and says 'Drive Slowly.' I see far ahead, on the other side of the hedge bordering the high road, a small notice-board. He sees it too. He keeps his eye on it. And in due course 'Trespassers,' he says, 'will be Prosecuted.' Poor man!—mentally a wreck.

MAX BEERBOHM *Going Out for a Walk*

Going for a walk

Comprehension

Explain in a sentence the purpose of the examples given by the author in lines 11–23 ('The man's face . . . Prosecuted').

Vocabulary

Explain the meaning of the following words and phrases as they are used in the passage: laudable (l. 1); professed (l. 3); confirmed (l. 5); partake (l. 6); thick and fast (l. 9); encyclopaedic (l. 10); kindling fancy (l. 10); vapidly (l. 17); inscription (l. 18); bordering (l. 21); in due course (l. 23); trespassers (l. 23).

The Paragraph

1. Drawing your information from lines 11–23 ('The man's face . . . Prosecuted.') write a list of points in note form to answer the following question: What effect did walking have on the author's friend?

2. Note that the style of writing in the essay by Max Beerbohm is humorous and satirical. The paragraph given below is taken from a composition entitled *On not climbing mountains* and is written in the same style. In about 200 words, write the paragraph that might have preceded this one:

Another equally unsatisfactory reason for climbing mountains is the desire to see the view. There is no doubt that the sight of snow-capped peaks and rugged scenery is impressive, but what climber is ever in a position to appreciate this as he sags under a heavy load of equipment? He is too busy fighting exhaustion to notice anything but the marks he makes in the snow as he wearily plods towards the summit. Even the most insensitive tourist is in a better position to enjoy mountain scenery—providing he has been sensible enough to make use of a ski-lift or funicular railway which provides a maximum of safety, speed and comfort.

Key Structures

1. Compare these two sentences:
Instead of saying: It is possible that walking for walking's sake *is* as highly laudable and exemplary a thing as it is held to be by those who practise it.
We can say: Walking for walking's sake *may be* (or *might be*) as highly laudable and exemplary a thing it is held to be by those who practise it. (ll. 1–2)
Write three sentences using *may* or *might* in the same way.

2. Study the words in italics in this sentence:
My objection to it is that it stops the brain. (ll. 2–3)
Complete the following sentences:
a My feeling about it is that . . .
b His view is that . . .
c Her impression is that . . .

3. Compare these two expressions:
Instead of saying: Many men have professed to me . . .
We can say: Many a man has professed to me . . . (l. 3)
Write sentences using the following phrases:
many a time; many a mile; many an hour.

4. Note the word in italics in the following:
'. . . *whatever* a fellow-guest may have of power to instruct . . .' (ll. 6–7)
Similar emphatic compounds can be formed with *why, how, when, where, who,* and *which*. Supply a suitable form with *-ever* in the following sentences:
a . . . happens, you must not agree to his terms.
b . . . did he do a thing like that?

c . . . did you learn that I arrived yesterday?
d Choose . . . one you like best.
e He gets terribly upset . . . he makes a mistake.
f . . . could believe a thing like that!
5. Note that the words *knowledge* (l. 10) and *lighting* (l. 11) have no plural. Write sentences using the following words: luggage, information, machinery, thunder, progress, advice.
6. Note how in lines 12–23 ('He says that A . . . Prosecuted.') the present tense has been used to describe vividly an occurrence that took place in the past. Write three or four sentences to continue this paragraph opening:
We stop at a village inn and I ask him if he would like a drink. He says that he never drinks. However, he agrees to accompany me to the bar. We both . . .

Special Difficulties

1. Write sentences to bring out the difference between the following pairs of words: objection (l. 2), objective; brain (l. 3), mind; confirm (l. 5), assure; topic (l. 11), local; charming (l. 15), enchanting; presently (l. 15), immediately; aloud (l. 17), allowed; license (l. 17), licence; ahead (l. 21), in front of; hedge (l. 21), fence.
2. Note the words in italics in the following sentences. Use these words again in sentences of your own, giving each word a different meaning from the one it has in the example:
a Where the *kindling* fancy that played like summer lightning over any topic that was started? (ll. 10–11)
b Gone is the *light* from his fine eyes. (l. 12)
c He says that A (our host) is a *thoroughly* good fellow. (ll. 12–13)
d Poor man!—mentally a *wreck*. (ll. 23–24)
3. Explain the meaning of the word *set* in these sentences:
a The man's face that was so mobile is *set* now. (ll. 11–12)
b The sun has *set*.
c He'll never change now. He's so *set* in his ways.
d Will you *set* the table please?
e Has that jelly *set* yet?
f Get *set*, ready, go!
4. Note the use of *fore* in this word:
I *foresee* that during the rest of the walk . . . (ll. 17–18)
Write sentences using the following words: forewarn; foretell; forecast; forebode.

25

How it came about that snakes manufactured poison is a mystery. Over the periods their saliva, a mild, digestive juice like our own, was converted into a poison that defies analysis even today. It was not forced upon them by the survival competition; they could have caught and lived on prey without using poison just as the thousands of non-poisonous snakes still do. Poison to a snake is merely a luxury; it enables it to get its food with very little effort, no more effort than one bite. And why only snakes? Cats, for instance, would be greatly helped; no running fights with large, fierce rats or tussles with grown rabbits— just a bite and no more effort needed. In fact, it would be an assistance to all the carnivorae—though it would be a two-edged weapon when they fought each other. But, of the vertebrates, unpredictable Nature selected only snakes (and one lizard). One wonders also why Nature, with some snakes concocted poison of such extreme potency.

In the conversion of saliva into poison one might suppose that a fixed process took place. It did not; some snakes manufactured a poison different in every respect from that of others, as different as arsenic is from strychnine, and having different effects. One poison acts on the nerves, the other on the blood.

The makers of the nerve poison include the mambas and the cobras and their venom is called neurotoxic. Vipers (adders) and rattlesnakes manufacture the blood poison, which is known as haemolytic. Both poisons are unpleasant, but by far the more unpleasant is the blood poison. It is said that the nerve poison is the more primitive of the two, that the blood poison is, so to speak, a newer

An Indian grass snake swallowing a frog

product from an improved formula. Be that as it may, the nerve poison does its
business with man far more quickly than the blood poison. This, however, means
25 nothing. Snakes did not acquire their poison for use against man but for use
against prey such as rats and mice, and the effects on these of viperine poison is
almost immediate.

JOHN CROMPTON *The Snake*

Comprehension

Answer these questions:
a Why does the author find it odd that snakes should be capable of manufacturing
poison?
b What is the difference between neurotoxic and haemolytic poison?

Vocabulary

Explain the meaning of the following words and phrases as they are used in the passage:
mild (l. 2); converted (l. 2); defies analysis (l. 3); the survival competition (ll. 3–4);
carnivorae (l. 10); a two-edged weapon (l. 10); concocted (l. 12); extreme potency
(l. 13); viperine (l. 26).

The Paragraph

1. Drawing your information from the first paragraph (lines 1–13) write a list of points
in note form to answer the following question: Why is the author justified in stating
that Nature behaved in an unpredictable way in allowing snakes to manufacture
poison?
2. Read the last paragraph again. (Lines 18–27). Then, using the list of points given
below, reconstruct the paragraph in your own words as far as possible. Do not refer
to the passage until you have finished the exercise.
a Nerve poison (e.g. mambas): neurotoxic.
b Blood poison (e.g. vipers): haemolytic.
c Blood poison the more unpleasant.
d Nerve poison possibly the more primitive.
e Blood poison a later development.
f But nerve poison acts more quickly on man.
g Purpose of poison: not against man, but snake's prey: e.g. rats.
3. Write a paragraph of about 200 words on one of the following subjects:
a Our fear of snakes.
b The survival competition.

Key Structures

1. Compare these two sentences:
Instead of saying: They had the ability to catch and live on prey without using poison if
they wanted to (but they didn't).
We can say: They could have caught and lived on prey without using poison. (ll. 4–5)
Write sentences using the following expressions:
could have succeeded; could have stayed; could have bought.
2. Write sentences using the following expressions:
force upon (l. 3); live on (l. 4); conversion into (l. 14); different from (ll. 15–16); act on
(l. 17); effect on (l. 26).

3. Compare these two sentences:
Instead of saying: They could have caught and lived on prey without using poison just as the thousands of non-poisonous snakes still *catch and live on prey without using poison.*
We can say: They could have caught and lived on prey without using poison just as the thousands of non-poisonous snakes still *do.* (ll. 4–5)
Complete the following sentences by adding the correct form of *do*:
a Even though he has retired, he still gets up early just as he always . . .
b He certainly enjoys music as much as you . . .
c If you act as he . . . you won't be very popular.
4. Study the following sentence:
Both poisons are unpleasant, but by far *the more unpleasant* is the blood poison. (ll. 20–21)
Why is *the more* used here and not *the most*?
Write two sentences using *the more* and *the most.*
5. Note how the word *far* has been added for emphasis in this sentence: Nerve poison does its business . . . *far more quickly* than . . . (ll. 23–24)
The word *much* may be used in the same way. We can say *much more quickly,* using *much* in an emphatic way. Write sentences using the following phrases: much more expensive; far more difficult; far less exciting; much less interesting.

Special Difficulties

1. Write sentences to bring out the difference between the following pairs of words: merely (l. 6), only; fierce (l. 8), furious; wonder (l. 12), wander; take place (l. 15), take part; prey (l. 26), pray.
2. Explain the verbs in italics in the following:
a How it *came about* that snakes manufacture poison is a mystery. (l. 1)
b I'm sorry I said that. I don't know what *came over* me.
c He *came up with* some very interesting ideas.
d I *came across* an old friend of yours while I was abroad.
3. Write sentences using the following words and phrases: enable (l. 6); running fights (l. 8); in fact (l. 9); in every respect (ll. 15–16); so to speak (l. 22); be that as it may (l. 23).
4. Supply full stops and commas where necessary in the following paragraph. Do not refer to the passage until you have finished the exercise:
The makers of the nerve poison include the mambas and the cobras and their venom is called neurotoxic vipers (adders) and rattlesnakes manufacture the blood poison which is known as haemolytic both poisons are unpleasant but by far the more unpleasant is the blood poison it is said that the nerve poison is the more primitive of the two that the blood poison is so to speak a newer product from an improved formula be that as it may the nerve poison does its business with man far more quickly than the blood poison this however means nothing snakes did not acquire their poison for use against man but for use against prey such as rats and mice and the effects on these of viperine poison is almost immediate. (ll. 18–27)

26

William S. Hart was, perhaps, the greatest of all Western stars, for unlike Gary
Cooper and John Wayne he appeared in nothing but Westerns. From 1914 to
1924 he was supreme and unchallenged. It was Hart who created the basic
formula of the Western film, and devised the protagonist he played in every film
5 he made, the good-bad man, the accidental, noble outlaw, or the honest but
framed cowboy, or the sheriff made suspect by vicious gossip; in short, the individual in conflict with himself and his frontier environment.

Unlike most of his contemporaries in Hollywood, Hart actually knew something of the old West. He had lived in it as a child when it was already disappear-
10 ing, and his hero was firmly rooted in his memories and experiences, and in both
the history and the mythology of the vanished frontier. And although no period
or place in American history has been more absurdly romanticized, myth and
reality did join hands in at least one arena, the conflict between the individual
and encroaching civilization.

15 Men accustomed to struggling for survival against the elements and Indians
were bewildered by politicians, bankers and business-men, and unhorsed by
fences, laws and alien taboos. Hart's good-bad man was always an outsider,
always one of the disinherited, and if he found it necessary to shoot a sheriff or
rob a bank along the way, his early audiences found it easy to understand and
20 forgive, especially when it was Hart who, in the end, overcame the attacking
Indians.

Audiences in the second decade of the twentieth century found it pleasant to

William S. Hart in an early Western

escape to a time when life, though hard, was relatively simple. We still do; living
in a world in which undeclared aggression, war, hypocrisy, chicanery, anarchy
5 and impending immolation are part of our daily lives, we all want a code to
live by.

CARL FOREMAN Virtue and a Fast Gun from The Observer

Comprehension

Answer these questions:
a What, according to the writer, is the basic formula of the Western film?
b How did the spread of civilization affect the old West?
c Why have Western films appealed so much to twentieth-century audiences?

Vocabulary

Explain the meaning of the following words and phrases as they are used in the passage:
supreme (l. 3); devised the protagonist (l. 4); framed (l. 6); in conflict (l. 7); environment (l. 7); contemporaries (l. 8); firmly rooted (l. 10); encroaching (l. 14); bewildered
(l. 16); impending immolation (l. 25).

The Paragraph

1. Drawing your information from the first three paragraphs (lines 1–21) write a list
of points in note form to answer the following question: With what justification can
the claim be made that William S. Hart was, perhaps, the greatest of all Western stars?
2. Read the fourth paragraph again. (Lines 22–26). Then, using the list of points given
below, reconstruct the paragraph in your own words as far as possible. Do not refer to
the passage until you have finished the exercise:
a Audiences—2nd decade 20th century—escape: appeal of hard and simple life.
b We still do: world of aggression, hypocrisy—want a code to live by.
3. Write a paragraph of about 200 words on one of the following subjects:
a A short appreciation of any actor or actress who took part in a Western film you have
seen.
b Westerns.

Key Structures

1. Which words could be omitted from the following sentences without affecting the
sense of the original? Do not refer to the passage until you have finished the exercise:
a It was Hart who created the basic formula of the Western film, and devised the
protagonist whom he played in every film which he made, the good-bad man, the
accidental, noble outlaw, or the honest but framed cowboy, or the sheriff who has been
made suspect by vicious gossip; in short, the individual who is in conflict with himself
and with his frontier environment. (ll. 3–7)
b Men who had been accustomed to struggling for survival against the elements and
Indians were bewildered by politicians, bankers and business-men. (ll. 15–16)
2. Compare these sentences:
Instead of saying: He appeared *only* in Westerns.
We can say: He appeared in *nothing but* Westerns. (l. 2)
Or: He *did not appear* in *anything but* Westerns.
Write three sentences using the phrase *nothing but*.
3. Supply *a* or *the* where necessary in the following paragraph. Do not refer to the
passage until you have finished the exercise:

Unlike . . . most of . . . his contemporaries in . . . Hollywood, . . . Hart actually knew something of . . . old West. He had lived in it as . . . child when it was already disappearing, and . . . his hero was firmly rooted in . . . his memories and . . . experiences, and in both . . . history and . . . mythology of . . . vanished frontier. And although no period or place in . . . American history has been more absurdly romanticized, . . . myth and . . . reality did join hands in at least one arena, . . . conflict between . . . individual and . . . encroaching civilization. (ll. 8–14)

4. Note the form of the verb in this sentence:

Myth and reality *did join* hands in at least one arena. (ll. 12–13)

We use this form when we wish to place particular emphasis on the verb.

Write these sentences again using this emphatic verb form:

a I *mentioned* it to him but he wasn't impressed.

b You *posted* my letter, didn't you?

c We *enjoyed* ourselves at the party.

5. Compare these two uses of *though*:

Life, *though* (even if it was) hard, was relatively simple. (l. 23)

I wish you had told me *though*. (however)

Write two sentences using *though* in the ways shown above.

6. Compare these two sentences:

Instead of saying : We all want a code *by which to live.*

We can say : We all want a code *to live by.* (ll. 25–26)

Write sentences which end with the following expressions:

to fight for; to talk about; to act on; to work with.

Special Difficulties

1. Write sentences to bring out the difference between the following pairs of words: appear (l. 2), seem; devise (l. 4), device; suspect (l. 6), suspicious; memory (l. 10), remembrance; history (l. 11), story; rob (l. 19), steal; especially (l. 20), specially.

2. Note this use of *unlike*:

Unlike Gary Cooper and John Wayne he appeared in nothing but Westerns (ll. 1–2)

Complete the following sentences in any way you wish:

a Unlike most of his contemporaries . . . (l. 8)

b Unlike some people . . .

c Unlike yourself . . .

3. Write sentences using the following phrases:

in short (l. 6); in conflict with (l. 7); at least (l. 13); in the end (l. 20).

27

Why does the idea of progress loom so large in the modern world? Surely because progress of a particular kind is actually taking place around us and is becoming more and more manifest. Although mankind has undergone no general improvement in intelligence or morality, it has made extraordinary progress in
5 the accumulation of knowledge. Knowledge began to increase as soon as the thoughts of one individual could be communicated to another by means of speech. With the invention of writing, a great advance was made, for knowledge could then be not only communicated but also stored. Libraries made education possible, and education in its turn added to libraries: the growth of knowledge
10 followed a kind of compound-interest law, which was greatly enhanced by the invention of printing. All this was comparatively slow until, with the coming of science, the *tempo* was suddenly raised. Then knowledge began to be accumulated according to a systematic plan. The trickle became a stream; the stream has now become a torrent. Moreover, as soon as new knowledge is acquired, it
15 is now turned to practical account. What is called 'modern civilization' is not the result of a balanced development of all man's nature, but of accumulated knowledge applied to practical life. The problem now facing humanity is: What is going to be done with all this knowledge? As is so often pointed out, knowledge is a two-edged weapon which can be used equally for good or evil. It is now being
20 used indifferently for both. Could any spectacle, for instance, be more grimly

American doctors remove a live grenade from the back of a South Vietnamese farmer. Saigon, 1966

whimsical than that of gunners using science to shatter men's bodies while, close. at hand, surgeons use it to restore them? We have to ask ourselves very seriously what will happen if this twofold use of knowledge, with its ever-increasing power, continues.

G. N. M. TYRRELL *The Personality of Man*

Comprehension

Answer these questions:
a How does the author define the word 'progress'?
b How was the spread of knowledge affected by the coming of science?
c What problem has the spread of knowledge given rise to?

Vocabulary

Explain the meaning of the following words and phrases as they are used in the passage: loom so large (l. 1); manifest (l. 3); accumulation (l. 5); enhanced (l. 10); indifferently (l. 20); spectacle (l. 20); grimly whimsical (ll. 20–21); twofold (l. 23).

The Paragraph

1. Drawing your information from lines 5–17 ('Knowledge began . . . practical life.') write a list of points in note form to answer the following question: How did the growth of knowledge follow 'a kind of compound-interest law'?
2. Read lines 17–24 again. ('The problem . . . continues.') Then, using the list of points given below, reconstruct the author's argument in your own words as far as possible. Do not refer to the passage until you have finished the exercise.
a Problem facing humanity: what to do with knowledge.
b Two-edged weapon: good and evil.
c Used for both.
d Ironical use of science. E.g. gunner—wounded men—surgeons.
e Where will this two-fold use lead?
3. Write a paragraph of about 200 words on one of the following subjects:
a Support the author's view that mankind has undergone no general improvement in intelligence or morality.
b Support the author's view that knowledge is a two-edged weapon.

Key Structures

1. Supply the correct form of the verbs in brackets in these sentences. Do not refer to the passage until you have finished the exercise:
a Knowledge began to increase as soon as the thoughts of one individual (can communicate) to another by means of speech. With the invention of writing, a great advance (make), for knowledge then not only (can communicate) but also (store). (ll. 5–8)
b The growth of knowledge followed a kind of compound-interest law, which greatly (enhance) by the invention of printing. All this was comparatively slow until, with the coming of science, the *tempo* suddenly (raise). Then knowledge began to (accumulate) according to a systematic plan. (ll. 9–13)
c Moreover, as soon as new knowledge (acquire), it now (turn) to practical account. (ll. 14–15)
d As so often (point) out, knowledge is a two-edged weapon which (can use) equally for good or evil. It now (use) indifferently for both. (ll. 18–20)

2. Study this sentence pattern:
Libraries *made education possible.* (ll. 8–9)
Write sentences using *make* in the same pattern with the following words: unnecessary; desirable; unrecognizable.
3. Compare these two sentences:
Instead of saying: The problem *which now faces* humanity . . .
We can say: The problem *now facing* humanity . . . (l. 17)
Complete the following sentences:
a People emigrating . . .
b All aeroplanes arriving . . .
c Ships sailing . . .
4. Compare the expressions in italics in these two sentences:
Instead of saying: What is called 'modern civilization' is not the result of a balanced development of all man's nature, but of accumulated *knowledge which has been applied* to practical life.
We can say: What is called 'modern civilization' is not the result of a balanced development of all man's nature, but of accumulated *knowledge applied* to practical life. (ll. 15–17)
Complete the following sentences:
a Photographs taken . . .
b Passports issued . . .
c Passengers delayed . . .

Special Difficulties

1. Write sentences to bring out the difference between the following pairs of words: surely (l. 1), certainly; extraordinary (l. 4), outstanding; printing (l. 11), typing; raise (l. 12), rise; spectacle (l. 20), view.
2. Write sentences using the following words and phrases:
more and more (l. 3); by means of (l. 6); in its turn (l. 9); a kind of (l. 10); comparatively (l. 11); according to (l. 13); at hand (l. 22).
3. What do you understand by the following metaphor:
The trickle became a stream; the stream has now become a torrent. (ll. 13–14)
4. Note the use of *ever-* in this phrase: its *ever-increasing* power. (ll. 23–24)
Write sentences using the following expressions:
ever-expanding; ever-changing; ever-diminishing.

28

No two sorts of birds practise quite the same sort of flight; the varieties are infinite; but two classes may be roughly seen. Any ship that crosses the Pacific is accompanied for many days by the smaller albatross, which may keep company with the vessel for an hour without visible or more than occasional movement of
5 wing. The currents of air that the walls of the ship direct upwards, as well as in the line of its course are enough to give the great bird with its immense wings sufficient sustenance and progress. The albatross is the king of the gliders, the class of fliers which harness the air to their purpose, but must yield to its opposition. In the contrary school the duck is supreme. It comes nearer to the engines
10 with which man has 'conquered' the air, as he boasts. Duck, and like them the pigeons, are endowed with steel-like muscles, that are a good part of the weight of the bird, and these will ply the short wings with irresistible power that they can bore for long distances through an opposite gale before exhaustion follows. Their humbler followers, such as partridges, have a like power of strong propul-
15 sion, but soon tire. You may pick them up in utter exhaustion, if wind over the sea has driven them to a long journey. The swallow shares the virtues of both schools in highest measure. It tires not nor does it boast of its power; but belongs to the air, travelling it may be six thousand miles to and from its northern nesting home feeding its flown young as it flies and slipping through a medium that
20 seems to help its passage even when the wind is adverse. Such birds do us good, though we no longer take omens from their flight on this side and that; and even the most superstitious villagers no longer take off their hats to the magpie and wish it good-morning.

WILLIAM BEACH THOMAS *A Countryman's Creed*

A flock of wild geese in flight

Comprehension

Answer these questions:
a Why is the albatross described as 'the king of the gliders'?
b Why does the author single out the swallow for special praise?

Vocabulary

Explain the meaning of the following words and phrases as they are used in the passage:
infinite (ll. 1–2); sufficient sustenance (l. 7); harness (l. 8); yield (l. 8); endowed (l. 11); irresistible power (l. 12); bore (l. 13); like (l. 14); utter (l. 15); adverse (l. 20); omens (l. 21).

The Paragraph

1. Drawing your information from lines 1–13 ('No two sorts . . . exhaustion follows.') write a list of points in note form to answer the following question: How does the flight of an albatross differ from that of a duck?
2. Read lines 16–23 again. ('The swallow shares . . . wish it good-morning.') Then, using the list of points given below, reconstruct the author's description in your own words as far as possible. Do not refer to the passage until you have finished the exercise.
a Swallow: the good qualities of both schools.
b Does not tire; has great power.
c Flies as much as 6,000 miles to and from nesting home.
d Feeds young in flight.
e Good progress in adverse conditions.
f Such birds do us good.
g No omens—even among superstitious villagers.
3. Write a paragraph of about 200 words on one of the following subjects:
a The power of flight.
b Birds.

Key Structures

1. Supply *a*, *an* or *the* where necessary in the following. Do not refer to the passage until you have finished the exercise:
No two sorts of . . . birds practise quite . . . same sort of . . . flight; . . . varieties are infinite; but . . . two classes may be roughly seen. Any ship that crosses . . . Pacific is accompanied for many days by . . . smaller albatross, which may keep company with . . . vessel for . . . hour without . . . visible or . . . more than occasional movement of . . . wing. . . . currents of . . . air that . . . walls of . . . ship direct upwards, as well as in . . . line of its course are enough to give . . . great bird with . . . its immense wings sufficient sustenance and . . . progress. . . . albatross is . . . king of . . . gliders, . . . class of . . . fliers which harness . . . air to their purpose, but must yield to its opposition. (ll. 1–9)
2. Note the form of the verbs in italics:
You *may pick* them up in utter exhaustion, if wind over the sea *has driven* them to a long journey. (ll. 15–16)
Complete the following sentences:
a If you have ever driven at a hundred miles an hour . . .
b If you have never been to New Zealand . . .
c If you have finished your work . . .
3. Supply the correct form of the verbs in brackets. Do not refer to the passage until you have finished the exercise:

The swallow (share) the virtues of both schools in highest measure. It (tire)* not nor (boast) of its power; but (belong) to the air, (travel) it may be six thousand miles to and from its northern nesting home (feed) its flown young as it (fly) and (slip) through a medium that (seem) to help its passage even when the wind (be) adverse. (ll. 16–20)

Special Difficulties

1. Write sentences to bring out the difference between the following pairs of words: practise (l. 1), practice; quite (l. 1), quiet; wing (l. 5), feather; course (l. 6), coarse; conquer (l. 10), defeat.

2. Note how the words *sort* and *kind* can be used in the singular and in the plural: No two *sorts* (or *kinds*) of *birds* practise quite the same *sort* (or *kind*) of *flight*. Write two sentences using the words *sort* and *sorts*.

3. Explain the meaning of *rough* and *roughly* in these sentences:
a Two classes may be *roughly* seen. (l. 2)
b The surface of this road is very *rough*.
c *Roughly* six hundred people attended the meeting.
d Last night the sea was very *rough*.

4. Write sentences using the following expressions:
keep company with (ll. 3–4); as well as (l. 5); take off their hats to (l. 22).

5. Note the use of *good* in this phrase: 'a *good* part of the weight of the bird' (ll. 11–12). Write sentences using the following phrases: a good fifteen minutes; a good twenty miles; a good five hundred people; a good many; a good few.

6. Note how *such as* may be used to introduce an example:
Their humbler followers, *such as* partridges . . . (l. 14)
Write two sentences using *such as* in this way.

7. Note the phrase *do us good* (l. 20). Which of the following words are used with *do* and which with *make*:
your duty; an excuse; a fortune; wrong; harm; an attempt; a bed; a proposal; sense; a speech; shopping; a problem; a lesson; a difference; a copy; an announcement; an agreement; work; a job; money; a mistake; a living; fun of; your best; business; an experiment; friends with; a favour; homework; trouble; sure; a will; a noise.
With which of the above words would it be possible to use either *do* or *make*?

8. Note the phrase: *wish it good-morning.* (l. 23)
Write sentences using the following phrases: wish me luck; wish me well; wish me good-night.

---

* The form given in the passage is archaic.

29

A young man sees a sunset and, unable to understand or to express the emotion that it rouses in him, concludes that it must be the gateway to a world that lies beyond. It is difficult for any of us in moments of intense aesthetic experience to resist the suggestion that we are catching a glimpse of a light that shines down
5 to us from a different realm of existence, different and, because the experience is intensely moving, in some way higher. And, though the gleams blind and dazzle, yet do they convey a hint of beauty and serenity greater than we have known or imagined. Greater too than we can describe; for language, which was invented to convey the meanings of this world, cannot readily be fitted to the uses of
10 another.

    That all great art has this power of suggesting a world beyond is undeniable. In some moods Nature shares it. There is no sky in June so blue that it does not point forward to a bluer, no sunset so beautiful that it does not waken the vision of a greater beauty, a vision which passes before it is fully glimpsed, and in
15 passing leaves an indefinable longing and regret. But, if this world is not merely a bad joke, life a vulgar flare amid the cool radiance of the stars, and existence an empty laugh braying across the mysteries; if these intimations of a something behind and beyond are not evil humour born of indigestion, or whimsies sent by the devil to mock and madden us, if, in a word, beauty means something, yet we
20 must not seek to interpret the meaning. If we glimpse the unutterable, it is unwise to try to utter it, nor should we seek to invest with significance that which we cannot grasp. Beauty in terms of our human meanings *is* meaningless.

C. E. M. JOAD *Pieces of Mind*

The Line of Beauty. A self portrait of
Hogarth (1697–1764) with his dog

Comprehension

Answer these questions:

a What, according to the author, have great art and certain moods of Nature in common?

b Why does the author feel that it is unwise to attempt to interpret beauty?

Vocabulary

Explain the meaning of the following words and phrases as they are used in the passage: rouses (l. 2); aesthetic (l. 3); realm (l. 5); moving (l. 6); convey (l. 7); indefinable longing (l. 15); radiance (l. 16); braying (l. 17); whimsies (l. 18); glimpse the unutterable (l. 20); invest with significance (l. 21).

The Paragraph

1. Drawing your information from the second paragraph (lines 11–22) write a list of points in note form to answer the following question: How does the author arrive at the conclusion that beauty in terms of our human meanings is meaningless?

2. Read the first paragraph again. (Lines 1–10). Then, using the list of points given below, reconstruct the author's argument in your own words as far as possible. Do not refer to the passage until you have finished the exercise:

a Effect of sunset on a young man: vision of another world.

b Aesthetic experiences: suggestion of the existence of a world in some way higher than our own.

c Hint of beauty and serenity we have never known.

d Impossible to describe: language ill-equipped.

3. Write a paragraph of about 200 words on one of the following subjects:

a What is beautiful to one individual is ugly to another.

b Beauty does have a meaning: it reflects the grandeur of God.

c Beauty has no meaning: it should be accepted for what it is.

d There is no such thing as 'beauty'. There are merely various phenomena, objects, etc. which we attempt to classify as 'beautiful', but this is a purely subjective evaluation on our part.

Key Structures

1. Compare the uses of *must* in these two sentences:

A young man sees a sunset and . . . concludes that it *must be* the gateway to a world that lies beyond. (ll. 1–3)

If . . . beauty means something . . . we *must not seek* to interpret the meaning. (ll. 19–20)

In which of the following sentences would it be possible to replace *must* by *has to*?

a I haven't seen Tom for some time; he *must* be ill.

b He *must* advertise for a new secretary now that Miss Perkins has left.

c He *must* stay in bed for at least a week.

d I'm afraid he *must* be mistaken.

2. Compare the use of *it is* and *there is* in these sentences:

It is difficult for any of us . . . to resist the suggestion. (ll. 3–4)

There is no sky in June so blue . . . (l. 12)

Supply *it* or *there* in the following sentences:

a . . . must have been after one o'clock when I arrived home.

b . . . must have been a large number of accidents over the Christmas holidays.

c You might be asked to make a speech, but I think . . . is highly unlikely.

d . . . will be difficult to dissuade him now that he has made up his mind.

e . . . will be difficult times ahead.

3. Compare these two sentences:

Instead of saying : It is undeniable that all great art has this power of suggesting a world beyond.

We can say : That all great art has this power of suggesting a world beyond is undeniable. (l. 11)

Write these sentences again so that each one begins with *That*.

a It is unbelievable that he wrote this story himself.

b It is astonishing to me that you should believe this to be true.

c It is quite true that we all feel depressed sometimes.

4. Complete the following sentence in any way you wish. Then compare what you have written with the sentence in the passage:

If we glimpse the unutterable . . . (l. 20)

Special Difficulties

1. Write sentences to bring out the difference between the following pairs of words: unable (l. 1), enable; rouse (l. 2), raise; lie (l. 2), lay; fit (l. 9), suit; indefinable (l. 15), undefined; vulgar (l. 16), common.

2. Note the words in italics in the following sentences. Use these words again in sentences of your own, giving each word a different meaning from the one it has in the example:

a A young man sees a sunset and . . . *concludes* that it must be the gateway to a world that lies beyond. (ll. 1–3)

b It is difficult for any of us in moments of intense aesthetic *experience* to resist the suggestion that we are catching a glimpse of a light that shines down to us from a different realm of existence. (ll. 3–5)

c And *though* the gleams blind and dazzle, yet do they convey a hint of beauty. (ll. 6–7)

d Nor should we seek to *invest* with significance that which we cannot *grasp*. (ll. 21–22)

e Beauty in *terms* of our human meanings is meaningless. (l. 22)

3. Note the use of *fully* in this phrase

'. . . before it is *fully* glimpsed'. (l. 14)

Write sentences using the following expressions:

fully realize; fully capable; explain fully.

4. Write sentences using the following phrases:

catch a glimpse (l. 4); in some way (l. 6); seek to (l. 21).

30

Each civilization is born, it culminates, and it decays. There is a widespread
testimony that this ominous fact is due to inherent biological defects in the
crowded life of cities. Now, slowly and at first faintly, an opposite tendency is
showing itself. Better roads and better vehicles at first induced the wealthier
5 classes to live on the outskirts of the cities. The urgent need for defence had also
vanished. This tendency is now spreading rapidly downwards. But a new set of
conditions is just showing itself. Up to the present time, throughout the eighteenth
and nineteenth centuries, this new tendency placed the home in the immediate
suburbs, but concentrated manufacturing activity, business relations, govern-
10 ment, and pleasure in the centres of the cities. Apart from the care of children
and periods of sheer rest, the active lives were spent in the cities. In some ways
the concentration of such activities was even more emphasized, and the homes
were pushed outwards even at the cost of the discomfort of commuting. But, if
we examine the trend of technology during the past generation, the reasons for
15 this concentration are largely disappearing. Still more, the reasons for the choice
of sites for cities are also altering. Mechanical power can be transmitted for
hundreds of miles, men can communicate almost instantaneously by telephone,
the chiefs of great organizations can be transported by airplanes, the cinemas can
produce plays in every village, music, speeches, and sermons can be broadcast.
20 Almost every reason for the growth of cities, concurrently with the growth of
civilization has been profoundly modified.

A. N. WHITEHEAD *Adventures of Ideas*

A traffic jam in the Place de la Concorde, Paris

Comprehension

Answer these questions:
a State two ways in which cities today differ from those of the past.
b State briefly why the reasons for the choice of sites for cities are altering.

Vocabulary

Explain the meaning of the following words and phrases as they are used in the passage:
culminates (l. 1); widespread testimony (ll. 1–2); inherent biological defects (l. 2); induced (l. 4); immediate suburbs (ll. 8–9); the discomfort of commuting (l. 13); sites (l. 16); transmitted (l. 16); instantaneously (l. 17); concurrently (l. 20); profoundly modified (l. 21).

The Paragraph

1. Drawing your information from lines 3–15 ('Now, slowly ... are largely disappearing.') write a list of points in note form to answer the following question: How has the pattern of life in cities slowly changed during the last three centuries?
2. Read lines 15–21 again. ('Still more, ... profoundly modified.') Then, using the list of points given below, reconstruct the author's argument in your own words as far as possible. Do not refer to the passage until you have finished the exercise.
a Reasons for choice of sites for cities altering.
b Mechanical power transmitted hundreds of miles—communication by telephone—transport by airplanes—cinemas—broadcasting.
c Growth of cities and civilization modified.
3. Write a paragraph of about 200 words on one of the following subjects:
a Modern cities.
b Modern means of communication.

Key Structures

1. Put the words in brackets in their right position in these sentences. In some cases more than one position is possible. Do not refer to the passage until you have finished the exercise:
a Now, slowly and faintly, an opposite tendency is showing itself. (at first) (ll. 3–4)
b Better roads and better vehicles induced the wealthier classes to live on the outskirts of the cities. (at first) (ll. 4–5)
c But a new set of conditions is showing itself. (just) (ll. 6–7)
d In some ways the concentration of such activities was emphasized, and the homes were pushed outwards at the cost of the discomfort of commuting. (even more, even) (ll. 11–13)
e The reasons for this concentration are disappearing. (largely) (ll. 14–15)
f The reasons for the choice of sites for cities are altering. (still more, also) (ll. 15–16)
g Men can communicate instantaneously by telephone. (almost) (l. 17)
h Every reason for the growth of cities, concurrently with the growth of civilization has been modified. (almost, profoundly) (ll. 20–21)
2. Supply *the* where necessary in the spaces below. Do not refer to the passage until you have finished the exercise:
Up to ... present time, throughout ... eighteenth and ... nineteenth centuries, this new tendency placed ... home in ... immediate suburbs, but concentrated ... manufacturing activity, ... business relations, ... government, and ... pleasure in ... centres of ... cities. Apart from ... care of ... children and ... periods of sheer rest, ... active lives were spent in ... cities. In some ways ... concentration of such activities

was even more emphasized, and . . . homes were pushed outwards even at . . . cost of
. . . discomfort of commuting. (ll. 7–13)

3. Supply the missing words in the following paragraph. Do not refer to the passage
until you have finished the exercise:

But, if we examine the trend . . . technology . . . the past generation, the reasons . . .
this concentration are largely disappearing. Still more, the reasons . . . the choice . . .
sites . . . cities are also altering. Mechanical power can be transmitted . . . hundreds . . .
miles, men can communicate almost instantaneously . . . telephone, the chiefs . . .
great organizations can be transported . . . airplanes, the cinemas can produce plays
. . . every village, music, speeches, and sermons can be broadcast. Almost every reason
. . . the growth . . . cities, concurrently . . . the growth . . . civilization has been profoundly modified. (ll. 13–21)

Special Difficulties

1. Write sentences to bring out the difference between the following pairs of words:
born (l. 1), borne; show (l. 4), point at; commute (l. 13), communicate.

2. Explain the meaning of the words *faint* and *faintly* in these sentences:
a Now, slowly and at first *faintly*, an opposite tendency is showing itself. (ll. 3–4)
b He drew a *faint* line on a piece of paper.
c I must go outside. I feel *faint*.
d I haven't the *faintest* idea how that happened.

3. Note the use of *-wards* to emphasize direction:
This tendency is now spreading rapidly *downwards*. (l. 6)
Write sentences using the following words: upwards, backwards, forwards, towards.

4. Compare these three sentences:
a *Apart from* the care of children and periods of sheer rest, the active lives were spent
in the cities. (ll. 10–11)
b *Except for* the care of children and periods of sheer rest, the active lives were spent
in the cities.
c I sent an invitation to everyone *except* George.
Apart from and *except for* are used in exactly the same way. *Except* cannot be used at
the beginning of a sentence unless it is followed by *for*.
Write sentences using *apart from*, *except for* and *except*.

IF YOU CAN DO THIS TEST GO ON TO PART 2

Read the following passage carefully, then do the exercises below:

Television is a method of communication. It is about as revolutionary as the invention of printing. Neither printing nor television is in itself an idea, or power, or good or bad. They are simply methods by which ideas and experiences can be communicated faster to more people. It is perhaps because the characteristics
5 of television, which determine what it can best communicate, are so different from those of printing, that professional educationists were reluctant for so long to interest themselves in the newer method.

Printing and television are certainly alike in that both are costly to the producers of the communication and relatively cheap to the receiver. They are both,
10 therefore, mass media which depend upon reaching great numbers. But whereas the printed word, being relatively permanent, can communicate to numbers of like minds over centuries, television is relatively ephemeral and communicates, using both pictures and words, to millions of unlike minds at the same moment in time. Moreover television appeals not only to those who can read but to those
15 who can't.

Professional educationists, accustomed to communication through words, and highly valuing reading and the quality of the like minds reachable through books, saw television, in its early years, not only as a rival for attention but as an enemy of the good. Some ten years ago a friend said to me: 'We in Oxford may be old
20 fashioned and fuddy-duddy,* but most of us think that television is actively detrimental.' Even that great pioneer of teaching by radio, the late Mary Somerville, had no faith in television. 'It won't last,' she said to me as recently as 1948. 'It's a flash in the pan.' And many in the world of education no doubt hoped that this was true.

25 The situation has now altered. It is clear that television is no flash in the pan. So educationists all over the world are trying to get access to its 'power', often by attempting to use traditional methods of academic teaching to inculcate, through television, the ideas and attitudes in which they devotedly believe. But one of the characteristics of television is that it has no power other than that
30 created by the wish of people to watch it. If nobody watches it, then television has no power.

Grace Wyndham Goldie Television and Education from The Listener

Comprehension

Answer these questions:
a Name two qualities which printing and television have in common.
b Name two ways in which television differs from printing.
c State two of the objections made by educationists against television.
d 'The situation has altered.' (l. 25) Which situation is the author referring to, and how has it altered?

* old-fashioned.

Vocabulary

Explain the meaning of the following words and phrases as they are used in the passage: a method of communication (l. 1); characteristics (l. 4); reluctant (l. 6); relatively (l. 9); mass media (l. 10); ephemeral (l. 12); rival (l. 18); detrimental (l. 21).

The Sentence

1. Combine the following sentences so as to make one complex statement out of each group. Make any changes you think necessary, but do not alter the sense of the original. Do not refer to the passage until you have finished the exercise:

a They are simply methods. By these methods ideas and experiences can be communicated faster to more people. (ll. 3–4)

b The characteristics of television are different from those of printing. The characteristics of television determine what it can best communicate. Because of this professional educationists were reluctant for so long to interest themselves in the newer method. (ll. 4–7)

c Printing and television are certainly alike in one respect. They are costly to the producers of the communication. They are relatively cheap to the receiver. (ll. 8–9)

d They are both, therefore, mass media. They depend on reaching great numbers. (ll. 9–10)

e The printed word is relatively permanent. It can communicate to numbers of like minds over centuries. Television is relatively ephemeral. It communicates to millions of unlike minds at the same moment in time. It uses both pictures and words. (ll. 11–14)

2. Supply the missing words in the following. Do not refer to the passage until you have finished the exercise:

a Professional educationists, accustomed to communication through words, ... highly valuing reading ... the quality of the like minds reachable through books, saw television, in its early years, ... as a rival for attention ... as an enemy of the good. (ll. 16–19)

b So educationists all over the world are trying to get access to its 'power', often ... attempting to use traditional methods of academic teaching ... inculcate, through television, the ideas and attitudes in ... they devotedly believe. (ll. 26–28)

The Paragraph

1. Which of the following words or phrases would best serve as a title for this passage. Give reasons for your choice:
Television; Television and Printing; Television and Education; Television as a Mass Medium; Mass Media; The Appeal of Television.

2. The following sentences have been taken from the first paragraph. (Lines 1–7). Arrange them in their correct order. Do not refer to the passage until you have finished the exercise:

a Television is a method of communication.

b It is perhaps because the characteristics of television, which determine what it can best communicate, are so different from those of printing, that professional educationists were reluctant for so long to interest themselves in the newer method.

c It is about as revolutionary as the invention of printing.

d They are simply methods by which ideas and experiences can be communicated faster to more people.

e Neither printing nor television is in itself an idea, or power, or good or bad.

3. Drawing your information from the second paragraph (lines 8–15) write a list of points in note form to answer the following question: In what ways are television and printing similar to each other, and in what ways do they differ from each other?

4. Read the last paragraph again. (Lines 25–31). Using the list of points given below, reconstruct the author's arguments in your own words as far as possible. Do not refer to the passage until you have finished the exercise:

a Situation altered.

b Television has come to stay.

c Educationists: access to its power.

d Traditional methods of teaching through television.

e But television can only have power if people watch it.

5. Write a paragraph of about 200 words on one of the following subjects:

a The use of television in education.

b How can television enrich our lives?

c What are the arguments against watching television?

Part 2

Unit 4

INSTRUCTIONS TO THE STUDENT

Content
This Unit consists of ten passages followed by exercises on Comprehension, Vocabulary, Précis, Composition, Key Structures and Special Difficulties.

Aim
To employ the skills you have acquired in constructing sentences and paragraphs in order to write Précis and Composition.

How to Work
1. Read each passage carefully two or three times.
2. Answer the questions in the order in which they are given.

Précis
In Part 1 you learnt how to write points in note form to answer a specific question on a passage. When writing précis, you will be required to do precisely the same thing. This time, however, you will join your points to reconstruct the main ideas of each passage in a limited number of words. Follow the instructions very carefully.

Composition
In Part 1 you learnt how to write a paragraph from notes which were provided. When writing a composition, you will be required to do precisely the same thing. This time, however, the notes given have not been derived from the passage. They are of a general nature and meant to be suggestions only. You may ignore them altogether if you wish. Follow the instructions very carefully.

31

Many people in industry and the Services, who have practical experience of noise, regard any investigation of this question as a waste of time; they are not prepared even to admit the possibility that noise affects people. On the other hand, those who dislike noise will sometimes use most inadequate evidence to support their pleas for a quieter society. This is a pity, because noise abatement really is a good cause, and it is likely to be discredited if it gets to be associated with bad science.

One allegation often made is that noise produces mental illness. A recent article in a weekly newspaper, for instance, was headed with a striking illustration of a lady in a state of considerable distress, with the caption 'She was yet another victim, reduced to a screaming wreck'. On turning eagerly to the text, one learns that the lady was a typist who found the sound of office typewriters worried her more and more until eventually she had to go into a mental hospital. Now the snag in this sort of anecdote is of course that one cannot distinguish cause and effect. Was the noise a cause of the illness, or were the complaints about noise merely a symptom? Another patient might equally well complain that her neighbours were combining to slander her and persecute her, and yet one might be cautious about believing this statement.

What is needed in the case of noise is a study of large numbers of people living under noisy conditions, to discover whether they are mentally ill more often than other people are. The United States Navy, for instance, recently examined a very large number of men working on aircraft carriers: the study was known as

An American aircraft carrier, USS *Hancock*

Project Anehin. It can be unpleasant to live even several miles from an aerodrome; if you think what it must be like to share the deck of a ship with several squad-
25 rons of jet aircraft, you will realize that a modern navy is a good place to study noise. But neither psychiatric interviews nor objective tests were able to show any effects upon these American sailors. This result merely confirms earlier American and British studies: if there is any effect of noise upon mental health it must be so small that present methods of psychiatric diagnosis cannot find it.
30 That does not prove that it does not exist; but it does mean that noise is less dangerous than, say, being brought up in an orphanage—which really is a mental health hazard.

D. E. BROADBENT *Non-auditory Effects of Noise* from *Science Survey*

Comprehension

Answer these questions:
a What does the author mean by the statement 'noise abatement really is a good cause, and it is likely to be discredited if it gets to be associated with bad science.'? (ll. 5–7)
b Why is a modern navy a good place to study noise?

Vocabulary

Explain the meaning of the following words and phrases as they are used in the passage: investigation (l. 2); inadequate evidence (l. 4); abatement (l. 5); allegation (l. 8); snag (l. 14); cautious (l. 18); hazard (l. 32).

Précis

1. Drawing your information from the first two paragraphs (lines 1–18) write a list of points in note form outlining the author's argument about noise abatement.
2. Using this list of points, reconstruct the author's argument in not more than 90 words. Your answer should be in one paragraph.

Composition

Write a composition of about 300 words on the following subject: Noise in modern life. You may use some or all of the ideas given below if you wish:
a We have grown accustomed to living and working against a background of noise: traffic in the streets; machines in the factory; office equipment; labour-saving devices in the home; aeroplanes overhead.
b In a modern industrial society hardly any place is free from noise; in cities, the problem is acute.
c Many people learn to live against this background and do not seem to be affected.
d Some people even seem to require noise as a necessary condition in which to work: e.g. music as a constant background.
e We seem to be helpless to do anything about noise and have come to accept it as one of the more unpleasant features of modern civilization.

Key Structures

1. Study this sentence:
Many people in industry and the Services, *who have practical experience of noise*, regard any investigation of this question as a waste of time. (ll. 1–2)

Expand the following sentences by inserting suitable clauses beginning with *who* or *which* after the words in italics:

a Many roads . . . were not built for such heavy traffic.

b The heavy snow . . . has now begun to melt.

c The party of tourists . . . left this morning.

d The clerk . . . apologized for the mistake.

2. Compare these two sentences:

Instead of saying: One allegation *that is often made* is that noise produces mental illness.

We can say: One allegation *often made* is that noise produces mental illness. (l. 8)

Write sentences using the following phrases:

frequently seen; sometimes heard; generally considered.

3. Note the use of *yet* in these sentences:

a Has he come *yet*?

b I haven't seen him *yet*.

c She was *yet* another victim. (ll. 10–11)

Write three sentences using *yet* in the ways shown above.

4. Compare these two sentences:

Instead of saying: When one turns eagerly to the text, one learns that the lady was a typist.

We can say: On turning eagerly to the text, one learns that the lady was a typist. (ll. 11–12)

Write these sentences again so that each one begins with *On*:

a When I opened the door, I got a surprise.

b When he saw me approaching, he ran towards me.

c When he was asked to leave the meeting, he got very angry.

d When she arrived at the station, she bought a ticket.

5. Write sentences using the following expressions:

reduced to (l. 11); cause of (l. 15); complaints about (l. 15); cautious about (l. 18); share with (l. 24); effects upon (l. 27); methods of (l. 29).

Special Difficulties

1. Write sentences to bring out the difference between the following pairs of words: regard (l. 2), look at; affects (l. 3), effects (l., 27); pleas (l. 5), please; objective (l. 26), objection; confirm (l. 27), assure.

2. The opposites of these words are to be found in the passage. What are they? like; adequate; credit; pleasant.

3. Explain the meaning of the verbs and expressions in italics:

a It does mean that noise is less dangerous than, say, being *brought up* in an orphanage—which really is a mental health hazard. (ll. 30–32)

b The question was recently *brought up* in Parliament.

c The boxer was knocked out in the first round. It took a long time to *bring him round*.

d The whole scene *brought back* the days of my childhood.

e Their wonderful performance *brought down the house*.

f Can you *bring to mind* what happened on the fourth of July?

g Difficult conditions will sometimes *bring out* a man's best qualities.

32

It is animals and plants which lived in or near water whose remains are most likely to be preserved, for one of the necessary conditions of preservation is quick burial, and it is only in the seas and rivers, and sometimes lakes, where mud and silt have been continuously deposited, that bodies and the like can be rapidly 5 covered over and preserved.

But even in the most favourable circumstances only a small fraction of the creatures that die are preserved in this way before decay sets in or, even more likely, before scavengers eat them. After all, all living creatures live by feeding on something else, whether it be plant or animal, dead or alive, and it is only by 10 chance that such a fate is avoided. The remains of plants and animals that lived on land are much more rarely preserved, for there is seldom anything to cover them over. When you think of the innumerable birds that one sees flying about, not to mention the equally numerous small animals like field mice and voles which you do not see, it is very rarely that one comes across a dead body, except, 15 of course, on the roads. They decompose and are quickly destroyed by the weather or eaten by some other creature.

It is almost always due to some very special circumstances that traces of land animals survive, as by falling into inaccessible caves, or into an ice crevasse, like the Siberian mammoths, when the whole animal is sometimes preserved, as in 20 a refrigerator. This is what happened to the famous Beresovka mammoth which was found preserved and in good condition. In his mouth were the remains of fir trees—the last meal that he had before he fell into the crevasse and broke his

The mammoth in the Palaeontological Museum in Leningrad. Photographed in 1860

back. The mammoth has now been restored in the Palaeontological Museum in
Leningrad. Other animals were trapped in tar pits, like the elephants, sabre-
25 toothed cats, and numerous other creatures that are found at Rancho la Brea,
which is now just a suburb of Los Angeles. Apparently what happened was that
water collected on these tar pits, and the bigger animals like the elephants ven-
tured out on to the apparently firm surface to drink, and were promptly bogged
in the tar. And then, when they were dead, the carnivores, like the sabre-toothed
30 cats and the giant wolves, came out to feed and suffered exactly the same fate.
There are also endless numbers of birds in the tar as well.

ERROL WHITE *The Past Life of the Earth* from *Discovery*

Comprehension

Answer these questions:
a Why are animals or plants which lived in or near water most likely to be preserved?
b What usually happens to the dead bodies of animals?
c How were the remains of the Beresovka mammoth accidentally preserved?

Vocabulary

Explain the meaning of the following words and phrases as they are used in the passage:
preservation (l. 2); the like (l. 4); a small fraction (l. 6); scavengers (l. 8); innumerable (l. 12); decompose (l. 15); inaccessible (l. 18); restored (l. 23); promptly bogged
(l. 28).

Précis

1. Drawing your information from the first two paragraphs (lines 1–16) write a list of
points in note form outlining the author's main ideas on the preservation of animals.
2. Using this list of points, reconstruct the author's account in not more than 80
words. Your answer should be in one paragraph.

Composition

Write a composition of about 300 words on the following subject: Extinct forms of
animal life. You may use some or all of the ideas given below if you wish:
a Fascination of a natural history museum where the skeletons and fossils of extinct
forms of life are on display.
b The sort of thing one can see: remains of animals that existed in pre-historic times.
E.g. Reptiles: dinosaurs, tyrannosaurs. Birds: pterodactyls. Fish: early sharks; fossi-
lized crustaceans. Mammals: perhaps the most fascinating: Neanderthal man.
c The remains of animals which became extinct recently: e.g. the dodo. Many forms
of animal life are in danger of becoming extinct today.
d A reference to 'living fossils'—primitive forms of life which have surprisingly sur-
vived: e.g. the coelacanth; the platypus.

Key Structures

1. Note the form of the verbs in italics:
Only a small fraction of the creatures that die are preserved in this way *before* decay
sets in or, even more likely, *before* scavengers *eat* them. (ll. 6–8)
Write sentences using the same construction with these words: until; after; as soon
as; when.

2. Compare the use of *for* in these two sentences:

a The remains of plants and animals that lived on land are much more rarely preserved, *for* there is seldom anything to cover them over. (ll. 10–12)

b I think this letter is *for* you.

Write two sentences using *for* in the ways illustrated above.

3. Supply the correct form of the verbs in the following. Do not refer to the passage until you have finished the exercise:

It is almost always due to some very special circumstances that traces of land animals survive, as by (fall) into inaccessible caves, or into an ice crevasse, like the Siberian mammoths, when the whole animal sometimes (preserve) as in a refrigerator. This is what (happen) to the famous Beresovka mammoth which (find) (preserve) and in good condition. In his mouth (be) the remains of fir trees—the last meal that he (have) before he (fall) into the crevasse and (break) his back. The mammoth now (restore) in the Palaeontological Museum in Leningrad. Other animals (trap) in tar pits, like the elephants, sabre-toothed cats, and numerous other creatures that (find) at Rancho la Brea. (ll. 17–25)

Special Difficulties

1. Write sentences to bring out the difference between the following pairs of words: continuously (l. 4), continually; favourable (l. 6), favourite; alive (l. 9), living; avoid (l. 10), prevent; fir (l. 22), fur.

2. Note the phrase in italics: Only a small fraction of the creatures that die are preserved *in this way*. (ll. 6–7)

Write sentences using the following phrases:

in the way; on the way; in a way; by the way.

3. Explain the meaning of *due to* and *due* in these sentences:

a It is almost always *due to* some very special circumstances that traces of land animals survive. (ll. 17–18)

b The train is *due to* arrive in three minutes.

c It is *due* to him to say what he did last night.

d Halifax lies *due* North from here.

4. Study the use of *as* and *like* in this sentence:

It is . . . due to some very special circumstances . . . *as* by falling into inaccessible caves, *like* the Siberian mammoths . . . (ll. 17–19)

Supply *like* or *as* in the following sentences:

a Please do . . . I say.

b He was white . . . a sheet.

c He left . . . suddenly . . . he came.

d Don't act . . . a baby.

e The carnivores, . . . the sabre-toothed cats came out to feed and suffered exactly the same fate. (ll. 29–30)

33

From the seventeenth-century empire of Sweden, the story of a galleon that sank at the start of her maiden voyage in 1628 must be one of the strangest tales of the sea. For nearly three and a half centuries she lay at the bottom of Stockholm harbour until her discovery in 1956. This was the *Vasa*, royal flagship of
5 the great imperial fleet.

King Gustavus Adolphus, 'The Northern Hurricane', then at the height of his military success in the Thirty Years' War, had dictated her measurements and armament. Triple gun-decks mounted sixty-four bronze cannon. She was intended to play a leading rôle in the growing might of Sweden.
10 As she was prepared for her maiden voyage on August 10, 1628, Stockholm was in a ferment. From the Skeppsbron and surrounding islands the people watched this thing of beauty begin to spread her sails and catch the wind. They had laboured for three years to produce this floating work of art; she was more richly carved and ornamented than any previous ship. The high stern castle was
15 a riot of carved gods, demons, knights, kings, warriors, mermaids, cherubs; and zoomorphic animal shapes ablaze with red and gold and blue, symbols of courage, power, and cruelty, were portrayed to stir the imaginations of the superstitious sailors of the day.

Then the cannons of the anchored warships thundered a salute to which the
20 *Vasa* fired in reply. As she emerged from her drifting cloud of gun smoke with the water churned to foam beneath her bow, her flags flying, pennants waving, sails filling in the breeze, and the red and gold of her superstructure ablaze with

The 'Vasa', now in dry dock in Stockholm

colour, she presented a more majestic spectacle than Stockholmers had ever seen before. All gun-ports were open and the muzzles peeped wickedly from them.

25 As the wind freshened there came a sudden squall and the ship made a strange movement, listing to port. The Ordnance Officer ordered all the port cannon to be heaved to starboard to counteract the list, but the steepening angle of the decks increased. Then the sound of rumbling thunder reached the watchers on the shore, as cargo, ballast, ammunition and 400 people went sliding and crashing
30 down to the port side of the steeply listing ship. The lower gun-ports were now below water and the inrush sealed the ship's fate. In that first glorious hour, the mighty *Vasa*, which was intended to rule the Baltic, sank with all flags flying—in the harbour of her birth.

ROY SAUNDERS *The Raising of the 'Vasa'* from *The Listener*

Comprehension

Answer these questions:
a Why was the *Vasa* regarded as an important ship when she was built?
b How long did it take to build the *Vasa*?
c Why is the *Vasa* described as a 'floating work of art'?

Vocabulary

Explain the meaning of the following words and phrases as they are used in the passage: galleon (l. 1); dictated (l. 7); might (l. 9); maiden voyage (l. 10); in a ferment (l. 11); zoomorphic (l. 16); portrayed (l. 17); churned (l. 21); ablaze (l. 22); freshened (l. 25); sudden squall (l. 25); ballast (l. 29); inrush (l. 31); sealed the ship's fate (l. 31).

Précis

1. Drawing your information from lines 10–33 ('As she prepared . . . her birth.') write a list of points in note form describing what the people in Stockholm harbour saw on August 10, 1628.
2. Using this list of points, reconstruct the author's description of the scene in not more than 100 words. Your answer should be in one paragraph.

Composition

Write a composition of about 300 words on the following subject: Recovering lost treasure from the sea. You may use some or all of the ideas given below if you wish:
a The difficulty of salvaging wrecks in the past.
b Modern techniques have made salvaging less difficult: skin diving.
c Hunting for treasure is carried out not only by experts but also by amateurs.
d Examples of treasure recovered: the Mediterranean: Roman ships; Greek works of art. Off the coast of Florida: gold from Spanish galleons.

Key Structures

1. Supply the correct form of the verbs in brackets in the following. Do not refer to the passage until you have finished the exercise:
King Gustavus Adolphus, 'The Northern Hurricane', then at the height of his military success in the Thirty Years' War, (dictate) her measurements and armament. Triple gun-decks (mount) sixty-four bronze cannon. She (intend) to play a leading rôle in the growing might of Sweden.

As she (prepare) for her maiden voyage on August 10, 1628, Stockholm (be) in a ferment. From the Skeppsbron and surrounding islands the people (watch) this thing of beauty begin to spread her sails and catch the wind. They (labour) for three years to produce this floating work of art; she more richly (carve) and (ornament) than any previous ship. (ll. 6–14)

2. Study this sentence pattern:

The people *watched* this thing of beauty *begin* to spread her sails and *catch* the wind. (ll. 11–12)

Complete these sentences using the same pattern:

a I heard him . . .

b I noticed someone . . .

c Did you see anyone . . .

3. Supply *for* or *since* in the following sentences:

a They had laboured . . . three years to produce this floating work of art. (ll. 12–13)

b . . . 1628 few attempts had been made to salvage the *Vasa*.

c . . . nearly three and a half centuries she lay at the bottom of Stockholm harbour. (ll. 3–4)

4. Note this construction:

As the wind freshened *there came* a sudden squall. (l. 25)

Write sentences using the following: there lived; there seemed.

5. Study the construction in italics:

. . . 400 people *went sliding and crashing* . . . (l. 29)

Write sentences using the following expressions:

go shopping; go swimming; go sailing.

Special Difficulties

1. Explain the meaning of *spread* in these sentences:

a The people watched this thing of beauty begin to *spread* her sails. (ll. 11–12)

b You should know better than to *spread* such rumours.

c *Spread* some jam on your bread.

d Help me to *spread* the tablecloth.

2. Explain the meaning of *produce* in these sentences:

a They had laboured for three years to *produce* this floating work of art. (ll. 12–13)

b The inspector asked me to *produce* my ticket.

c Who *produced* this play?

d This country does not *produce* enough wheat for its needs.

3. Explain the meaning of the words in italics:

a All gun-ports were open and the muzzles *peeped* wickedly from them. (l. 24)

b I opened the door and *peered* into the darkness.

c I've been so busy, I haven't even *glanced* at today's newspapers.

d I just *caught a glimpse* of a face at the window.

34

This is a sceptical age, but although our faith in many of the things in which our forefathers fervently believed has weakened, our confidence in the curative properties of the bottle of medicine remains the same as theirs. This modern faith in medicines is proved by the fact that the annual drug bill of the Health
5 Services is mounting to astronomical figures and shows no signs at present of ceasing to rise. The majority of the patients attending the medical out-patients departments of our hospitals feel that they have not received adequate treatment unless they are able to carry home with them some tangible remedy in the shape of a bottle of medicine, a box of pills, or a small jar of ointment, and the doctor
10 in charge of the department is only too ready to provide them with these require-ments. There is no quicker method of disposing of patients than by giving them what they are asking for, and since most medical men in the Health Services are overworked and have little time for offering time-consuming and little-appre-ciated advice on such subjects as diet, right living, and the need for abandoning
15 bad habits, etc., the bottle, the box, and the jar are almost always granted them.
  Nor is it only the ignorant and ill-educated person who has such faith in the bottle of medicine, especially if it be wrapped in white paper and sealed with a dab of red sealing-wax by a clever chemist. It is recounted of Thomas Carlyle that when he heard of the illness of his friend, Henry Taylor, he went off
20 immediately to visit him, carrying with him in his pocket what remained of a bottle of medicine formerly prescribed for an indisposition of Mrs Carlyle's. Carlyle was entirely ignorant of what the bottle in his pocket contained, of the

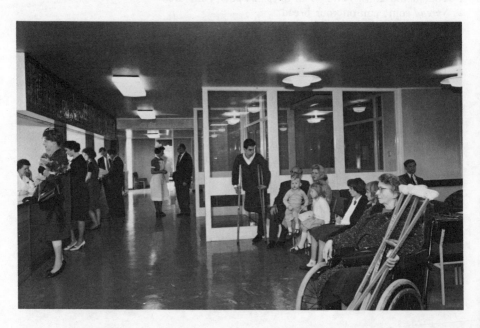

The Out-patients Department at Queen Mary's Hospital, Roehampton

nature of the illness from which his friend was suffering, and of what had pre-
viously been wrong with his wife, but a medicine that had worked so well in one
25 form of illness would surely be of equal benefit in another, and comforted by
the thought of the help he was bringing to his friend, he hastened to Henry
Taylor's house. History does not relate whether his friend accepted his medical
help, but in all probability he did. The great advantage of taking medicine is that
it makes no demands on the taker beyond that of putting up for a moment with a
30 disgusting taste, and that is what all patients demand of their doctors—to be
cured at no inconvenience to themselves.

KENNETH WALKER *Patients and Doctors*

Comprehension

Answer these questions:
a Why do doctors readily provide their patients with medicines?
b How does the anecdote about Thomas Carlyle illustrate the author's argument?

Vocabulary

Explain the meaning of the following words and phrases as they are used in the passage:
sceptical (l. 1); fervently (l. 2); curative properties (ll. 2–3); astronomical figures (l. 5);
tangible (l. 8); disposing (l. 11); granted (l. 15); indisposition (l. 21); putting up
with (l. 29); inconvenience (l. 31).

Précis

1. Drawing your information from the first paragraph (lines 1–15) write a list of points
in note form outlining the author's argument that we have great faith in the power of
medicine.
2. Using this list of points, reconstruct the author's argument in not more than 80
words. Your answer should be in one paragraph.

Composition

Write a composition of about 300 words on the following subject: 'A public health
service is an essential part of social welfare.' Argue for or against this idea. You may
use some or all of the ideas given below if you wish:
a No one should have the right to buy good health.
b A public health service is expensive to run and is often abused.
c No one objects to a public health service more than the doctors.
d Example of a country where a public health service seems to be an impossibility:
America.
e Examples of countries with successful services: Sweden, Britain, Israel.

Key Structures

1. Note the phrase in italics in this sentence:
Our confidence in the curative properties of the bottle of medicine remains *the same as*
theirs. (ll. 2–3)
Write two sentences using *the same as* and *different from*.
2. Read this sentence:
The fact that the annual drug bill of the Health Service is mounting to astronomical
figures proves *this modern faith in medicines.*

Write this sentence again so that it begins with the words in italics. Then compare what you have written with lines 3–5.

3. Supply the correct form of the verbs in brackets in the following sentences. Do not refer to the passage until you have finished the exercise:

a It shows no signs at present of (cease) to rise. (ll. 5–6)

b The majority of the patients (attend) the medical out-patients departments feel that they have not received adequate treatment . . . (ll. 6–7)

c There is no quicker method of (dispose) of patients than by (give) them what they are asking for, and since most medical men in the Health Services are overworked and have little time for (offer) time-consuming and little-appreciated advice on such subjects as diet, right living, and the need for (abandon) bad habits, etc., the bottle, the box, and the jar are almost always granted them. (ll. 11–15)

4. Note the form of the verb in italics in this sentence:

Nor *is it* only the ignorant and ill-educated person who has such faith in the bottle of medicine. (ll. 16–17)

Write sentences which begin with the following words:

Not only; Never; Only now.

5. Write sentences using the following expressions:

believe in (l. 2); confidence in (l. 2); in charge of (l. 10); dispose of (l. 11); advice on (l. 14); the need for (l. 14); sealed with (l. 17); prescribed for (l. 21); ignorant of (l. 22); suffer from (l. 23); wrong with (l. 24); benefit in (l. 25); demand of (l. 30); inconvenience to (l. 31).

Special Difficulties

1. Write sentences to bring out the difference between the following pairs of words: cease (l. 6), seize; rise (l. 6), raise; receive (l. 7), take; ask for (l. 12), ask; advice (l. 14), advise; especially (l. 17), specially; prescribed (l. 21), proscribed; accept (l. 27), agree.

2. Explain the meaning of the words and phrases in italics:

a The doctor *in charge of* the department is only too ready to provide them with these requirements. (ll. 9–11)

b The soldiers *charged* at the enemy.

c He was arrested and *charged* with murder.

d How much did they *charge* you for installing this boiler?

3. Note the use of *ill-* in this phrase: ill-educated (l. 16)

Write sentences using the following phrases:

ill-advised; ill-informed; ill-prepared.

35

Many strange new means of transport have been developed in our century, the strangest of them being perhaps the hovercraft. In 1953, a former electronics engineer in his fifties, Christopher Cockerell, who had turned to boat-building on the Norfolk Broads, suggested an idea on which he had been working for
5 many years to the British Government and industrial circles. It was the idea of supporting a craft on a 'pad', or cushion, of low-pressure air, ringed with a curtain of higher pressure air. Ever since, people have had difficulty in deciding whether the craft should be ranged among ships, planes, or land vehicles—for it is something in between a boat and an aircraft. As a shipbuilder, Cockerell was
10 trying to find a solution to the problem of the wave resistance which wastes a good deal of a surface ship's power and limits its speed. His answer was to lift the vessel out of the water by making it ride on a cushion of air, no more than one or two feet thick. This is done by a great number of ring-shaped air jets on the bottom of the craft. It 'flies', therefore, but it cannot fly higher—its action de-
15 pends on the surface, water or ground, over which it rides.

The first tests on the Solent in 1959 caused a sensation. The hovercraft travelled first over the water, then mounted the beach, climbed up the dunes, and sat down on a road. Later it crossed the Channel, riding smoothly over the waves, which presented no problem.

20 Since that time, various types of hovercraft have appeared and taken up regular service—cruises on the Thames in London, for instance, have become an annual attraction. But we are only at the beginning of a development that may transform

A hovercraft takes to the water at Cowes

sea and land transport. Christopher Cockerell's craft can establish transport networks in large areas with poor communications such as Africa or Australia; it
25 can become a 'flying fruit-bowl', carrying bananas from the plantations to the ports; giant hovercraft liners could span the Atlantic; and the railway of the future may well be the 'hovertrain', riding on its air cushion over a single rail, which it never touches, at speeds up to 300 m.p.h.—the possibilities appear unlimited.

EGON LARSEN *The Pegasus Book of Inventors*

Comprehension

a State briefly how a hovercraft works.
b Name two ways in which the hovercraft may transform sea and land transport.

Vocabulary

Explain the meaning of the following words and phrases as they are used in the passage: a former (l. 2); ringed with (l. 6); ranged (l. 8); a solution to the problem (l. 10); caused a sensation (l. 16); riding smoothly (l. 18); cruises (l. 21); annual (l. 21); networks (ll. 23–24); span (l. 26).

Précis

1. Drawing your information from the first two paragraphs (lines 1–19) write a list of points in note form describing how the hovercraft was developed.
2. Using this list of points, reconstruct the author's account in not more than 90 words. Your answer should be in one paragraph.

Composition

Write a composition of about 300 words on the following subject: Modern means of transport. You may use some or all of the ideas given below if you wish:
a The main emphasis in all forms of transport is speed and comfort. The world has become a smaller place.
b Air travel: the jet aeroplane; the helicopter; future possibilities in the rocket.
b Sea: Ocean liners; the hydrofoil; the hovercraft.
d Land: Electric trains; automatic control (e.g. Japan); the car; the building of motorway networks.
e Of all modern means of transport, the car is creating most problems as it is causing serious congestion in cities. No satisfactory solution to this problem has yet been found.

Key Structures

1. Note the use of *being* in this sentence:
Many strange new means of transport have been developed in our century, the strangest of them *being* perhaps the hovercraft. (ll. 1–2)
Complete these sentences using the same construction:
a Many international exhibitions have been held, the most recent one . . .
b New York is full of skyscrapers, the tallest one . . .
2. Supply the correct form of the verbs in brackets in the following. Do not refer to the passage until you have finished the exercise:
In 1953, a former electronics engineer in his fifties, Christopher Cockerell, who (turn) to boat-building on the Norfolk Broads, (suggest) an idea on which he (work) for many

years to the British Government and industrial circles. It (be) the idea of (support) a craft on a 'pad', or cushion, of low-pressure air, (ring) with a curtain of higher pressure air. Ever since, people (have) difficulty in (decide) whether the craft (should range) among ships, planes, or land vehicles. (ll. 2–8)

3. Supply *among* or *between* in the following sentences:

a People have had difficulty in deciding whether the craft should be ranged . . . ships, planes, or land vehicles. (ll. 7–8)

b It is something in . . . a boat and an aircraft. (ll. 8–9)

c Diplomatic relations . . . the two countries have been broken.

d Strictly . . . ourselves, this whole business is beginning to get me down.

4. Note the phrase *a good deal of* in this sentence:

'. . . wave resistance . . . wastes *a good deal of* a surface ship's power . . .' (ll. 10–11)

Write sentences using the following phrases: a great deal of; a great many; a good many; a good few.

5. Note the form of the verbs in italics:

His answer was to lift the vessel out of the water by *making* it *ride* on a cushion of air. (ll. 11–12)

Complete the following sentences:

a I made him . . .

b The teacher made the class . . .

c He trained the team by making them . . .

6. Compare these two sentences:

Instead of saying: It is quite likely that the railway of the future will be the 'hovertrain'
We can say; The railway of the future *may* (or *might*) well be the 'hovertrain'. (ll. 26–27)

Write two sentences using *may* (or *might*) *well* in this way.

Special Difficulties

1. Write sentences to bring out the difference between the following pairs of words: engineer (l. 3), mechanic; solution (l. 10), solvent; waste (l. 10), waist; at the beginning (l. 22), at first.

2. Explain the meaning of the verbs in italics:

a He had *turned to* boat-building on the Norfolk Broads. (ll. 3–4)

b Please *turn off* the tap.

c Aunt Matilda *turned up* unexpectedly last night.

d The soldiers marched to the other side of the park, *turned about*, and marched back.

3. Note the use of the verb *ride* in this sentence:

It crossed the Channel, *riding* smoothly over the waves. (ll. 18–19)

Write sentences using the following expressions:

ride a horse; go for a ride (in a car, on a bicycle); give someone a ride.

36

Our knowledge of the oceans a hundred years ago was confined to the two-dimensional shape of the sea-surface and the hazards of navigation presented by the irregularities in depth of the shallow water close to the land. The open sea was deep and mysterious, and anyone who gave more than a passing thought to the
5 bottom confines of the oceans probably assumed that the sea-bed was flat. Sir James Clark Ross had obtained a sounding of over 2,400 fathoms in 1839, but it was not until 1869, when H.M.S. *Porcupine* was put at the disposal of the Royal Society for several cruises, that a series of deep soundings was obtained in the Atlantic and the first samples were collected by dredging the bottom.
10 Shortly after this the famous H.M.S. *Challenger* expedition established the study of the sea-floor as a subject worthy of the most qualified physicists and geologists. A burst of activity associated with the laying of submarine cables soon confirmed the Challenger's observation that many parts of the ocean were two to three miles deep, and the existence of underwater features of considerable magnitude.
15   Today enough soundings are available to enable a relief map of the Atlantic to be drawn and we know something of the great variety of the sea-bed's topography. Since the sea covers the greater part of the earth's surface it is quite reasonable to regard the sea-floor as the basic form of the crust of the earth, with superimposed upon it the continents, together with the islands and other features
20 of the oceans. The continents form rugged tablelands which stand nearly three miles above the floor of the open ocean. From the shore-line out to a distance which may be anywhere from a few miles to a few hundred miles runs the gentle

H.M.S. *Challenger* at St. Paul's Rocks near the Equator

slope of the continental shelf, geologically part of the continents. The real
dividing-line between continents and oceans occurs at the foot of a steeper slope.
25   This continental slope usually starts at a place somewhere near the 100-fathom
mark and in the course of a few hundred miles reaches the true ocean-floor at
2,500–3,000 fathoms. The slope averages about 1 in 30, but contains steep,
probably vertical, cliffs, and gentle sediment-covered terraces, and near its lower
reaches there is a long tailing-off which is almost certainly the result of material
30 transported out to deep water after being eroded from the continental masses.

T. F. GASKELL Exploring the Sea-floor from Science Survey

Comprehension

Answer these questions:
a What does the author mean by the phrase 'the two-dimensional shape of the sea-surface'? (ll. 1–2)
b Which sentence in the first paragraph suggests that before the expedition of H.M.S. *Challenger* the sea-bed was not considered as an object for serious study?
c What lies immediately between the continental slope and the true ocean floor?

Vocabulary

Explain the meaning of the following words and phrases as they are used in the passage:
hazards of navigation (l. 2); dredging (l. 9); submarine (l. 12); considerable magnitude
(l. 14); relief (l. 15); crust (l. 18); superimposed (l. 19); vertical (l. 28); tailing-off
(l. 29); eroded (l. 30).

Précis

1. Drawing your information from the first two paragraphs (lines 1–24) write a list
of points in note form outlining the author's account of the study of the sea-bed.
2. Using this list of points, reconstruct the author's account in not more than 120
words. Your answer should be in one paragraph.

Composition

Write a composition of about 300 words on the following subject:
Man has done relatively little to exploit the wealth of the sea. You may use some or all
of the ideas given below if you wish:
a The intensive study of the sea is comparatively recent.
b The sea as a source of power: harnessing the tides to provide electricity.
c The sea as a source of food; distilling water from the sea; fish; plankton as a source
of protein to feed growing world population; 'cultivating' the sea-bed.
d The sea as a source of wealth: obtaining minerals; oil or gas under the sea (e.g.
the North Sea).
e The setting up of permanent villages under the sea; the pioneer work of Com-mander Cousteau.

Key Structures

1. Supply the correct form of the verbs in brackets. Do not refer to the passage until
you have finished the exercise:
a Our knowledge of the oceans a hundred years ago (confine) to the two-dimensional
shape of the sea-surface. (ll. 1–2)

b It was not until 1869, when H.M.S. *Porcupine* (put) at the disposal of the Royal Society for several cruises, that a series of deep soundings (obtain) in the Atlantic and the first samples (collect) by dredging the bottom. (ll. 7–9)

c Today enough soundings are available to enable a relief map of the Atlantic (draw) and we know something of the great variety of the sea-bed's topography. (ll. 15–17)

2. Compare these two sentences:

Instead of saying: It was *only in 1869* . . . that a series of deep soundings was obtained in the Atlantic.

We can say: It was *not until 1869* . . . that a series of deep soundings was obtained in the Atlantic. (ll. 7–9)

Change the following sentences in the same way:

a I only understood what had happened when I read the report in the newspaper.

b The plane will only take off again when the engine has been checked.

c Tom only got home at four o'clock this morning.

d I shall return this book to the library only after I have read it.

e He agreed to deliver the goods only after I had paid for them.

3. Compare the uses of *since* in these two sentences:

a Since the sea covers the greater part of the earth's surface it is quite reasonable to regard the sea-floor as the basic form of the crust of the earth. (ll. 17–18)

b I have not seen him *since* last week.

Write two sentences illustrating these two uses of *since*.

Special Difficulties

1. Write sentences to bring out the difference between the following pairs of words: flat (l. 5), level; disposal (l. 7), disposition; worthy (l. 11), valuable; laying (l. 12), lying; confirm (l. 12), assure; rugged (l. 20), ragged.

2. Write two sentences using the phrases 'the open sea' (l. 3) and 'the open air'.

3. Note that the word *series* (l. 8) is singular. Write sentences using the following words: mathematics, news, physics, billiards.

4. Write sentences using the following words and phrases: shortly after (l. 10); shortly before; shortly.

5. Explain the meaning of the word *feature* in these sentences:

a A burst of activity . . . soon confirmed . . . the existence of underwater *features* of considerable magnitude. (ll. 12–14)

b I never enjoy *feature* films.

c The present world tour of the President of the United States *is featured* prominently in all today's newspapers.

d I hardly recognized him when I saw him again: his *features* have changed with the years.

6. What do you understand by the phrase: 'The slope averages about *1 in 30* . . .'? (l. 27)

Write sentences using the following expressions: 1 in 10; 1 in 1,000.

37

The Victorians, realizing that the greatest happiness accorded to man is that provided by a happy marriage, endeavoured to pretend that all their marriages were happy. We, for our part, admitting the fact that no feat of intelligence and character is so exacting as that required of two people who desire to live per-
5 manently together on a basis of amity, are obsessed by the problem of how to render the basic facts of cohabitation simpler and more reasonable, in order that unhappy marriages may less frequently result. The Victorians would have considered it 'painful' or 'unpleasant' were one to point out that only four marriages out of every ten are anything but forced servitudes. We ourselves start from this
10 very assumption and try to build from it a theory of more sensible relations between the sexes. Of all forms of arrant untruthfulness Victorian optimism appears to me to have been the most cowardly and the most damaging.

Truth, therefore, is an attitude of the mind. It is important, if one does not wish to inconvenience and to bore one's friends, not to tell lies. But it is more
15 important not to think lies, or to slide into those mechanical and untruthful habits of thought which are so pleasant and so easy as descents to mental ineptitude. The Victorian habit of mind (which I consider to have been a bad habit of mind) was unduly preoccupied by what was socially and morally convenient. Convenience is, however, in all affairs of life, an execrable test of value. One
20 should have the courage to think uncomfortably, since it is only by rejecting the convenient that one can come to think the truth.

Not, after all, that there is any such thing as truth. At best we can approach

A scene from the film of Edward Albee's play, *Who's Afraid of Virginia Woolf?*

to some relative approximation. On the other hand, there is surely such a thing as untruth. One is generally aware when one has said something, or acted in some
25 way which has left on other people an impression not strictly in accordance with the facts. One is generally aware, also, when one has thrust aside an inconvenient thought and slid into its place another thought which is convenient. One's awareness in the former case is in general more acute than in the latter, since we are more on the look-out for the lies we utter than for those we merely think. In
30 fact, however, it is the untruthful thought which is the more vicious of the two. Spoken lies are invariably tiresome and may actually be dishonest. But continuous lying in the mind, a disease to which the Anglo-Saxon is peculiarly exposed, spells the destruction of human thought and character.

HAROLD NICOLSON On Telling the Truth from Small Talk

Comprehension

Answer these questions:
a How does our attitude to marriage differ from that of the Victorians?
b Explain in a sentence what you think the author means by the phrase 'lying in the mind'. (l. 32)

Vocabulary

Explain the meaning of the following words and phrases as they are used in the passage: accorded to (l. 1); endeavoured to pretend (l. 2); fact (l. 3); obsessed (l. 5); cohabitation (l. 6); forced servitudes (l. 9); assumption (l. 10); ineptitude (ll. 16–17); execrable (l. 19); rejecting the convenient (ll. 20–21); relative approximation (l. 23); thrust aside (l. 26); invariably (l. 31).

Précis

1. Drawing your information from the first two paragraphs (lines 1–21) write a list of points to answer the following question: Why, according to the author, was the Victorian attitude to truth hypocritical?
2. Using this list of points, reconstruct the author's argument in not more than 100 words. Your answer should be in one paragraph.

Composition

Write a composition of about 300 words on the following subject: 'No feat of intelligence and character is so exacting as that required by two people who desire to live permanently together.' Argue for or against this idea. You may use some or all of the ideas given below if you wish:
a People often marry for the wrong reasons: divorce rates are high.
b Marriage may bring great happiness but requires qualities of selflessness, sacrifice and the continuous need for compromise.
c The personal relationship of two adults becomes enormously complicated after the arrival of children.
d A perfect marriage may be an unattainable ideal, but a marriage that works is certainly possible.

Key Structures

1. Note the pattern in italics:

We . . . are obsessed by the problem of how to render the basic facts of cohabitation simpler and more reasonable, *in order that* unhappy marriages *may* less frequently *result*. (ll. 3–7)

Write three sentences using the pattern *in order that . . . may*.

2. Compare these two sentences:

Instead of saying: The Victorians would have considered it 'painful' or 'unpleasant' *if one were to point out* that only four marriages out of every ten are anything but forced servitudes.

We can say: The Victorians would have considered it 'painful' or 'unpleasant' *were one to point out* that only four marriages out of every ten are anything but forced servitudes. (ll. 7–9)

Complete the following sentences:

a Were there to be a General Election this year . . .

b Were he to change his mind . . .

3. Compare these two sentences:

Instead of saying: One should have the courage to think uncomfortably. (ll. 19–20)

We can say: You should have the courage to think uncomfortably.

Write two sentences using *one* and *you* in this way.

4. Study this sentence:

Continuous lying in the mind, *a disease to which the Anglo-Saxon is peculiarly exposed,* spells the destruction of human thought and character. (ll. 31–33)

Complete the following sentences:

a Travelling by air, a thing . . .

b Learning how to drive a car, a skill . . .

c Editing a newspaper, a job . . .

Special Difficulties

1. Write sentences to bring out the difference between the following pairs of words: reasonable (l. 6), logical; sensible (l. 10), sensitive; habit (l. 16), custom; continuous (ll. 31–32), continual.

2. Write sentences using the following words and phrases: accorded to (l. 1); unduly (l. 18); at best (l. 22); on the other hand (l. 23); in accordance with (l. 25); the former . . . the latter (l. 28).

3. Note this phrase: *only four marriages out of every ten* (ll. 8–9). Write sentences using the following expressions:

ninety out of every hundred people; seven out of twenty-four candidates.

4. Compare the phrases in italics:

a Not, after all, that there is *any such thing* as truth. (l. 22)

b There is *no such thing* as truth.

Write two sentences using the phrases *any such thing* and *no such thing*.

38

Appreciation of sculpture depends upon the ability to respond to form in three dimensions. That is perhaps why sculpture has been described as the most difficult of all arts; certainly it is more difficult than the arts which involve appreciation of flat forms, shape in only two dimensions. Many more people are
5 'form-blind' than colour-blind. The child learning to see, first distinguishes only two-dimensional shape; it cannot judge distances, depths. Later, for its personal safety and practical needs, it has to develop (partly by means of touch) the ability to judge roughly three-dimensional distances. But having satisfied the requirements of practical necessity, most people go no further. Though they may attain
10 considerable accuracy in the perception of flat form, they do not make the further intellectual and emotional effort needed to comprehend form in its full spatial existence.

This is what the sculptor must do. He must strive continually to think of, and use, form in its full spatial completeness. He gets the solid shape, as it were, in-
15 side his head—he thinks of it, whatever its size, as if he were holding it completely enclosed in the hollow of his hand. He mentally visualizes a complex form *from all round itself*; he knows while he looks at one side what the other side is like; he identifies himself with its centre of gravity, its mass, its weight; he realizes its volume, as the space that the shape displaces in the air.
20 And the sensitive observer of sculpture must also learn to feel shape simply as shape, not as description or reminiscence. He must, for example, perceive an egg as a simple single solid shape, quite apart from its significance as food, or

Henry Moore and his sculpture, *Reclining Figure*

from the literary idea that it will become a bird. And so with solids such as a shell, a nut, a plum, a pear, a tadpole, a mushroom, a mountain peak, a kidney, a carrot, a tree-trunk, a bird, a bud, a lark, a ladybird, a bulrush, a bone. From these he can go on to appreciate more complex forms or combinations of several forms.

HENRY MOORE *The Sculptor Speaks* from *The Listener*

Comprehension

Answer these questions:
a What does the author mean when he says that many people are 'form-blind'? (l. 5)
b What do you understand by the following statement: 'the sensitive observer of sculpture must also learn to feel shape simply as shape, not as a description or reminiscence.'? (ll. 20–21)

Vocabulary

Explain the meaning of the following words and phrases as they are used in the passage: in three dimensions (ll. 1–2); involve (l. 3); distinguishes (l. 5); roughly (l. 8); they may attain considerable accuracy in the perception (ll. 9–10); strive (l. 13); visualizes (l. 16); combinations (l. 26).

Précis

1. Drawing your information from the first two paragraphs (lines 1–19) write a list of points in note form to answer the following question: How does a sculptor's appreciation of form differ from that of an ordinary person?
2. Using this list of points, reconstruct the author's argument in not more than 90 words. Your answer should be in one paragraph.

Composition

Write a composition of about 300 words on the following subject: 'The arts (music, literature, painting and sculpture) cannot be enjoyed unless one has a specialized knowledge of them.' Argue against this statement. You may use some or all of the ideas given below if you wish:
a Many people enjoy listening to music, reading novels or poetry, looking at pictures or sculpture without knowing anything about the technical difficulties involved in creating works of art.
b There is a difference between appreciation and enjoyment: in order to appreciate a work of art, one should have a great deal of specialized knowledge; in order to enjoy a work of art, no such knowledge is necessary.
c Specialized knowledge can increase one's enjoyment: a trained mind knows what to look for.
d Specialized knowledge can diminish one's enjoyment: it may make you hypercritical and interfere with your response.
e Artists do not create works of art for those who have specialized knowledge only: often they attempt to communicate to large numbers of people.
f If specialized knowledge were necessary to enjoy the arts, then only those engaged in the arts would be in a position to enjoy them—something which is demonstrably untrue.

Key Structures

1. Supply the missing words in the following sentences. Do not refer to the passage until you have finished the exercise:

a That is perhaps why sculpture has been described as . . . . . . difficult . . . all arts; certainly it is . . . difficult . . . the arts which involve appreciation of flat forms. (ll. 2–4)

b . . . . . . people are 'form-blind' . . . colour blind. (ll. 4–5)

c But having satisfied the requirements of practical necessity, . . . people go no . . . (ll. 8–9)

2. Compare these two sentences:

Instead of saying: When they have satisfied the requirements of practical necessity, most people go no further.

We can say: Having satisfied the requirements of practical necessity, most people go no further. (ll. 8–9)

Write three sentences beginning with *Having*.

3. Rewrite each of these sentences replacing *has to* by *must*:

a This is what the sculptor has to do. (l. 13)

b He has to strive continually to think of, and use, form in its full spatial completeness. (ll. 13–14)

c And the sensitive observer of sculpture also has to learn to feel shape simply as shape, not as description or reminiscence. (ll. 20–21)

d He has, for example, to perceive an egg as a simple single solid shape. (ll. 21–22)

4. Note the construction in italics:

He thinks of it . . . *as if he were holding* it completely enclosed in the hollow of his hand. (ll. 15–16)

Complete the following sentences using the same construction:

a He acted as if . . .

b He talked as if . . .

c It looked as if . . .

Special Difficulties

1. Write sentences to bring out the difference between the following pairs of words: appreciation (l. 1), estimation; distinguish (l. 5), perceive (l. 21); depths (l. 6), deeps; continually (l. 13), continuously; displace (l. 19), replace; single (l. 22), unique.

2. Explain the meaning of the word *form* in these sentences:

a It is more difficult than the arts which involve appreciation of flat *forms*. (ll. 3–4)

b A new golf club has just been *formed* in our district.

c How many children are there in your *form*?

d I don't feel like playing tennis. I haven't been in very good *form* lately.

e There were not enough chairs to go round so we had to sit on *forms*.

f Would you please fill up this *form*?

3. Explain the meaning of the phrases in italics:

a He knows while he looks at one side what the other side *is like*. (l. 17)

b What *is* your new school *like*?

c What *was* the weather *like* yesterday?

39

In his own lifetime Galileo was the centre of violent controversy; but the scientific dust has long since settled, and today we can see even his famous clash with the Inquisition in something like its proper perspective. But, in contrast, it is only in modern times that Galileo has become a problem child for historians of
5 science.

    The old view of Galileo was delightfully uncomplicated. He was, above all, a man who experimented: who despised the prejudices and book learning of the Aristotelians, who put his questions to nature instead of to the ancients, and who drew his conclusions fearlessly. He had been the first to turn a telescope to the
10 sky, and he had seen there evidence enough to overthrow Aristotle and Ptolemy together. He was the man who climbed the Leaning Tower of Pisa and dropped various weights from the top, who rolled balls down inclined planes, and then generalized the results of his many experiments into the famous law of free fall.

    But a closer study of the evidence, supported by a deeper sense of the period,
15 and particularly by a new consciousness of the philosophical undercurrents in the scientific revolution, has profoundly modified this view of Galileo. Today, although the old Galileo lives on in many popular writings, among historians of science a new and more sophisticated picture has emerged. At the same time our sympathy for Galileo's opponents has grown somewhat. His telescopic observa-
20 tions are justly immortal; they aroused great interest at the time, they had important theoretical consequences, and they provided a striking demonstration of the potentialities hidden in instruments and apparatus. But can we blame those

The 200-inch Hale telescope at Palomar
Observatory, California

who looked and failed to see what Galileo saw, if we remember that to use a
telescope at the limit of its powers calls for long experience and intimate famili-
25 arity with one's instrument? Was the philosopher who refused to look through
Galileo's telescope more culpable than those who alleged that the spiral nebulae
observed with Lord Rosse's great telescope in the eighteen-forties were scratches
left by the grinder? We can perhaps forgive those who said the moons of Jupiter
were produced by Galileo's spy-glass if we recall that in his day, as for centuries
30 before, curved glass was the popular contrivance for producing not truth but
illusion, untruth; and if a single curved glass would distort nature, how much
more would a pair of them?

MICHAEL HOSKIN *Galileo Reborn* from *The Listener*

Comprehension

Answer these questions:
a State in a sentence the main difference between the old and modern view of Galileo.
b How does the author justify Galileo's contemporaries for failing to see what he saw?

Vocabulary

Explain the meaning of the following words and phrases as they are used in the passage:
violent controversy (l. 1); clash (l. 2); proper perspective (l. 3); despised the preju-
dices (l. 7); consciousness (l. 15); profoundly modified (l. 16); consequences (l. 21);
potentialities (l. 22); culpable (l. 26); contrivance (l. 30); distort (l. 31).

Précis

1. Drawing your information from the last paragraph (lines 14–32) write a list of points
in note form to answer the following question: How has a closer study of the evidence
profoundly modified the old view of Galileo?
2. Using this list of points, reconstruct the author's argument in not more than 90
words. Your answer should be in one paragraph.

Composition

Write a composition of about 300 words on the following subject: 'New ideas can
never be readily accepted by those who cling to old beliefs.' Argue in favour of this
statement. You may use some or all of the ideas given below if you wish:
a Why new ideas are resisted: prejudice, fear, narrow sensibilities. Examples: the
length of time the views of Aristotle and Ptolemy persisted. Copernicus' reluctance to
publish his work.
b New ideas which are resisted when they first make their appearance are gradually
assimilated until they finally become commonplace. Examples: The observation of
Copernicus that the earth goes round the sun; the views of Galileo: the scientific
method; Kepler's ideas on planetary motions; Darwin's idea of evolution; Freud's ideas
on psychology.
c There are, however, exceptions. Some great ideas have been accepted almost without question from the time they made their appearance: Newton's ideas on gravitation
were acclaimed in the eighteenth century just as Einstein's ideas on relativity were
acclaimed in the twentieth.

Key Structures

1. Supply the missing words in the following paragraph. Do not refer to the passage until you have finished the exercise:

He had been the first to turn a telescope . . . the sky, and he had seen there evidence enough to overthrow Aristotle and Ptolemy together. He was the man who climbed the Leaning Tower . . . Pisa and dropped various weights . . . the top, who rolled balls . . . inclined planes, and then generalized the results . . . his many experiments . . . the famous law . . . free fall. (ll. 9–13)

2. Supply *a* or *the* where necessary in the following paragraph. Do not refer to the passage until you have finished the exercise:

But . . . closer study of . . . evidence, supported by . . . deeper sense of . . . period, and particularly by . . . new consciousness of . . . philosophical undercurrents in . . . scientific revolution, has profoundly modified this view of . . . Galileo. Today, although . . . old Galileo lives on in . . . many popular writings, among . . . historians of . . . science . . . new and more sophisticated picture has emerged. (ll. 14–18)

3. Compare these two sentences:

Instead of saying: Using a telescope at the limit of its powers calls for long experience and intimate familiarity with one's instrument.

We can say: To use a telescope at the limit of its powers calls for long experience and intimate familiarity with one's instrument. (ll. 23–25)

Write sentences which begin with the following words: To build; Reading; To eat; Smoking.

Special Difficulties

1. Write sentences to bring out the difference between the following pairs of words: plane (l. 12), plain; popular (l. 17), folk; sympathy (l. 19), affection; arouse (l. 20), arise; blame (l. 22), accuse; refuse (l. 25), deny; scratch (l. 27), scrape.

2. Explain the meaning of the verb *settle* in these sentences:

b Have you *settled down* in your new house yet?

c I *settled down* in an armchair to read a book.

d I shall *settle* my account next week.

e We must *settle* this problem once for all.

f His ancestors *settled* in Boston in the eighteen fifties.

3. Note the use of *on* in this sentence to indicate continuity:

The old Galileo lives *on* in many popular writings. (l. 17)

Write sentences using the following verbs: keep on; carry on; go on; drive on; walk on; read on.

4. Explain the verbs in italics:

a To use a telescope . . . *calls for* long experience. (ll. 23–24)

b I'll *call on* you on my way home from work.

c I'll *call you up* at the office tomorrow morning.

d It's impossible to have a party tomorrow. Why don't we *call* the whole thing *off*?

e May I leave this suitcase here? I'll *call for* it later.

f I think you'd better *call in* a doctor.

40

Populations increase and decrease relatively not only to one another, but also to natural resources. In most parts of the world, the relation between population and resources is already unfavourable and will probably become even more unfavourable in the future. This growing poverty in the midst of growing poverty
5 constitutes a permanent menace to peace. And not only to peace, but also to democratic institutions and personal liberty. For overpopulation is not compatible with freedom. An unfavourable relationship between numbers and resources tends to make the earning of a living almost intolerably difficult. Labour is more abundant than goods, and the individual is compelled to work long hours
10 for little pay. No surplus of accumulated purchasing power stands between him and the tyrannies of unfriendly nature or of the equally unfriendly wielders of political and economic power. Democracy is, among other things, the ability to say 'no' to the boss. But a man cannot say 'no' to the boss, unless he is sure of being able to eat when the boss's favour has been withdrawn. And he cannot be
15 certain of his next meal unless he owns the means of producing enough wealth for his family to live on, or has been able to accumulate a surplus out of past wages, or has a chance of moving to virgin territories, where he can make a fresh start. In an overcrowded country, very few people own enough to make them financially independent; very few are in a position to accumulate purchasing
20 power; and there is no free land. Moreover, in any country where population presses hard upon natural resources, the general economic situation is apt to be so precarious that government control of capital and labour, production and con-

Russian immigrants pass the
Statue of Liberty in 1892

sumption, becomes inevitable. It is no accident that the twentieth century should
be the century of highly centralized governments and totalitarian dictatorships;
25 it had to be so for the simple reason that the twentieth century is the century of
planetary overcrowding.

ALDOUS HUXLEY Themes and Variations

Comprehension

Answer these questions:

a What do you understand by the following: 'the relation between population and
resources is already unfavourable'? (ll. 2–3)

b What do you understand by the phrase 'surplus of accumulated purchasing power'?
(l. 10)

c Why does the author consider over-population to constitute a threat to democracy?

d Why, according to the author, is it no accident that the twentieth century should be
the century of highly centralized governments and totalitarian dictatorships?

Vocabulary

Explain the meaning of the following words and phrases as they are used in the passage:
a permanent menace (l. 5); personal liberty (l. 6); compatible (ll. 6–7); intolerably (l. 8);
abundant (l. 9); wielders (l. 11); withdrawn (l. 14); virgin territories (l. 17); apt (l. 21);
precarious (l. 22); inevitable (l. 23); totalitarian (l. 24).

Précis

1. Drawing your information from the passage write a list of points in note form outlining the undesirable effects of over-population.

2. Using this list of points, reconstruct the author's argument in not more than 120
words.

Composition

Write a composition of about 300 words on the following subject: The Ideals of
Democracy. You may use some or all of the ideas given below if you wish:

a The right of the people to elect a government of their choice.

b Freedom of the individual: thought and action; religious beliefs.

c Freedom of the press.

d Democratic ideals will not work in conditions of poverty and extreme social unrest.

e Democratic ideals presuppose a fair distribution of wealth; equality of opportunity
in education; full employment; insurance against illness and unemployment.

Key Structures

1. Supply *a(n)* or *the* where necessary in the following. Do not refer to the passage
until you have finished the exercise:

. . . populations increase and decrease relatively not only to one another, but also to . . .
natural resources. In . . . most parts of . . . world, . . . relation between . . . population
and . . . resources is already unfavourable and will probably become even more unfavourable in . . . future. This growing poverty in . . . midst of growing poverty constitutes . . . permanent menace to . . . peace. And not only to . . . peace, but also to . . .
democratic institutions and . . . personal liberty. For . . . overpopulation is not compatible with . . . freedom. . . . unfavourable relationship between . . . numbers and . . .

133

resources tends to make . . . earning of . . . living almost intolerably difficult. . . . labour is more abundant than . . . goods, and . . . individual is compelled to work long hours for . . . little pay. (ll. 1–10)

2. Put the words in brackets in their correct positions in these sentences. In some cases more than one position is possible. Do not refer to the passage until you have finished the exercise:

a The relation between population and resources is unfavourable and will become more unfavourable in the future. (in most parts of the world, already, probably, even) (ll. 2–4)

b An unfavourable relationship between numbers and resources tends to make the earning of a living difficult. (almost intolerably) (ll. 7–8)

c No surplus of accumulated purchasing power stands between him and the tyrannies of unfriendly nature or of the unfriendly wielders of political and economic power. (equally) (ll. 10–12)

3. Compare the use of *being* and *been* in this sentence:

A man cannot say 'no' to the boss, unless he is sure of *being* able to eat when the boss's favour has *been* withdrawn. (ll. 13–14)

Supply *being* or *been* in these sentences:

a An inquiry is . . . made into the cause of the fire.

b I have . . . waiting for you for over half an hour.

c You should have . . . more careful.

d Now that the strike has ended, the ships are . . . unloaded.

e After . . . held up for over half an hour, the plane finally took off.

f After having . . . questioned by the police, the man was allowed to go home.

Special Difficulties

1. Write sentences to bring out the difference between the following pairs of words: parts (l. 2), places; peace (l. 5), piece; earn (l. 8), win.

2. Explain the meaning of the verbs in italics:

a He cannot be certain of . . . producing enough wealth for his family to *live on*. (ll. 14–16)

b Up to the end of the nineteenth century, the people of Ireland *lived* mainly *on* potatoes.

c Even though he's thirty years old, he can't support himself. He still *lives on* his parents.

d We are a long-established firm and must *live up to* our high reputation.

e She was involved in a scandal many years ago and has never been able to *live it down*.

3. Note that the word *wages* (l. 17) is plural and is followed by a plural verb: His wages *are* very high.

Write sentences using the following words: scissors, clothes, people, police, trousers.

Unit 5

INSTRUCTIONS TO THE STUDENT

Content

This Unit consists of ten passages followed by exercises on Comprehension, Vocabulary, Précis, Composition, Key Structures and Special Difficulties.

Aim

To carry the skills acquired in the previous Unit a stage further.

How to Work

1. Read each passage carefully two or three times.
2. Answer the questions in the order in which they are given.

Précis

You will be required to write a summary of a part of each passage in a limited number of words. Your work should fall into three distinct parts:

1. Write a list of points in note form deriving the specific information required by the question.
2. Join these points to write a draft précis in your own words as far as possible. When you have completed the draft, correct and amend it making sure you have not exceeded the word limit.
3. Write a fair copy of your précis. At the end, state the number of words you have used.

Composition

You will be required to write a composition of about 400 words on a subject connected in some way with the passage. Your work should fall into two distinct parts:

1. Write a list of ideas in note form which might be used to discuss the subject.
2. Write a composition based on these ideas.

41

Education is one of the key words of our time. A man without [...],
many of us believe, is an unfortunate victim of adverse circumsta[...]
of one of the greatest twentieth-century opportunities. Convinc[...] [...] [...]
portance of education, modern states 'invest' in institutions of learning to get
5 back 'interest' in the form of a large group of enlightened young men and women
who are potential leaders. Education, with its cycles of instruction so carefully
worked out, punctuated by text-books—those purchasable wells of wisdom—
what would civilization be like without its benefits?

So much is certain: that we would have doctors and preachers, lawyers and
10 defendants, marriages and births—but our spiritual outlook would be different.
We would lay less stress on 'facts and figures' and more on a good memory, on
applied psychology, and on the capacity of a man to get along with his fellow-
citizens. If our educational system were fashioned after its bookless past we
would have the most democratic form of 'college' imaginable. Among the people
15 whom we like to call savages all knowledge inherited by tradition is shared by
all; it is taught to every member of the tribe so that in this respect everybody is
equally equipped for life.

It is the ideal condition of the 'equal start' which only our most progressive
forms of modern education try to regain. In primitive cultures the obligation to
20 seek and to receive the traditional instruction is binding to all. There are no
'illiterates'—if the term can be applied to peoples without a script—while our
own compulsory school attendance became law in Germany in 1642, in France

The library at the University of Sussex

_06, and in England in 1876, and is still non-existent in a number of 'civi-
_ed' nations. This shows how long it was before we deemed it necessary to
make sure that all our children could share in the knowledge accumulated by the
'happy few' during the past centuries.

Education in the wilderness is not a matter of monetary means. All are entitled
to an equal start. There is none of the hurry which, in our society, often hampers
the full development of a growing personality. There, a child grows up under
30 the ever-present attention of his parents; therefore the jungles and the savannahs
know of no 'juvenile delinquency.' No necessity of making a living away from
home results in neglect of children, and no father is confronted with his inability
to 'buy' an education for his child.

JULIUS E. LIPS *The Origin of Things*

Comprehension

Answer these questions:
a In what way can education be said to be 'an investment'?
b Give one reason why the author appears to be opposed to formal education.
c Give one reason why, according to the author, a primitive society is superior to a
civilized society.

Vocabulary

Explain the meaning of the following words and phrases as they are used in the passage:
key (l. 1); adverse circumstances (l. 2); enlightened (l. 5); potential (l. 6); lay less stress
(l. 11); binding (l. 20); illiterates (l. 21); compulsory (l. 22); monetary means (l. 27);
entitled (l. 27); juvenile delinquency (l. 31).

Précis

Drawing your information from lines 9–33 ('So much . . . for his child.') write a
summary of the author's argument that real equality of opportunity is only to be found
in a primitive society. Do not write more than 100 words. Your answer should be in
one paragraph.

Composition

1. Write a list of ideas in note form which could be used to discuss this subject: 'A
man without an education, many of us believe, is an unfortunate victim of adverse
circumstances deprived of one of the greatest twentieth-century opportunities.'
2. Drawing on your list of ideas, write a composition of about 400 words.

Key Structures

1. Supply the missing words in the following paragraph. Do not refer to the passage
until you have finished the exercise:
Education is one . . . the key words . . . our time. A man . . . an education, many . . .
us believe, is an unfortunate victim . . . adverse circumstances deprived . . . one . . .
the greatest twentieth-century opportunities. Convinced . . . the importance . . . education, modern states 'invest' . . . institutions . . . learning to get back 'interest' . . .
the form . . . a large group . . . enlightened young men and women who are potential
leaders. Education, . . . its cycles . . . instruction so carefully worked . . ., punctuated

... text-books—those purchasable wells ... wisdom—what would civilization be like ... its benefits? (ll. 1–8)

2. A great many words and phrases are enclosed in inverted commas in this passage. What purpose do the inverted commas serve? Justify your answer with reference to three phrases.

3. Supply *less* or *fewer* in the following sentences:

a We would lay [*less*] stress on 'facts and figures'. (l. 11)

b There were [*fewer*] opportunities to get a good education in the past.

c [*Fewer*] people die of tuberculosis these days.

d I have [*less*] time now than I used to have.

e If there were [*fewer*] buses on the roads it would be easier to drive to work.

4. Supply *who*, *whom* or *which* in the following sentences. Do not refer to the passage until you have finished the exercise:

a Modern states get back 'interest' in the form of a large group of enlightened young men and women ... are potential leaders. (ll. 4–6)

b Among the people ... we like to call savages all knowledge inherited by tradition is shared by all. (ll. 14–16)

c It is the ideal condition of the 'equal start' ... only our most progressive forms of modern education try to regain. (ll. 18–19)

5. Study the pattern in italics:

This shows how long it was before we *deemed it necessary* to make sure that all our children could share in the knowledge accumulated by the 'happy few' during the past centuries. (ll. 24–26)

Write sentences using the same pattern with the following verbs:

consider, find, think, feel, believe.

Special Difficulties

1. Write sentences to bring out the difference between the following pairs of words: opportunities (l. 3), chances; potential (l. 6), potent; lay (l. 11), lie; memory (l. 11), remembrance; imaginable (l. 14), imaginative; tribe (l. 16), race; compulsory (l. 22), necessary.

2. Explain the meaning of the words in italics:

a Our spiritual *outlook* would be different. (l. 10)

b He's usually such a quiet person. I can't account for this *outburst*, can you?

c There was an *outbreak* of dysentery among the troops.

d One unexpected *outcome* of the new policy has been a fall in prices.

3. Comment on the use of *all* in these sentences:

All knowledge ... *is* shared by *all*. (ll. 15–16)

All are entitled to an equal start. (ll. 27–28)

42

Parents are often upset when their children praise the homes of their friends and regard it as a slur on their own cooking, or cleaning, or furniture, and often are foolish enough to let the adolescents see that they are annoyed. They may even accuse them of disloyalty, or make some spiteful remark about the friends'
5 parents. Such a loss of dignity and descent into childish behaviour on the part of the adults deeply shocks the adolescents, and makes them resolve that in future they will not talk to their parents about the places or people they visit. Before very long the parents will be complaining that the child is so secretive and never tells them anything, but they seldom realize that they have brought this on
10 themselves.

Disillusionment with the parents, however good and adequate they may be both as parents and as individuals, is to some degree inevitable. Most children have such a high ideal of their parents, unless the parents themselves have been unsatisfactory, that it can hardly hope to stand up to a realistic evaluation. Parents
15 would be greatly surprised and deeply touched if they realized how much belief their children usually have in their character and infallibility, and how much this faith means to a child. If parents were prepared for this adolescent reaction, and realized that it was a sign that the child was growing up and developing valuable powers of observation and independent judgment, they would not be so hurt,
20 and therefore would not drive the child into opposition by resenting and resisting it.

The adolescent, with his passion for sincerity, always respects a parent who

An English family at home

admits that he is wrong, or ignorant, or even that he has been unfair or unjust.
What the child cannot forgive is the parents' refusal to admit these charges if the
25 child knows them to be true.

Victorian parents believed that they kept their dignity by retreating behind an
unreasoning authoritarian attitude; in fact they did nothing of the kind, but
children were then too cowed to let them know how they really felt. Today we
tend to go to the other extreme, but on the whole this is a healthier attitude both
30 for the child and the parent. It is always wiser and safer to face up to reality,
however painful it may be at the moment.

DORIS ODLUM *Journey Through Adolescence*

Comprehension

Answer these questions:
a What sort of behaviour among parents does the author characterize as 'childish'?
b Why, according to the author, is it inevitable that adolescents should become dis-
illusioned with their parents?
c How does our attitude towards adolescents differ from that of the Victorians?

Vocabulary

Explain the meaning of the following words and phrases as they are used in the passage:
slur (l. 2); spiteful remark (l. 4); resolve (l. 6); disillusionment (l. 11); to some degree
inevitable (l. 12); evaluation (l. 14); touched (l. 15); infallibility (l. 16); resenting (l. 20);
charges (l. 24); retreating behind an unreasoning authoritarian attitude (ll. 26–27).

Précis

Drawing your information from lines 1–21 ('Parents . . . resisting it.') write a summary
of the author's argument that it is inevitable that adolescents should react against their
parents. Do not write more than 100 words. Your answer should be in one paragraph.

Composition

1. Write a list of ideas in note form which could be used to discuss this subject:
Account for the fact that children seem to grow up more quickly today than they did
in the past.
2. Drawing on your list of ideas, write a composition of about 400 words.

Key Structures

1. Put the words in brackets in their correct position in these sentences. In many cases
more than one position is possible. Do not refer to the passage until you have finished
the exercise:
a Parents are upset when their children praise the homes of their friends. (often)
(l. 1)
b Such a loss of dignity and descent into childish behaviour on the part of the adults
shocks the adolescents. (deeply) (ll. 5–6)
c They realize that they have brought this on themselves. (seldom) (ll. 9–10)
d Parents would be surprised and touched if they realized how much belief their children have in their character and infallibility. (greatly, deeply, usually) (ll. 14–16)

2. Compare the uses of *enough* in these two sentences:
a Parents are often . . . *foolish enough* to let the adolescents see that they are annoyed. (ll. 1–3)
b Have you had *enough tea*, or would you like some more?
Write two sentences using *enough* in the ways shown above.
3. Note the form of the verbs used after *let* and *make* in these two sentences:
a They often are foolish enough to *let* the adolescents *see* that they are annoyed. (ll. 2–3)
b Such a loss of dignity . . . *makes* them *resolve* that in future they will not talk to their parents. (ll. 5–7)
Complete the following sentences:
a They let us . . .
b We made them . . .
c Will you let him . . .
d Why make me . . .
4. Supply the correct form of the verbs in brackets in these sentences. Do not refer to the passage until you have finished the exercise:
a Parents greatly (surprise) . . . if they realized . . . how much this faith means to a child. (ll. 14–17)
b If parents were prepared for this adolescent reaction, and (realize) that it (be) a sign that the child (grow) up and (develop) valuable powers of observation and independent judgment, they not (be) so hurt, and therefore not (drive) the child into opposition by resenting and resisting it. (ll. 17–21)
5. Compare these two sentences:
Instead of saying: The thing the child cannot forgive is the parents' refusal to admit these charges.
We can say: What the child cannot forgive is the parents' refusal to admit these charges. (l. 24)
Write three statements similar in form to the one above beginning with *What*.

Special Difficulties

1. Write sentences to bring out the difference between the following pairs of words: enough (l. 3), fairly; loss (l. 5), lose; descent (l. 5), decent; belief (l. 15), loyalty; grow up (l. 18), grow; hurt (l. 19), pain; refusal (l. 24), denial.
2. Write sentences using the following phrases:
on the part of (l. 5); before very long (ll. 7–8); to stand up to (l. 14); nothing of the kind (l. 27); on the whole (l. 29); to face up to (l. 30); at the moment (l. 31).

43

Faith in controlled nuclear fission is now being shown by the construction of atomic power stations. In Britain, Calder Hall on the coast of Cumberland first made its contribution to the National Electricity grid in 1957. Subsequently a chain of nuclear power stations was planned. Of necessity they are sited near the coasts or tidal water because of the need of much water for cooling and a certain discharge of possible radioactive effluent. Atomic power is associated in the public mind with the destructive force of atom bombs and partly for this reason, though it is claimed that there is no danger to be associated with atomic power stations, they are being sited away from populous centres.

The present position is that the three main sources of power are coal, oil and water power. We sometimes refer to electricity, gas or petrol as if they were the actual sources of power, forgetting that electricity must be generated by the consumption of coal or oil or by the utilization of water power, whilst coke, gas and petrol are examples of secondary fuels by which coal and oil may be more effectively used.

Where alternative sources of power are available there are some marked contrasts in handling. The bulk and weight of coal required in the majority of manufacturing industries is large in comparison with the bulk and weight of other raw materials. This is not always true—as with the manufacture of pig iron and steel from low-grade iron ores—but it did lead to the concentration of industrial developments on the coal-fields, a phenomenon well seen in such countries as Britain where the Industrial Revolution came before the days of oil or electricity. Coal being a solid must be distributed mainly by rail or water.

Coal-carrying barges on the Grand Union Canal at Watford

The Esso Oil Refinery at Milford Haven

By way of contrast oil can be transported large distances by pipeline but over-
25 seas movement has involved building of large numbers of tankers, including now
some of the largest vessels afloat. Unless suitable on other grounds oilfields have
not become industrial regions; on the contrary the oil industry is marked by a
certain amount of smell and an element of danger, hence the siting of refineries
at a distance from population centres. It is not always realized that the owners of
30 pipelines can handle the oil of different customers, sending it through at different periods. Natural gas can also be transported large distances by pipe. Early
in 1959 Britain received the first ship cargo of natural gas—liquefied for the
purpose of transport.

L. DUDLEY STAMP Our Developing World

Comprehension

Answer these questions:
a Why are nuclear power stations sited near the coasts?
b What led to the concentration of industrial developments on the coal-fields?
c Why are oil refineries sited at a distance from population centres?

Vocabulary

Explain the meaning of the following words and phrases as they are used in the passage:
subsequently (l. 3); populous centres (l. 9); generated (l. 12); consumption (l. 13);
utilization (l. 13); marked contrasts (ll. 16–17); hence (l. 28).

Précis

Drawing your information from the passage, explain why certain sources of power are
sited in particular areas. Do not write more than 120 words. Your answer should be in
one paragraph.

Composition

1. Write a list of ideas in note form which could be used to discuss this subject:
Despite the construction of atomic power stations, oil is likely to remain the world's
chief source of power for many years to come.
2. Drawing on your list of ideas, write a composition of about 400 words.

Key Structures

1. Supply the missing words in the following sentences. Do not refer to the passage
until you have finished the exercise:
a Faith . . . controlled nuclear fission is now being shown . . . the construction . . .
atomic power stations. (ll. 1–2)
b . . . Britain, Calder Hall . . . the coast . . . Cumberland first made its contribution . . .
the National Electricity grid . . . 1957. (ll. 2–3)
c . . . necessity they are sited . . . the coasts or tidal water because . . . the need of
much water . . . cooling and a certain discharge . . . possible radioactive effluent.
(ll. 4–6)
d Atomic power is associated . . . the public mind . . . the destructive force . . . atom
bombs. (ll. 6–7)
e The bulk and weight . . . coal required . . . the majority . . . manufacturing industries is large . . . comparison . . . the bulk and weight . . . other raw materials.
(ll. 17–19)

f This is not always true—as . . . the manufacture . . . pig iron and steel . . . low-grade iron ores—but it did lead . . . the concentration . . . industrial developments . . . the coal-fields, a phenomenon well seen . . . such countries as Britain where the Industrial Revolution came . . . the days . . . oil or electricity. (ll. 19–23)

b . . . way . . . contrast oil can be transported large distances . . . pipeline but overseas movement has involved building . . . large numbers . . . tankers, including now some . . . the largest vessels afloat. (ll. 24–26)

2. Compare the four sentences given below:

a Electricity *must be* generated by the consumption of coal.

b Electricity *had to be* generated by the consumption of coal or oil.

c Tom hasn't come to work today. He *must be* ill.

d Tom didn't come to work yesterday. He *must have been* ill.

Supply *had to* or *must have been* with the correct form of the verbs in brackets in the following sentences:

a This letter . . . (write) several days before it was posted.

b I'm sorry I couldn't come earlier. I . . . (go) to the bank.

c We . . . (sell) our house because my husband was posted overseas.

d This church . . . (build) in Norman times.

e I . . . (drive) at eighty miles an hour to get here on time.

f The last time I went to the National Gallery, the Virgin of the Rocks was not on display. It . . . (remove) for cleaning.

Special Difficulties

1. Write sentences to bring out the difference between the following pairs of words: control (l. 1), check; construction (l. 1), manufacture (l. 19); contribution (l. 3), offering; claim (l. 8), believe; populous (l. 9), popular; petrol (l. 14), benzine; effectively (l. 15), efficiently; lead (l. 20), guide; suitable (l. 26), convenient.

2. Explain the meaning of *claim* in these sentences:

a He *claims* that he is the author of this book.

b How much money did you *claim* from the insurance company?

c A packet containing a large sum of money was taken to the police station. So far no one has *claimed* it.

3. Explain the meaning of the words and expressions in italics:

a The Industrial Revolution came before the *days* of oil or electricity. (ll. 22–23)

b I'd like to *end my days* in a small cottage by the sea.

c *These days* schools have changed a great deal. *In my day*, teachers were far more strict.

d *Every dog has his day.*

44

If a nation is essentially disunited, it is left to the government to hold it together. This increases the expense of government, and reduces correspondingly the amount of economic resources that could be used for developing the country. And it should not be forgotten how small those resources are in a poor and back-
5 ward country. Where the cost of government is high, resources for development are correspondingly low.

This may be illustrated by comparing the position of a nation with that of a private business enterprise. An enterprise has to incur certain costs and expenses in order to stay in business. For our purposes, we are concerned only with one
10 kind of cost—the cost of managing and administering the business. Such adminis-trative overhead in a business is analogous to the cost of government in a nation. The administrative overhead of a business is low to the extent that everyone working in the business can be trusted to behave in a way that best promotes the interests of the firm. If they can each be trusted to take such responsibilities,
15 and to exercise such initiative as falls within their sphere, then administrative overhead will be low. It will be low because it will be necessary to have only one man looking after each job, without having another man to check upon what he is doing, keep him in line, and report on him to someone else. But if no one can be trusted to act in a loyal and responsible manner towards his job, then the
20 business will require armies of administrators, checkers, and foremen, and ad-ministrative overhead will rise correspondingly. As administrative overhead rises, so the earnings of the business, after meeting the expense of administration, will fall; and the business will have less money to distribute as dividends or invest directly in its future progress and development.
25 It is precisely the same with a nation. To the extent that the people can be

The Ministry of Natural Resources
and Local Government, Zomba, Malawi

The Home Office, Whitehall, London

relied upon to behave in a loyal and responsible manner, the government does not require armies of police and civil servants to keep them in order. But if a nation is disunited, the government cannot be sure that the actions of the people will be in the interests of the nation; and it will have to watch, check, and control
30 the people accordingly. A disunited nation therefore has to incur unduly high costs of government.

RAYMOND FROST *The Backward Society*

Comprehension

Answer these questions:
a Why is the expense of government increased if a nation is disunited?
b What do you understand by the phrase 'administrative overhead'? (ll. 10–11)

Vocabulary

Explain the meaning of the following words and phrases as they are used in the passage: reduces correspondingly the amount of economic resources (ll. 2–3); incur (l. 8); analogous (l. 11); promotes (l. 13); distribute as dividends (l. 23); precisely (l. 25); unduly (l. 30).

Précis

Drawing your information from lines 7–31 ('This may be ... costs of government') show how the running of a business enterprise can be compared with the running of a country. Do not write more than 120 words. Your answer should be in one paragraph.

Composition

1. Write a list of ideas in note form which could be used to discuss this subject: Ideally, a civil service should consist of a permanently appointed body of men who are not necessarily affiliated to the political party that is in power at any particular time.
2. Drawing on your list of ideas, write a composition of about 400 words.

Key Structures

1. Supply the correct form of the verbs in brackets in the following sentences. Do not refer to the passage until you have completed the exercise:
a This ... reduces ... the amount of economic resources that could be used for (develop) the country. (ll. 2–3)
b This may be illustrated by (compare) the position of a nation with that of a private business enterprise. (ll. 7–8)
c We are concerned only with ... the cost of (manage) and (administer) the business. (ll. 9–10)
d It will be low because it will be necessary to have only one man (look) after each job, without (have) another man to check upon what he is doing. (ll. 16–18)
e The earnings of the business, after (meet) the expense of administration, will fall. (ll. 22–23)
2. Write these sentences again so that they begin with the words given in brackets. Make any other necessary changes. Do not refer to the passage until you have completed the exercise:
a We should not forget how small these resources are. (It) (l. 4)
b We may illustrate this by comparing the position of a nation with that of a private business enterprise. (This) (ll. 7–8)

c Only one kind of cost concerns us. (We) (ll. 9–10)

d We can trust each of them to take such responsibilities. (They) (l. 14)

e We cannot trust anyone to act in a loyal and responsible manner. (No one) (ll. 18–19)

f We can rely upon the people to behave in a loyal and responsible manner. (The people) (ll. 25–26)

3. In which of the following sentences would it be possible to use *in order to* in place of *to*? Do not refer to the passage until you have completed the exercise:

a An enterprise has to incur certain costs and expenses *to* stay in business. (ll. 8–9)

b They can be trusted *to* take such responsibilities. (l. 14)

c No one can be trusted *to* act in a loyal and responsible manner. (ll. 18–19)

d The government does not require armies of police and civil servants *to* keep them in order. (ll. 26–27)

3. Note the use of *best* in this sentence:

Everyone working in the business can be trusted to behave in a way that *best promotes* the interest of the firm. (ll. 12–14)

Write sentences using the following expressions:

best illustrates; best describes; best explains.

Special Difficulties

1. Write sentences to bring out the difference between the following pairs of words: job (l. 17), work; rise (l. 21), raise; earnings (l. 22), profits; watch (l. 29), follow; check (l. 29), control (l. 29).

2. Explain the meaning of the words in italics:

a It should not be forgotten how small those resources are in a poor and *backward* country. (ll. 4–5)

b The train had to go *backwards* for half a mile.

c She is concerned with the care of *backward* children.

3. How does the position of *only* affect the meaning of the following sentences:

a We are concerned *only* with one kind of cost. (ll. 9–10)

b We *only* are concerned.

c We are concerned with *only* one kind of cost.

d We are concerned with one kind of cost *only*.

45

At the age of twelve years, the human body is at its most vigorous. It has yet to reach its full size and strength, and its owner his or her full intelligence; but at this age the likelihood of death is least. Earlier, we were infants and young children, and consequently more vulnerable; later, we shall undergo a progressive loss
5 of our vigour and resistance which, though imperceptible at first, will finally become so steep that we can live no longer, however well we look after ourselves, and however well society, and our doctors, look after us. This decline in vigour with the passing of time is called ageing. It is one of the most unpleasant discoveries which we all make that we *must* decline in this way, that if we escape
10 wars, accidents and diseases we shall eventually 'die of old age', and that this happens at a rate which differs little from person to person, so that there are heavy odds in favour of our dying between the ages of sixty-five and eighty. Some of us will die sooner, a few will live longer—on into a ninth or tenth decade. But the chances are against it, and there is a virtual limit on how long we can hope
15 to remain alive, however lucky and robust we are.

Normal people tend to forget this process unless and until they are reminded of it. We are so familiar with the fact that man ages, that people have for years assumed that the process of losing vigour with time, of becoming more likely to die the older we get, was something self-evident, like the cooling of a hot kettle
20 or the wearing-out of a pair of shoes. They have also assumed that all animals, and probably other organisms such as trees, or even the universe itself, must in the nature of things 'wear out'. Most animals we commonly observe do in fact

Two tortoises, both from the Seychelles;
the small one is a year old, the large one
is over a hundred

age as we do if given the chance to live long enough; and mechanical systems like
a wound watch, or the sun, do in fact run out of energy in accordance with the
25 second law of thermodynamics (whether the whole universe does so is a moot
point at present). But these are not analogous to what happens when man ages.
A run-down watch is still a watch and can be rewound. An *old* watch, by contrast, becomes so worn and unreliable that it eventually is not worth mending.
But a watch could never repair itself—it does not consist of living parts, only of
30 metal, which wears away by friction. We could, at one time, repair ourselves—
well enough, at least, to overcome all but the most instantly fatal illnesses and
accidents. Between twelve and eighty years we gradually lose this power; an
illness which at twelve would knock us over, at eighty can knock us out, and into
our grave. If we could stay as vigorous as we are at twelve, it would take about
35 700 years for half of us to die, and another 700 for the survivors to be reduced
by half again.

ALEX COMFORT *The Process of Ageing*

Comprehension

Answer these questions:
a Why is the likelihood of death least when we are twelve years old?
b Why are there heavy odds in favour of our dying between the ages of sixty-five and
eighty?
c Which power do we gradually lose between the ages of twelve and eighty?

Vocabulary

Explain the meaning of the following words and phrases as they are used in the passage:
likelihood (l. 3); vulnerable (l. 4); imperceptible (l. 5); decline in vigour (l. 7); rate
(l. 11); robust (l. 15); self-evident (l. 19); moot (l. 25); fatal (l. 31).

Précis

Drawing your information from the second paragraph (lines 16–36) write a summary of
the author's description of the process of ageing. Do not write more than 100 words.
Your answer should be in one paragraph.

Composition

1. Write a list of ideas in note form which could be used to discuss the following subject: Suggest reasons why we in the twentieth century can expect to live longer than
people who lived in bygone times.
2. Drawing on your list of ideas, write a composition of about 400 words.

Key Structures

1. Supply *the* where necessary in the following sentences:
a It is one of . . . most unpleasant discoveries which we all make. (ll. 8–9)
b . . . most animals we commonly observe do in fact age as we do. (ll. 22–23)
c Death is something which . . . most people fear.
d Make . . . most of what you've got.
e . . . most of the things I've got were bought overseas.

2. Compare the use of *however* in these sentences.

a There is a virtual limit on how long we can hope to remain alive, *however* lucky and robust we are.

b No one will deny that many of the programmes shown on television are very poor. There are, *however*, a fair number which are very fine indeed.

Write two sentences using *however* in the ways shown above.

3. Complete these sentences in any way you wish. Then compare what you have written with the sentences in the passage:

a We shall undergo a progressive loss of our vigour and resistance which will finally become so steep that . . . (ll. 4–6)

b We are so familiar with the fact that man ages, that . . . (l. 17)

c An *old* watch, by contrast, becomes so worn and unreliable that . . . (ll. 27–28)

Special Difficulties

1. Write sentences to bring out the difference between the following pairs of words: strength (l. 2), force; infant (l. 3), baby; imperceptible (l. 5), unperceived; alive (l. 15), living; pair (l. 20), pear.

2. Explain the meaning of the verbs in italics:

a We shall undergo a progressive loss of our vigour . . . however well we *look after* ourselves. (ll. 4–6)

b *Look out!* There's a bus coming!

c I am *looking forward to* the summer holidays.

d Everybody *looks on* him as a leader.

e If there are any words in the passage you don't understand, *look* them *up* in the dictionary.

f Business was very slack before Christmas, but things are *looking up* now.

g I shall certainly *look up* all my old friends when I go back home.

h Why don't you *look in* next week. I'm sure he'll be back by then.

3. Explain the meaning of the verbs in italics:

a Mechanical systems . . . *run out of* energy. (ll. 23–24)

b My new car hasn't been *run in* yet.

c That little boy was nearly *run over* by a bus.

d He *ran through* all the money he had inherited in less than a year.

e While on holiday in Spain, we *ran into* our next door neighbours.

f Look at that lamp post. It looks as if a car *ran into* it.

4. Explain the meaning of the verbs in italics:

a An illness which at twelve would *knock* us *over*, at eighty can *knock* us *out*. (ll. 32–33)

b There's so much work to do in the office these days, I never *knock off* before six o'clock.

46

After millennia of growth so slow that each generation hardly noticed it, the cities are suddenly racing off in every direction. The world population goes up by two per cent a year, city population goes up by four per cent a year, but in big cities the rate may be as much as five and six per cent a year. To give only
5 one example of almost visible acceleration, Athens today grows by three dwellings and 100 square metres of road every hour. There is no reason to believe that this pace will slacken. As technology gradually swallows up all forms of work, industrial and agricultural, the rural areas are going to shrink, just as they have shrunk in Britain, and the vast majority of their people will move into the city. In fact,
10 in Britain now only about four or five per cent of people live in rural areas and depend upon them; all through the developing world the vanguard of the rural exodus has reached the urban fringes already, and there they huddle, migrants in the favellas and barrios of Latin America, in shanty towns in Africa, in those horrifying encampments one sees on the outskirts of Calcutta and Bombay. We
15 are heading towards an urban world.

    This enormous increase will go ahead whatever we do, and we have to remember that the new cities devour space. People now acquire far more goods and things. There is a greater density of household goods; they demand more services such as sewage and drainage. Above all the car changes everything: rising
20 incomes and rising populations can make urban car density increase by something like four and five per cent in a decade; traffic flows rise to fill whatever scale of highways are provided for them. The car also has a curious ambivalence:

Traffic at night on an American highway

it creates and then it destroys mobility. The car tempts people further out and
then gives them the appalling problem of getting back. It makes them believe
25 they can spend Sunday in Brighton, but makes it impossible for them to return
before, say, two in the morning. People go further and further away to reach
open air and countryside which continuously recedes from them, and just as
their working weeks decline and they begin to have more time for leisure, they
find they cannot get to the open spaces or the recreation or the beaches which
30 they now have the time to enjoy.

Recently some studies were made in the behaviour of mice when exposed to
more than a certain degree of density, frustration, and noise, and the mice just
became deranged. I think some sociologists wonder whether it might not be the
same for men. This combination of very high density of population, goods and
35 services, and machines, all increasing with almost brutal speed, does account for
some really antisocial tendencies in modern urban growth.

BARBARA WARD *The Menace of Urban Explosion* from *The Listener*

Comprehension

Answer these questions:
a What use does the author make of statistical evidence to support her statement that
'the cities are suddenly racing off in every direction'? (ll. 1–2)
b What does the author mean by the statement 'we are heading towards an urban
world'? (ll. 14–15)

Vocabulary

Explain the meaning of the following words and phrases as they are used in the passage:
millennia (l. 1); visible acceleration (l. 5); rural areas are going to shrink (l. 8); exodus
(l. 12); urban fringes (l. 12); a curious ambivalence (l. 22); appalling (l. 24); recedes
(l. 27); deranged (l. 33).

Précis

Drawing your information from the second paragraph (lines 16–30) describe how our
lives are affected by 'rising incomes and rising populations'. Do not write more than 90
words. Your answer should be in one paragraph.

Composition

1. Write a list of ideas in note form which could be used to discuss the following subject: The Population Explosion.
2. Drawing on your list of ideas, write a composition of about 400 words.

Key Structures

1. Note the use of *by* in this sentence:
The world population goes up *by* two per cent a year. (ll. 2–3)
Write sentences using the following expressions: by three feet; by $100; by three
million.
2. Study this sentence pattern:
To give only one example of almost visible acceleration, Athens today grows by three
dwellings and 100 square metres of road every hour. (ll. 4–6)

Complete the following sentences:

a To sum up . . .

b To illustrate . . .

3. Supply *the* where necessary in the following. Do not refer to the passage until you have finished the exercise:

As . . . technology gradually swallows up all . . . forms of . . . work, . . . industrial and . . . agricultural, . . . rural areas are going to shrink, just as they have shrunk in . . . Britain, and . . . vast majority of their people will move into . . . city. In fact, in . . . Britain now only about four or five per cent of . . . people live in . . . rural areas and depend on them. (ll. 7–11)

4. Choose the correct words in brackets in the following. Do not refer to the passage until you have finished the exercise:

The car tempts people further (off, out) and then gives them the appalling problem (of, in) getting back. It makes them believe they can spend Sunday (to, in) Brighton, but makes it impossible (to, for) them to return (about, before) say, two (of, in) the morning. (ll. 23–26)

Special Difficulties

1. Write sentences to bring out the difference between the following pairs of words: notice (l. 1), remark; rate (l. 4), pace; tempt (l. 23), attract; countryside (l. 27), country.

2. Explain the meaning of the verbs in italics.

a The world population *goes up* by two per cent a year. (ll. 2–3)

b The fire will *go out* if you don't put some more coal on it.

c Be careful, or that gun might *go off*.

d I haven't *gone into* the problem in any detail yet.

e Now let's *go over* these points again.

f Prices keep *going up* all the time.

g Why don't you *go in for* this short story competition?

h Do you think there's enough cake to *go round*?

3. Explain the meaning of *space* in these sentences:

a We have to remember that new cities devour *space*. (ll. 16–17)

b Great progress has been made in the conquest of *space*.

c He arrived after a short *space* of time.

4. Find other words which could be used to replace *just* in these sentences:

a The mice *just* became deranged. (ll. 32–33)

b He has *just* arrived.

c He ran all the way to the station and *just* managed to catch the train.

d This is *just* what I wanted.

e You went to all this trouble *just* for us.

f As a magistrate, he was always *just*, kind and wise.

47

The modern Plato, like his ancient counterpart, has an unbounded contempt for politicians and statesmen and party leaders who are not university men. He finds politics a dirty game, and only enters them reluctantly because he knows that at the very least he and his friends are better than the present gang. Brought up in
5 the traditions of the ruling classes, he has a natural pity for the common people whom he has learnt to know as servants, and observed from a distance at their work in the factory, at their play in the parks and holiday resorts. He has never mixed with them or spoken to them on equal terms, but has demanded and generally received a respect due to his position and superior intelligence. He
10 knows that if they trust him, he can give them the happiness which they crave. A man of culture, he genuinely despises the self-made industrialist and news-paper-king: with a modest professional salary and a little private income of his own, he regards money-making as vulgar and avoids all ostentation. Industry and finance seem to him to be activities unworthy of gentlemen, although, alas,
15 many are forced by exigencies of circumstance to take some part in them. An intellectual, he gently laughs at the superstitions of most Christians, but he attends church regularly because he sees the importance of organized religion for the maintenance of sound morality among the lower orders, and because he dislikes the scepticism and materialism of radical teachers. His genuine passions
20 are for literature and the philosophy of science and he would gladly spend all his time in studying them. But the plight of the world compels his unwilling atten-tion, and when he sees that human stupidity and greed are about to plunge

'Peace in our time.' Neville Chamberlain is greeted by crowds on his return from Munich, September, 1938

Europe into chaos and destroy the most glorious civilization which the world has
known, he feels that it is high time for men of good sense and good will to inter-
25 vene and to take politics out of the hands of the plutocrats of the Right and the
woolly-minded idealists of the Left. Since he and his kind are the only represen-
tatives of decency combined with intelligence, they must step down into the
arena and save the masses for themselves.

R. H. S. CROSSMAN *Plato Today*

Comprehension

Answer these questions:
a Why does the 'modern Plato' reluctantly enter politics?
b Why does the 'modern Plato' despise the self-made industrialist and newspaper-
king?
c Why is the 'modern Plato' neither a true Christian nor a true atheist?

Vocabulary

Explain the meaning of the following words and phrases as they are used in the passage:
counterpart (l. 1); unbounded contempt (l. 1); the present gang (l. 4); crave (l. 10);
self-made (l. 11); private income (l. 12); exigencies of circumstance (l. 15); radical
(l. 19); his genuine passions (l. 19); plight (l. 21); intervene (ll. 24–25); woolly-minded
(l. 26).

Précis

Drawing your information from the passage describe the main qualities of the 'modern
Plato'. Do not write more than 130 words. Your answer should be in one paragraph.

Composition

1. Write a list of ideas in note form which could be used to discuss this subject:
To what extent is the 'modern Plato' (in the author's definition of the phrase) a fit
person to 'save the masses for themselves'?
2. Drawing on your list of ideas, write a composition of about 400 words.

Key Structures

1. Study this sentence pattern:
He finds politics a dirty game. (ll. 2–3)
Write sentences using the same pattern with the following verbs: *consider* and *think*.
2. Put the words in brackets in their correct position in these sentences. In some cases
more than one position is possible. Do not refer to the passage until you have finished
the exercise:
a He enters them because he knows that he and his friends are better than the present
gang. (only, reluctantly, at the very least) (ll. 3–4)
b He has demanded and received a respect due to his position and superior intelligence.
(generally) (ll. 8–9)
c He despises the self-made industrialist and newspaper-king. (genuinely) (ll. 11–12)
d He laughs at the superstitions of most Christians, but attends church because he sees
the importance of organized religion for the maintenance of sound morality. (gently,
regularly) (ll. 16–18)
e His genuine passions are for literature and the philosophy of science and he would
spend all his time in studying them. (gladly) (ll. 19–21)

3. Study the form of this sentence:
Brought up in the tradition of the ruling classes, he has a natural pity for the common people. (ll. 4–5)
Complete the following sentences:
a Educated at the best schools in the country . . .
b Established in 1896 . . .
c Filled with horror at what he saw . . .
4. Supply a(n) or the where necessary in the following. Do not refer to the passage until you have finished the exercise:
. . . industry and . . . finance seem to him to be . . . activities unworthy of . . . gentlemen, although, alas, many are forced by . . . exigencies of . . . circumstance to take some part in them. . . . intellectual, he gently laughs at . . . superstitions of . . . most Christians, but he attends . . . church regularly because he dislikes . . . scepticism and . . . materialism of . . . radical teachers. (ll. 13–19)
5. Note the absence of the before church: 'He attends church regularly.' (ll. 16–17)
Write sentences using the following words in the same way: school, hospital, prison, market, breakfast.
6. Study the expression in italics in the following:
When he sees that human stupidity and greed are *about to plunge* Europe into chaos and destroy the most glorious civilization which the world has known, he feels . . . it is high time . . . to intervene. (ll. 22–25)
Write sentences using the following expressions: *is going to; is sure to; is about to; is to.*

Special Difficulties

1. Write sentences to bring out the difference between the following pairs of words: common (l. 5), vulgar (l. 13); salary (l. 12), wages; avoid (l. 13), prevent; laugh at (l. 16), laugh; attention (ll. 21–22), care.
2. Compare these two sentences:
He only *enters them* reluctantly. (ll. 2–3)
Britain has *entered into a new agreement* with Holland.
Write two sentences using 'enter' with and without *into.*
3. Note the words in italics in the following sentences. Use these words again in sentences of your own, giving each word a different meaning from the one it has in the example:
a He has never *mixed* with them or spoken to them. (ll. 7–8)
b He has received a respect *due* to his position. (l. 9)
c With a *modest* professional salary . . . he regards money-making as vulgar. (ll. 12–13)
d He sees the importance of organized religion for the maintenance of sound morality among the lower *orders*. (ll. 17–18)
e He sees that human stupidity and greed are about to *plunge* Europe into chaos. (ll. 22–23)

48

I have known very few writers, but those I have known, and whom I respect, confess at once that they have little idea where they are going when they first set pen to paper. They have a character, perhaps two; they are in that condition of eager discomfort which passes for inspiration; all admit radical changes of
5 destination once the journey has begun; one, to my certain knowledge, spent nine months on a novel about Kashmir, then reset the whole thing in the Scottish Highlands. I never heard of anyone making a 'skeleton', as we were taught at school. In the breaking and remaking, in the timing, interweaving, beginning afresh, the writer comes to discern things in his material which were not con-
10 sciously in his mind when he began. This organic process, often leading to moments of extraordinary self-discovery, is of an indescribable fascination. A blurred image appears; he adds a brushstroke and another, and it is gone; but something was there, and he will not rest till he has captured it. Sometimes the yeast within a writer outlives a book he has written. I have heard of writers who
15 read nothing but their own books; like adolescents they stand before the mirror, and still cannot fathom the exact outline of the vision before them. For the same reason, writers talk interminably about their own books, winkling out hidden meanings, super-imposing new ones, begging response from those around them. Of course a writer doing this is misunderstood: he might as well try to explain a
20 crime or a love affair. He is also, incidentally, an unforgivable bore.

This temptation to cover the distance between himself and the reader, to

A scene from the film of John le Carré's book, *The Spy who Came in from the Cold*

study his image in the sight of those who do not know him, can be his undoing: he has begun to write to please.

A young English writer made the pertinent observation a year or two back 25 that the talent goes into the first draft, and the art into the drafts that follow. For this reason also the writer, like any other artist, has no resting place, no crowd or movement in which he may take comfort, no judgment from outside which can replace the judgment from within. A writer makes order out of the anarchy of his heart; he submits himself to a more ruthless discipline than any critic dreamed 30 of, and when he flirts with fame, he is taking time off from living with himself, from the search for what *his* world contains at its inmost point.

JOHN LE CARRÉ *What Every Writer Wants* from *Harper's*

Comprehension

Answer these questions:
a What do you understand by this sentence: 'all admit radical changes of destination once the journey has begun.'? (ll. 4–5)
b What do you understand by the phrase 'organic process'? (l. 10)
c Quote a sentence from the passage from which you could deduce that a writer must be a lonely person.

Vocabulary

Explain the meaning of the following words and phrases as they are used in the passage: eager discomfort (l. 4); passes for (l. 4); skeleton (l. 7); beginning afresh (ll. 8–9); discern (l. 9); a blurred image (ll. 11–12); fathom (l. 16); interminably (l. 17); winkling out (l. 17); anarchy (l. 28); ruthless (l. 29); taking time off (l. 30).

Précis

Drawing your information from the first paragraph (lines 1–20) write a summary of the author's account of how a writer works. Do not write more than 100 words. Your answer should be in one paragraph.

Composition

1. Write a list of ideas in note form which could be used to discuss this subject: Which do you prefer reading: novels, plays, poetry or non-fiction? Give reasons for your choice.
2. Drawing on your list of ideas, write a composition of about 400 words.

Key Structures

1. Supply *who*, *whom* or *which* where necessary in the following sentences. Do not refer to the passage until you have finished the exercise:
a I have known very few writers, but those . . . I have known, and . . . I respect confess at once that they have little idea where they are going when they first set pen to paper. (ll. 1–3)
b The writer comes to discern things in his material . . . were not consciously in his mind when he began. (ll. 9–10)
c Sometimes the yeast within a writer outlives a book . . . he has written. (ll. 13–14)
d I have heard of writers . . . read nothing but their own books. (ll. 14–15)

2. Note the use of *little* in this sentence: they have *little idea* where they are going. (l. 2) Write sentences using the following expressions: little expectation; little appreciation; little improvement.

3. Compare these two sentences:

Instead of saying: I never heard of anyone *who made* a 'skeleton' as we were taught at school.

We can say: I have never heard of *anyone making* a 'skeleton' as we were taught at school. (ll. 7–8)

Change the following sentences in the same way:

a This organic process, *which often leads* to moments of extraordinary self-discovery, is of indescribable fascination. (ll. 10–11)

b I have often heard of writers *who read* nothing but their own books. (ll. 14–15)

c A writer *who does* this is misunderstood. (l. 19)

4. Note the use of *may/might as well* in the following sentences:

a Of course a writer doing this is misunderstood: he *might* (or *may*) *as well* try to explain a crime or love affair. (ll. 19–20)

b I haven't got anything else to do so I *might* (or *may*) *as well* do some gardening.

Write two sentences using *may/might as well* in the ways shown above.

5. Note the use of *back* in place of *ago* in the following:

A young English writer made the pertinent observation a year or two *back* ... (l. 24)

Write two sentences using *back* in this way.

Special Difficulties

1. Write sentences to bring out the difference between the following pairs of words: destination (l. 5), destiny; indescribable (l. 11), undescribed; capture (l. 13), arrest; misunderstood (l. 19), not understood; draft (l. 25), draught; judgment (l. 27), criticism.

2. The words in italics in the following sentences are used metaphorically. What is their literal meaning?

a He adds a *brushstroke* and another, and it is gone. (l. 12)

b Sometimes the *yeast* within a writer outlives a book he has written. (ll. 13–14)

c Like adolescents they stand before the mirror and still cannot *fathom* the exact outline of the vision before them. (ll. 15–16)

d When he *flirts* with fame, he is taking time off from living with himself. (l. 30)

49

Rockets and artificial satellites can go far above the ionosphere, and even escape from the Earth. Yet they are complex and expensive, and in their present stage of development they cannot lift massive telescopes, keep them steady while the observations are being carried out, and then return them safely. Balloons are
5 much easier to handle, and are also vastly cheaper. Their main limitation is that they are incapable of rising to the ionosphere. A height of between 80,000 and 90,000 feet is as much as can reasonably be expected, and so balloon-borne instruments can contribute little to either ultra-violet astronomy or X-ray astronomy. All the same, the balloon has much to be said in its favour, since it can at least
10 carry heavy equipment above most of the atmospheric mass—thus eliminating blurring and unsteadiness of the images. Moreover, water-vapour and carbon dioxide in the lower air absorb most of the infra-red radiations sent to us from the planets. Balloon ascents overcome this hazard with ease.

Hot-air balloons date back to the year 1783, and within a few months of the
15 first flight a French scientist, Charles, went up two miles in a free balloon. Yet there is little resemblance between these crude vehicles and a modern scientific balloon, which has by now become an important research tool.

The main development has been carried out by M. Schwarzschild and his team at Princeton University in the United States, in collaboration with the
20 United States Navy, the National Science Foundation, and the National Aeronautics and Space Administration. The 'Stratoscope' flights of 1959, concerned mainly with studies of the Sun, were remarkably successful, and the project has

Three inflating tubes send helium into
Stratoscope II shortly before lift-off

now been extended. With Stratoscope II, the overall height from the telescope
to the top of the launch balloon is 660 feet; the balloons together weigh over two
25 tons, and another two tons of ballast are carried for later release if height has to
be maintained during the night. The telescope, plus its controls, weighs three-
and-a-half tons. Two large parachutes are also carried; in case of emergency, the
instruments and their records can be separated from the main balloon system,
and brought down gently. Many of the radio and electronic devices used are
30 similar to those of artificial satellites.

Patrick Moore Balloon Astronomy from The Listener

Comprehension

Answer these questions:
a Why is it impracticable at present to use rockets and artificial satellites to carry
telescopes?
b Why can balloon-borne instruments contribute little to ultra-violet astronomy and
X-ray astronomy?
c What advantage have balloons over rockets and artificial satellites?

Vocabulary

Explain the meaning of the following words and phrases as they are used in the passage:
massive (l. 3); vastly cheaper (l. 5); eliminating blurring and unsteadiness of the images
(ll. 10–11); hazard (l. 13); resemblance (l. 16); crude (l. 16); overall (l. 23); maintained
(l. 26)

Précis

Drawing your information from lines 14–30 ('Hot-air balloons . . . artificial satellites.')
write an account of how balloons have been used in the past and how they are used in
the present to enable scientists to study the sky. Do not write more than 80 words.
Your answer should be in one paragraph.

Composition

1. Write a list of ideas in note form which could be used to discuss this subject:
Recent developments in astronomy.
2. Drawing on your list of ideas, write a composition of about 400 words.

Key Structures

1. Supply the correct form of the verbs in brackets in the following sentences. Do not
refer to the passage until you have finished the exercise:
a They cannot lift massive telescopes, keep them steady while the observations (carry)
out, and then return them safely. (ll. 3–4)
b A height of between 80,000 and 90,000 feet is as much as reasonably (can expect).
(ll. 6–7)
c All the same, the balloon has much to (say) in its favour. (l. 9)
d The main development (carry) out by M. Schwarzschild and his team at Princeton
University. (ll. 18–19)
e The 'Stratoscope' flights of 1959, concerned mainly with studies of the Sun, were
remarkably successful, and the project now (extend). (ll. 21–23)

f The balloons together weigh over two tons, and another two tons of ballast (carry) for later release if height has to (maintain) during the night. (ll. 24–26)

g Two large parachutes also (carry); in case of emergency, the instruments and their records (can separate) from the main balloon system and (bring) down gently. (ll. 27–29)

2. Note the use of *much* in this sentence:

Balloons are *much easier* to handle. (ll. 4–5)

Write sentences using the following expressions:

much more difficult; much less expensive; much lighter.

3. Supply the missing words in the following sentences. Do not refer to the passage until you have finished the exercise:

a They are incapable . . . rising . . . the ionosphere. (l. 6)

b A height . . . . . . 80,000 and 90,000 feet is as much as can reasonably be expected. (ll. 6–7)

c Balloon-borne instruments can contribute little . . . either ultra-violet astronomy or X-ray astronomy. (ll. 7–8)

d The main development has been carried out . . . M. Schwarzschild and his team . . . Princeton University . . . the United States, . . . collaboration . . . the United States Navy. (ll. 18–20)

e . . . case . . . emergency, the instruments and their records can be separated . . . the main balloon system and brought . . . gently. Many . . . the radio and electronic devices used are similar . . . those . . . artificial satellites. (ll. 27–30)

Special Difficulties

1. Write sentences to bring out the difference between the following pairs of words: steady (l. 3), firm; limitation (l. 5), limit; expect (l. 7), wait for; instrument (ll. 7–8), tool; equipment (l. 10), supplies; remarkably (l. 22), noticeably; emergency (l. 27), need; electronic (l. 29), electric.

2. Which adjectives can be formed from the following nouns:

expense (l. 2); mass (l. 3); incapability (l. 6); science (l. 16); similarity (l. 30).

3. Explain the words in italics in these sentences:

a Balloon ascents *overcome* this hazard with ease. (l. 13)

b I drove behind a huge lorry for over an hour before *overtaking* it.

c My room *overlooks* a courtyard.

d This is a detail he *overlooked*.

e I daren't write another cheque; my bank account is already *overdrawn*.

f My watch won't work. I think I *overwound* it.

g I always have the tendency to *oversleep* on Monday mornings.

4. Explain the words and phrases in italics:

a *In case of* emergency, the instruments . . . can be separated from the main balloon system. (ll. 27–28)

b I think we can make an exception in your *case*.

c Have you packed your *case* yet?

d I bought a whole *case* of oranges at the market.

50

In mediaeval times rivers were the veins of the body politic as well as economic. Boundaries between states or shires, they were crossed by fords which became the sites of towns, or by bridges which were often points of battle. Upon rivers the people of that time depended for food, power and transport.

5 In our day fish are caught in the sea and brought to us by rail and lorry; only the angler still thinks fresh-water fish important, and pollution of rivers drives him into smaller and smaller reaches in which to practise his sport. But in earlier times, when sea fish were eaten only by those who lived on the sea coast, when meat was obtainable only for part of the year, and when fasts were frequent and
10 universally practised, river fish played an important part in the national life. Every abbey and great man's house had its fish pond, and across the rivers great and small stretched the fish weirs, usually made of stakes and nets or basket-work. Between the owners of the fisheries and the bargemaster who needed an unimpeded passage continuous war was fought, till the importance of fresh-
15 water fish lessened as the practice of fasting ceased to be universal, as meat became available all the year round, and as the transport of sea fish inland became practicable.

Rivers were also the most important source of power. Every stream had its mills, not only for grinding corn, but for all the other industrial processes of the
20 time, such as fulling* cloth or driving the hammers of ironworks. Placed down the bank wherever a head of water could be got, these mills were to be found on the tiny stream that ran through a village, or on the bigger river that was also

* Cleansing and thickening.

A flash-lock which is still in use today

used for navigation. An artificial cut was made from the river to bring the water at proper height to the water-wheel, and, in order to make sure of a supply of water at all seasons, the mill-owner usually built a weir across the river to hold back the water and so form an artificial reservoir. If the river were navigable, the centre of such a weir was made of planks held vertically by cross beams so that they could be removed when it was necessary to pass a barge, or was fitted with a single pair of gates. Such weirs were called staunches or flash-locks; they did not disappear from the bigger rivers till present times, and may still be seen in the Fens.

CHARLES HADFIELD British Canals

Comprehension

Answer these questions:
a What do you understand by this sentence: 'rivers were the veins of the body politic as well as economic.'? (l. 1)
b Why are rivers no longer an important source of fish in modern times?
c Why were the owners of fisheries and the bargemasters continuously at war in mediaeval times?

Vocabulary

Explain the meaning of the following words and phrases as they are used in the passage: sites (l. 3); angler (l. 6); pollution (l. 6); unimpeded passage (l. 14); artificial reservoir (l. 26); vertically (l. 27).

Précis

Drawing your information from the passage explain why rivers were extremely important in mediaeval times. Do not write more than 140 words. Your answer should be in one paragraph.

Composition

1. Write a list of ideas in note form which could be used to discuss this subject: Rivers may no longer be 'the veins of the body politic and economic' but they are still of enormous importance.
2. Drawing on your list of ideas, write a composition of about 400 words.

Key Structures

1. Supply the missing words in the following. Do not refer to the passage until you have finished the exercise:
... mediaeval times rivers were the veins ... the body politic as well as economic. Boundaries ... states or shires, they were crossed ... fords which became the sites ... towns, or ... bridges which were often points ... battle. ... rivers the people ... that time depended ... food, power and transport.
... our day fish are caught ... the sea and brought ... us ... rail and lorry; only the angler still thinks fresh-water fish important, and pollution ... rivers drives him ... smaller and smaller reaches ... which to practise his sport. But ... earlier times, when sea fish were eaten only ... those who lived ... the sea coast, when meat was obtainable only ... part of the year, and when fasts were frequent and universally practised, river fish played an important part ... the national life. Every abbey and

great man's house had its fish pond, and . . . the rivers great and small stretched the fish weirs, usually made of stakes and nets or basket-work. . . . the owners . . . the fisheries and the barge-masters who needed an unimpeded passage continuous war was fought, . . . the importance . . . fresh-water fish lessened as the practice . . . fasting ceased to be universal. (ll. 1–15)

2. Join these sentences to make one complete statement. You may add or omit any words you please but you must not alter the sense of the original. Do not refer to the passage until you have completed the exercise:

a These mills were placed down the bank wherever a head of water could be got. These mills were to be found on the tiny stream that ran through a village. They were to be found on the bigger river. The bigger river was also used for navigation. (ll. 21–23)

b An artificial cut was made from the river. This was done to bring the water at proper height to the water-wheel. In order to make sure of a supply of water at all seasons, the mill-owner usually built a weir across the river. He did this to hold back the water and so form an artificial reservoir. (ll. 23–26)

Special Difficulties

1. Write sentences to bring out the difference between the following pairs of words: boundary (l. 2), frontier; practise (l. 7), practice (l. 15); meat (l. 9), flesh; house (l. 11), home; pond (l. 11), pool; stake (l. 12), steak; continuous (l. 14), continual; lessen (l. 15), lesson; practicable (l. 17), practical; source (l. 18), sauce.

2. Explain the meaning of the words in italics:

a The pollution of rivers *drives* him into smaller and smaller reaches. (ll. 6–7)

b Yesterday I *drove* over 400 miles.

c After a prolonged battle, they managed to *drive out* the invaders.

d The farmer *drove* his cattle to market.

e There is a long *drive* leading to our house.

f He is quite a capable person, but he lacks *drive* and initiative.

3. Explain the meaning of *stretch* in these sentences:

a Across the rivers great and small *stretched* the fish weirs. (ll. 11–12)

b Unlike ordinary rope, nylon rope *stretches*.

c I could tell little Tommy was tired from the way he began to *stretch* and yawn.

d There's a very bad *stretch* of road between these two villages.

e As I passed him, the beggar *stretched* out his hand for money.

Unit 6

INSTRUCTIONS TO THE STUDENT

Content

This Unit consists of ten passages followed by exercises on Comprehension, Vocabulary, Précis, Composition, Key Structures and Special Difficulties.

Aim

To provide more advanced practice in précis and composition.

How to Work

1. Read each passage carefully two or three times.
2. Answer the questions in the order in which they are given.

Précis and Composition

Carry out the instructions given in the introduction to Unit 5.

51

Two main techniques have been used for training elephants, which we may ⌐ respectively the tough and the gentle. The former method simply consists ⌐ setting an elephant to work and beating him until he does what is expected of him. Apart from any moral considerations this is a stupid method of training, for
5 it produces a resentful animal who at a later stage may well turn man-killer. The gentle method requires more patience in the early stages, but produces a cheerful, good-tempered elephant who will give many years of loyal service.

The first essential in elephant training is to assign to the animal a single mahout who will be entirely responsible for the job. Elephants like to have one
10 master just as dogs do, and are capable of a considerable degree of personal affection. There are even stories of half-trained elephant calves who have refused to feed and pined to death when by some unavoidable circumstance they have been deprived of their own trainer. Such extreme cases must probably be taken with a grain of salt, but they do underline the general principle that the relation-
15 ship between elephant and mahout is the key to successful training.

The most economical age to capture an elephant for training is between fifteen and twenty years, for it is then almost ready to undertake heavy work and can begin to earn its keep straight away. But animals of this age do not easily become subservient to man, and a very firm hand must be employed in the early stages.
20 The captive elephant, still roped to a tree, plunges and screams every time a man approaches, and for several days will probably refuse all food through anger and fear. Sometimes a tame elephant is tethered nearby to give the wild one confidence, and in most cases the captive gradually quietens down and begins to

A wild Indian elephant is roped to two trained ones during the first few days of training

accept its food. The next stage is to get the elephant to the training establishment,
25 a ticklish business which is achieved with the aid of two tame elephants roped to
the captive on either side.

When several elephants are being trained at one time it is customary for the
new arrival to be placed between the stalls of two captives whose training is
already well advanced. It is then left completely undisturbed with plenty of food
30 and water so that it can absorb the atmosphere of its new home and see that
nothing particularly alarming is happening to its companions. When it is eating
normally its own training begins. The trainer stands in front of the elephant
holding a long stick with a sharp metal point. Two assistants, mounted on tame
elephants, control the captive from either side, while others rub their hands over
35 his skin to the accompaniment of a monotonous and soothing chant. This is
supposed to induce pleasurable sensations in the elephant, and its effects are rein-
forced by the use of endearing epithets, such as 'ho! my son', or 'ho! my father',
or 'my mother', according to the age and sex of the captive. The elephant is not
immediately susceptible to such blandishments, however, and usually lashes
40 fiercely with its trunk in all directions. These movements are controlled by the
trainer with the metal-pointed stick, and the trunk eventually becomes so sore
that the elephant curls it up and seldom afterwards uses it for offensive purposes.

RICHARD CARRINGTON *Elephants*

Comprehension

Answer these questions:
a Why does the author consider the 'tough' method of training elephants to be stupid?
b In what way can elephants be compared with dogs?
c What, according to the author, is the key to successful elephant training?
d What is the main advantage of training an elephant of between fifteen and twenty
years old?
e What is the main disadvantage of training an elephant of between fifteen and twenty
years old?
f How can tame elephants be used to help in the training of wild elephants?

Vocabulary

Explain the meaning of the following words and phrases as they are used in the passage:
moral considerations (l. 4); turn (l. 5); assign (l. 8); capable of a considerable degree
of personal affection (ll. 10–11); pined to death (l. 12); underline (l. 14); subservient
(l. 19); tethered (l. 22); particularly alarming (l. 31); monotonous and soothing chant
(l. 35); blandishments (l. 39); lashes fiercely (ll. 39–40).

Précis

Drawing your information from the last paragraph (lines 27–42) write an account of
the method used for training several elephants at one time. Use your own words as far
as possible. Do not write more than 80 words. Your answer should be in one paragraph.

Composition

Write a composition of about 600 words on one of the following subjects:
a Pets.
b Animals in scientific research.
c 'It is cruel to train animals to perform tricks for our amusement.' Discuss.

Key Structures

1. Note the use of the word *who* in this sentence:

The gentle method ... produces a cheerful, good-tempered elephant *who* will give many years of loyal service. (ll. 5–7)

Write two sentences in which it would be preferable to use *who* instead of *which* when referring to animals.

2. Rewrite the sentences given below using the opening words or phrases provided. Do not refer to the passage until you have finished the exercise:

a The two main techniques which have been used for training elephants we may call respectively the tough and the gentle.

Two main techniques ... (ll. 1–2)

b We must probably take such extreme cases with a grain of salt.

Such extreme cases ... (ll. 13–14)

c When training several elephants at one time we usually place the new arrival between the stalls of two captives whose training is already well advanced.

When several elephants ... it is customary for ... (ll. 27–29)

d The trainer controls these movements with the metal-pointed stick.

These movements ... (ll. 40–41)

Special Difficulties

1. Write sentences to bring out the difference between the following pairs of words: train (l. 1), educate; apart from (l. 4), except; degree (l. 10), rank; effects (l. 36), affects; afterwards (l. 42), after.

2. Use the following expressions in sentences of your own:

must ... be taken with a grain of salt (ll. 13–14); a ticklish business (l. 25).

52

An earthquake comes like a thief in the night, without warning. It was necessary, therefore, to invent instruments that neither slumbered nor slept. Some devices were quite simple. One, for instance, consisted of rods of various lengths and thicknesses which would stand up on end like ninepins. When a shock came it
5 shook the rigid table upon which these stood. If it were gentle, only the more unstable rods fell. If it were severe, they all fell. Thus the rods by falling, and by the direction in which they fell, recorded for the slumbering scientist the strength of a shock that was too weak to waken him and the direction from which it came.

But instruments far more delicate than that were needed if any really serious
10 advance was to be made. The ideal to be aimed at was to devise an instrument that could record with a pen on paper the movements, of the ground or of the table, as the quake passed by. While I write my pen moves, but the paper keeps still. With practice, no doubt, I could in time learn to write by holding the pen still while the paper moved. That sounds a silly suggestion, but that was precisely
15 the idea adopted in some of the early instruments (seismometers) for recording earthquake waves. But when table, penholder and paper are all moving how is it possible to write legibly? The key to a solution of that problem lay in an everyday observation. Why does a person standing in a bus or train tend to fall when a sudden start is made? It is because his feet move on, but his head stays still.
20 A simple experiment will help us a little further. Tie a heavy weight at the end of a long piece of string. With the hand held high in the air hold the string so that the weight nearly touches the ground. Now move the hand to and fro and around

The Shaw seismograph at the
Science Museum, London

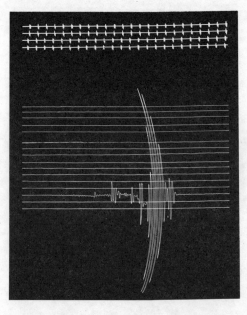

An earthquake recorded on a seismograph

but not up and down. It will be found that the weight moves but slightly or not at all. Imagine a pen attached to the weight in such a way that its point rests upon 25 a piece of paper on the floor. Imagine an earthquake shock shaking the floor, the paper, you and your hand. In the midst of all this movement the weight and the pen would be still. But as the paper moved from side to side under the pen point its movement would be recorded in ink upon its surface. It was upon this principle that the first instruments were made, but the paper was wrapped round a 30 drum which rotated slowly. As long as all was still the pen drew a straight line, but while the drum was being shaken the line that the pen was drawing wriggled from side to side. The apparatus thus described, however, records only the horizontal component of the wave movement, which is, in fact, much more complicated. If we could actually see the path described by a particle, such as a sand 35 grain in the rock, it would be more like that of a bluebottle buzzing round the room; it would be up and down, to and fro and from side to side. Instruments have been devised and can be so placed that all three elements can be recorded in different graphs.

When the instrument is situated at more than 700 miles from the earthquake 40 centre, the graphic record shows three waves arriving one after the other at short intervals. The first records the arrival of longitudinal vibrations. The second marks the arrival of transverse vibrations which travel more slowly and arrive several minutes after the first. These two have travelled through the earth. It was from the study of these that so much was learnt about the interior of the 45 earth. The third, or main wave, is the slowest and has travelled round the earth through the surface rocks.

H. H. SWINNERTON *The Earth Beneath Us*

Comprehension

Answer these questions:
a Explain how the device consisting of rods of various lengths and thicknesses could be used to indicate the extent of an earthquake.
b Why was this simple seismometer worked by rods unsatisfactory?
c Which everyday observation enabled scientists to improve seismometers?
d 'Instruments have been devised and can be so placed that all three elements can be recorded in different graphs.' (ll. 36–38) What are these 'elements'?
e Why, during an earthquake, is the third wave the last to be recorded?

Vocabulary

Explain the meaning of the following words and phrases as they are used in the passage: rigid (l. 5); slumbering (l. 7); delicate (l. 9); silly suggestion (l. 14); legibly (l. 17); everyday (ll. 17–18); tend (l. 18); to and fro (l. 22); slightly (l. 23); rotated (l. 30); wriggled (l. 31); the path described by a particle (l. 34); bluebottle (l. 35).

Précis

Drawing your information from lines 10–32 ('The ideal ... side to side.') describe how the seismometer used for recording the horizontal component of wave movements works. Do not write more than 120 words. Use your own words as far as possible. Your answer should be in one paragraph.

Composition

Write a composition of about 600 words on one of the following subjects:

a A description, real or imaginary, of an earthquake.

b The hidden forces of nature.

c Man's efforts to understand and control natural calamities. (E.g. earthquakes, floods, hurricanes, tornadoes, tidal waves, volcanic eruptions, avalanches, forest fires.)

Key Structures

1. Complete the following sentences in any way you wish. Then compare what you have written with the sentences in the passage:

a When a shock came it shook the rigid table upon which these stood. If it were gentle . . . (ll. 4–5)

b . . . if any really serious advance was to be made. (ll. 9–10)

c If we could actually see the path described by a particle . . . (l. 34)

2. Rewrite the sentences given below using the opening phrases provided. Do not refer to the passage until you have finished the exercise:

a Though that sounds a silly suggestion, that was precisely the idea adopted in some of the early instruments.

That sounds . . . (ll. 14–15)

b The reason for this is that his feet move on, but his head stays still.

It is because . . . (l. 19)

c Imagine that an earthquake shock shook the floor.

Imagine an . . . (l. 25)

d However, only the horizontal component of the wave movement, which is, in fact, far more complicated, is recorded by the apparatus thus described.

The apparatus thus described, however, . . . (ll. 32–34)

Special Difficulties

1. Write sentences to bring out the difference between the following pairs of words: device (l. 2), devise (l. 10); adopted (l. 15), adapted; lay (l. 17), laid; principle (ll. 28–29), principal; travel (l. 42), trip.

2. Note that the word *record* is differently pronounced in each of these sentences:

a The graphic record shows three waves. (l. 40)

b The first records the arrival of longitudinal vibrations. (l. 41)

Write pairs of sentences using the following words as *nouns* and as *verbs*: export; import; produce; conduct. In each sentence indicate the syllable which should be stressed.

53

The French Foreign Legion was founded by a Royal Ordinance, written on a small piece of official French War Office notepaper dated March 9th, 1831, and signed by the then reigning monarch of France, Louis-Philippe. He had been on the throne for barely eight months when he authorized this measure, which was
5 as much a product of necessity as of careful planning, although there may be divided views on this.

The reasons for forming the French Foreign Legion were probably twofold. In the first place the men of the disbanded royal bodyguard and the Regiment of Hohenlohe, suddenly turned loose on to the street of a capital seething with un-
10 rest, unemployed and perhaps disgruntled at their abrupt dismissal, were a potentially dangerous element. They were trained to the use of arms, and should they become tools of the politically ambitious or discontented they would present a distinct menace to the new régime, not yet too firmly established and sure of itself.
15 For some time Paris had been swarming with countless other discharged foreign soldiers who had served in the French army at various times under the Empire and the Republic, many of whom were in needy circumstances and open to suggestion, whilst others were openly looking for trouble and always ready to take part in any disturbance. It was clearly both expedient and desirable to re-
20 move these dangers as far away from the capital as possible.

Next, the Algerian adventure had begun, and it appeared that this might prove expensive in lives. The more Frenchmen killed in North Africa, the less popular

Soldiers from the Legion in an off-duty moment

the government at home would be, so if foreign cannon fodder was available so much the better. The Algerian landing had been viewed with mixed feelings in a politically divided France, but there does not seem to have been any marked indication on the part of the politicians that they were unanimous that the occupation should be abruptly terminated; most were wary and many apprehensive as to how the Algerian business would turn out.

The formation of a foreign legion seemed therefore to be an ideal method of killing these two birds with one stone. Once the conditions were made clear there does not seem to have been any serious opposition.

Marshal Soult was reputed to be the man behind the scheme both for removing and using the unemployed foreign ex-soldiers. He could not have failed to recognize, once they were formed into disciplined units, how useful they would be, both for garrison duty and for active operations in Algeria, nor the fact that if their casualties were heavy or their conditions not of the best, there would be no embarrassing reaction for agitation in France on their behalf.

The Royal Ordinance decreed that there should be a legion formed of foreigners for service outside France, which was to be called the 'Foreign Legion' and it was to be part of the French army and under the control of the War Minister. It laid down that as far as possible companies should be composed of men of the same nationality or who spoke a common language. Algeria was not specifically mentioned but as it was the only scrap of foreign territory of any size possessed by France at that moment, there was no doubt as to the meaning of the phrase 'outside France'.

In the anxiety to get dubious, restless characters out of the country no questions were asked as to nationality, previous record or history, and no proof of identity was required. The name and particulars given by the recruit were accepted at face value and many gave *noms de guerre*,* for understandable reasons. Thus the practice began, and the tradition started of 'asking no questions'. This tradition of guaranteeing anonymity began to develop quickly, although it was not until later that it was carried to the extreme of denying all knowledge of any individuals who were in its ranks and of refusing point blank to answer questions or to allow any outside contact with the legionnaires.

EDGAR O'BALLANCE *The Story of the French Foreign Legion*

* Pseudonyms.

Comprehension

Answer these questions:
a Who authorized the founding of the French Foreign Legion?
b What do you understand by this statement: 'The formation of the foreign legion seemed therefore to be an ideal method of killing these two birds with one stone.'? (ll. 29–30)
c What immediate advantages would result from forming the foreign legion?
d Whom was the foreign legion responsible to?
e Why was there no doubt as to the meaning of the phrase 'outside France', contained in the Royal Ordinance?
f What do you understand by this statement: 'the practice began . . . of "asking no questions"' (l. 50)

Vocabulary

Explain the meaning of the following words and phrases as they are used in the passage: reigning monarch (l. 3); authorized (l. 4); seething with unrest (ll. 9–10); disgruntled (l. 10); discharged (l. 15); expedient (l. 19); cannon fodder (l. 23); unanimous (l. 26); abruptly terminated (l. 27); apprehensive (l. 27); decreed (l. 38); scrap (l. 43); recruit (l. 48).

Précis

Drawing your information from lines 1–31 ('The French Foreign Legion . . . serious opposition.') explain how and why the French Foreign Legion came to be formed. Do not write more than 130 words. Use your own words as far as possible. Your answer should be in one paragraph.

Composition

Write a composition of about 600 words on one of the following subjects:
a Military Service.
b Pacifism.
c 'Our attitude to war has changed profoundly in recent times.' Discuss.

Key Structures

Rewrite the sentences given below using the opening words or phrases provided. Do not refer to the passage until you have finished the exercise:
a After having been on the throne for barely eight months he authorized this measure. He . . . when (ll. 3–4)
b If they became tools of the politically ambitious or discontented they would present a distinct menace to the new regime. Should . . . (ll. 11–13)
c It was decreed by the Royal Ordinance that there should be a legion formed of foreigners for service outside France.
    The Royal Ordinance . . . (ll. 38–39)

Special Difficulties

1. Write sentences to bring out the difference between the following pairs of words: to found (l. 1), to find; view (l. 6), aspect; loose (l. 9), lose; understandable (l. 49), understanding; deny (l. 52), refuse (l. 53).
2. Explain the meaning of the verbs in italics:
a It *laid down* that as far as possible companies should be composed of men of the same nationality. (ll. 41–42)
b This issue may *bring down* the government.
c The reporters *took down* what he said.
d You say you admire him, yet you are always *running* him *down*.
e I expected him to help me, but he *let* me *down*.
f The government is doing its best to *keep down* prices.
g He took part in a students' demonstration and was *sent down*.

54

We must conclude from the work of those who have studied the origin of life, that given a planet only approximately like our own, life is almost certain to start. Of all the planets in our own solar system we are now pretty certain the Earth is the only one on which life can survive. Mars is too dry and poor in
5 oxygen, Venus far too hot, and so is Mercury, and the outer planets have temperatures near absolute zero and hydrogen-dominated atmospheres. But other suns, stars as the astronomers call them, are bound to have planets like our own, and as the number of stars in the universe is so vast, this possibility becomes virtual certainty. There are one hundred thousand million stars in our own
10 Milky Way alone, and then there are three thousand million other Milky Ways, or Galaxies, in the universe. So the number of stars that we know exist is now estimated at about 300 million million million.

Although perhaps only 1 per cent of the life that has started somewhere will develop into highly complex and intelligent patterns, so vast is the number of
15 planets that intelligent life is bound to be a natural part of the universe.

If then we are so certain that other intelligent life exists in the universe, why have we had no visitors from outer space yet? First of all, they may have come to this planet of ours thousands or millions of years ago, and found our then prevailing primitive state completely uninteresting to their own advanced knowledge.
20 Professor Ronald Bracewell, a leading American radio-astronomer, argued in *Nature* that such a superior civilization, on a visit to our own solar system, may have left an automatic messenger behind to await the possible awakening of an

This photograph of unidentified lights was taken by a Coast Guard. Salem, Mass., USA, 1952

advanced civilization. Such a messenger, receiving our radio and television sig-
nals, might well re-transmit them back to its home-planet, although what im-
25 pression any other civilization would thus get from us is best left unsaid.

But here we come up against the most difficult of all obstacles to contact with
people on other planets—the astronomical distances which separate us. As a
reasonable guess, they might, on an average, be 100 light years away. (A light
year is the distance which light travels at 186,000 miles per second in one year,
30 namely 6 million million miles.) Radio waves also travel at the speed of light,
and assuming such an automatic messenger picked up our first broadcasts of the
1920's, the message to its home planet is barely half-way there. Similarly, our
own present primitive chemical rockets, though good enough to orbit men, have
no chance of transporting us to the nearest other star, four light years away, let
35 alone distances of tens or hundreds of light years.

Fortunately, there is a 'uniquely rational way' for us to communicate with
other intelligent beings, as Walter Sullivan has put it in his excellent recent book,
We are not alone. This depends on the precise radio-frequency of the 21-cm
wavelength, or 1420 megacycles per second. It is the natural frequency of emis-
40 sion of the hydrogen atoms in space and was discovered by us in 1951; it must
be known to any kind of radio-astronomer in the universe.

Once the existence of this wave-length had been discovered, it was not long
before its use as the uniquely recognizable broadcasting frequency for interstellar
communication was suggested. Without something of this kind, searching for
45 intelligences on other planets would be like trying to meet a friend in London
without a pre-arranged rendezvous and absurdly wandering the streets in the
hope of a chance encounter.

ANTHONY MICHAELIS *Are There Strangers in Space?*
from *The Weekend Telegraph*

Comprehension

Answer these questions:
a What do you understand by the word 'galaxy'?
b Why, according to the author, is it highly probable that life exists in other parts of
the universe?
c Why would it be extremely difficult to visit another planet even if one were travelling
at 186,000 miles per second?
d How might it be possible to accomplish interstellar communication?

Vocabulary

Explain the meaning of the following words and phrases as they are used in the passage:
approximately (l. 2); prevailing primitive state (ll. 18–19); automatic messenger (l. 22);
obstacles (l. 26); orbit (l. 33); interstellar (l. 43); chance encounter (l. 47).

Précis

Drawing your information from lines 26–47 ('But here . . . chance encounter.') write
an account of the difficulties of interstellar communication. Do not write more than
100 words. Use your own words as far as possible. Your answer should be in one
paragraph.

Composition

Write a composition of about 600 words on one of the following subjects:
a The universe.
b Flying saucers.
c If an outside observer were given the opportunity to spend a year on earth, what impression might he get of its inhabitants?

Key Structures

1. Note the form of the verb in italics:
But other suns . . . *are bound to* have planets like our own. (ll. 6–7)
Write sentences using the following expressions:
sure to; about to; due to.
2. Rewrite the sentences given below using the opening phrases provided. Do not refer to the passage until you have finished the exercise:
a As the number of planets is so vast intelligent life is bound to be a natural part of the universe.
   So vast . . . (ll. 14–15)
b First of all, it is possible that they came to this planet of ours thousands or millions of years ago.
   First of all, they may . . . (ll. 17–18)
c It was argued in *Nature* by professor Ronald Bracewell, a leading American radio-astronomer, that such a superior civilization, on a visit to our own solar system, may have left an automatic messenger behind.
   Professor Ronald Bracewell, . . . (ll. 20–22)
d Even if our own present primitive chemical rockets are good enough to orbit men, they have no chance of transporting us to the nearest other star.
   Our own present . . . though . . . (ll. 32–34)

Special Difficulties

1. Write sentences to bring out the difference between the following pairs of words:
planet (l. 2), star (l. 7); estimated (l. 12), esteemed; natural (l. 15), physical; unsaid (l. 25), untold; search for (l. 44), search.
2. Note the use of *let alone* in this sentence:
Similarly, our own present primitive chemical rockets, though good enough to orbit men, have no chance of transporting us to the nearest other star, four light years away, *let alone* distances of tens or hundreds of light years. (ll. 32–35)
Complete the following sentences:
a He's incapable of adding up a simple list of figures, let alone . . .
b He doesn't earn enough to support himself, let alone . . .

55

Custom has not been commonly regarded as a subject of any great moment. The inner workings of our own brains we feel to be uniquely worthy of investigation, but custom, we have a way of thinking, is behaviour at its most commonplace. As a matter of fact, it is the other way around. Traditional custom, taken the world
5 over, is a mass of detailed behaviour more astonishing than what any one person can ever evolve in individual actions, no matter how aberrant. Yet that is a rather trivial aspect of the matter. The fact of first-rate importance is the predominant rôle that custom plays in experience and in belief, and the very great varieties it may manifest.
10 No man ever looks at the world with pristine eyes. He sees it edited by a definite set of customs and institutions and ways of thinking. Even in his philosophical probings he cannot go behind these stereotypes; his very concepts of the true and the false will still have reference to his particular traditional customs. John Dewey has said in all seriousness that the part played by custom in
15 shaping the behaviour of the individual as over against any way in which he can affect traditional custom, is as the proportion of the total vocabulary of his mother tongue over against those words of his own baby talk that are taken up into the vernacular of his family. When one seriously studies the social orders that have had the opportunity to develop autonomously, the figure becomes no
20 more than an exact and matter-of-fact observation. The life history of the individual is first and foremost an accommodation to the patterns and standards traditionally handed down in his community. From the moment of his birth the

A Padaung girl from Burma
in her brass necklace

customs into which he is born shape his experience and behaviour. By the time
he can talk, he is the little creature of his culture, and by the time he is grown and
25 able to take part in its activities, its habits are his habits, its beliefs his beliefs, its
impossibilities his impossibilities. Every child that is born into his group will
share them with him, and no child born into one on the opposite side of the globe
can ever achieve the thousandth part. There is no social problem it is more incumbent upon us to understand than this of the rôle of custom. Until we are
30 intelligent as to its laws and varieties, the main complicating facts of human life
must remain unintelligible.

The study of custom can be profitable only after certain preliminary propositions have been accepted, and some of these propositions have been violently
opposed. In the first place any scientific study requires that there be no preferen-
35 tial weighting of one or another of the items in the series it selects for its consideration. In all the less controversial fields like the study of cacti or termites or
the nature of nebulae, the necessary method of study is to group the relevant
material and to take note of all possible variant forms and conditions. In this way
we have learned all that we know of the laws of astronomy, or of the habits of the
40 social insects, let us say. It is only in the study of man himself that the major
social sciences have substituted the study of one local variation, that of Western
civilization.

Anthropology was by definition impossible as long as these distinctions between ourselves and the primitive, ourselves and the barbarian, ourselves and
45 the pagan, held sway over people's minds. It was necessary first to arrive at that
degree of sophistication where we no longer set our own belief over against our
neighbour's superstition. It was necessary to recognize that these institutions
which are based on the same premises, let us say the supernatural, must be considered together, our own among the rest.

RUTH BENEDICT *Patterns of Culture*

Comprehension

Answer these questions:
a What do you understand by this statement: 'No man ever looks at the world with
pristine eyes'? (l. 10)
b How has the study of man differed from the study of less controversial subjects?
c What criterion must the anthropologist accept before he can undertake the study of
man objectively?

Vocabulary

Explain the meaning of the following words and phrases as they are used in the passage:
moment (l. 1); aberrant (l. 6); predominant rôle (ll. 7–8); manifest (l. 9); probings
(l. 12); vernacular (l. 18); autonomously (l. 19); incumbent (ll. 28–29); intelligent
(l. 30); unintelligible (l. 31); preferential weighting (ll. 34–35); controversial (l. 36);
held sway (l. 45).

Précis

Drawing your information from lines 1–28 ('Custom has not . . . achieve the thousandth part.') describe how our attitude to life is shaped by custom. Do not write more

than 100 words. Use your own words as far as possible. Your answer should be in one paragraph.

Composition

Write a composition of about 600 words on one of the following subjects:
a Tradition and the individual.
b How can the study of cultures different from our own lead to a better understanding of man's nature?
c 'There can be no absolute standards of right and wrong since our moral attitudes are conditioned by the society in which we live.' Discuss.

Key Structures

Rewrite the sentences given below using the opening words and phrases provided. Do not refer to the passage until you have finished the exercise:
a We have not commonly regarded custom as a subject of any great moment.
  Custom . . . (l. 1)
b We feel that the inner working of our own brains are uniquely worthy of investigation.
  The inner workings of our own brains we feel to . . . (ll. 1–2)
c What he sees is edited by a definite set of customs and institutions and ways of thinking.
  He sees . . . (ll. 10–11)
d From the moment of his birth his experience and behaviour are shaped by the customs into which he is born.
  From the moment of his birth the customs . . . (ll. 22–23)
e We had to arrive first at that degree of sophistication where we no longer set our own belief over against our neighbour's superstition.
  It was necessary . . . (ll. 45–47)

Special Difficulties

1. Write sentences to bring out the difference between these pairs of words:
custom (l. 1), habit; aspect (l. 7), view; proportion (l. 16), percentage; unintelligible (l. 31), unintelligent; controversial (l. 36), argumentative.
2. Write sentences using the following words differently from the way in which they have been used in the passage:
accommodation (l. 21); creature (l. 24); globe (l. 27); intelligent (l. 30).

56

Science and technology have come to pervade every aspect of our lives and, as a result, society is changing at a speed which is quite unprecedented. There is a great technological explosion around us, generated by science. This explosion is already freeing vast numbers of people from their traditional bondage to nature,
5 and now at last we have it in our power to free mankind once and for all from the fear which is based on want. Now, for the first time, man can reasonably begin to think that life can be something more than a grim struggle for survival. But even today, in spite of the high standard of living which has become general in the more fortunate West, the majority of people in the world still spend nearly
10 all their time and energy in a never-ending struggle with nature to secure the food and shelter they need. Even in this elementary effort millions of human beings each year die unnecessarily and wastefully from hunger, disease, or flood.

Yet, in the West, science and technology have made it possible for us to have a plentiful supply of food, produced by only a fraction of the labour that was
15 necessary even a few decades ago. In the United States, for instance, one man on the land produces more than enough food to feed fifteen men in the cities, and, in fact, there is a surplus of food grown even by this small proportion of the American labour force. We have considerably extended our expectation of life. We have enriched our lives by creating physical mobility through the motor-car,
20 the jet aeroplane, and other means of mechanical transport; and we have added to our intellectual mobility by the telephone, radio, and television. Not content with these advances, we are now thrusting forward to the stars, and the conquest

American astronaut, Edward White, walking in space. June, 1965

of space no longer strikes us as Wellsian or Jules Vernian. And with the advent
of the new phase of technology we call automation, we have the promise both of
25 greater leisure and of even greater material and intellectual riches.

But this is not inevitable. It depends on automation being adequately exploited. We shall need to apply our scientific and technological resources to
literally every aspect of our society, to our commerce, our industry, our medicine,
our agriculture, our transportation.
30 It is fascinating and encouraging to observe the development of this immense
process, a process in which man appears all the time to be engaged in the act of
creating an extension of himself. In his new technological successes this appears
particularly true. He is extending his eyes with radar; his tongue and his ear
through telecommunications; his muscle and body structure through mechaniza-
35 tion. He extends his own energies by the generation and transmission of power
and his nervous system and his thinking and decision-making faculties through
automation. If this observation is accurate, as I believe it is, the implications are
far-reaching. It might be reasonable to conclude that the direction of modern
science and technology is towards the creation of a series of machine-systems
40 based on man as a model.

LEON BAGRIT *The Age of Automation* from *The Listener*

Comprehension

Answer these questions:
a Name one important way in which science and technology may affect our lives.
b What do you understand by the term 'elementary effort'? (l. 11)
c How do the examples given in the second paragraph ('In the United States . . .
Jules Vernian.') illustrate the author's argument?
d What do you understand by this statement: 'It depends on automation being adequately exploited.'? (ll. 26–27)
e What do you understand by this statement: 'man appears all the time to be engaged
in the act of creating an extension of himself.'? (ll. 31–32)

Vocabulary

Explain the meaning of the following words and phrases as they are used in the passage:
pervade every aspect (l. 1); unprecedented (l. 2); bondage (l. 4); once and for all (l. 5);
grim struggle for survival (l. 7); secure (l. 10); a fraction of the labour (l. 14); surplus
(l. 17); thrusting (l. 22); faculties (l. 36); implications (l. 37).

Précis

Drawing your information from lines 13–40 ('Yet, in the West, . . . man as a model.')
write an account of man's technological successes. Do not write more than 130 words.
Use your own words as far as possible. Your answer should be in one paragraph.

Composition

Write a composition of about 600 words on one of the following subjects:
a Automation.
b Science and art.
c '"More pay for less work" has become one of the most frequently heard slogans of
our time.' Discuss.

Key Structures

Rewrite the sentences given below using the opening phrases provided. Do not refer to the passage until you have finished the exercise:

a The great technological explosion around us has been generated by science.

There is a great . . . (ll. 2–3)

b Vast numbers of people are already being freed from their traditional bondage to nature by this explosion.

This explosion . . . (ll. 3–4)

c Our expectation of life has been considerably extended.

We . . . (l. 18)

d Our scientific and technological resources will have to be applied to literally every aspect of our society, to our commerce, our industry, our medicine, our agriculture, our transportation.

We shall . . . (ll. 27–29)

e Nothing can be more fascinating and encouraging than to observe the development of this immense process, a process in which man appears all the time to be engaged in the act of creating an extension of himself.

It is . . . (ll. 30–32)

Special Difficulties

1. Write sentences to bring out the difference between the following pairs of words: pervade (l. 1), invade; technological (l. 3), technical; at last (l. 5), finally; reasonably (l. 6), logically; struggle (l. 7), agony; energy (l. 10), activity; material (l. 25), substantial.

2. Note the words in italics in the following sentences. Use these words again in sentences of your own, giving each word a different meaning from the one it has in the example:

a There is a great technological *explosion* around us. (ll. 2–3)

b We have a plentiful supply of food, *produced* by only a fraction of the labour. (ll. 13–14)

c He extends his own energies by the generation and transmission of power and his *nervous* system and his thinking and decision-making faculties through automation. (ll. 35–37)

3. Note how *through* has been used to mean *by means of* in this sentence: He extends his own energies . . . *through* automation. (ll. 35–37)

Write two sentences using *through* in this way.

57

In man's early days, competition with other creatures must have been critical.
But this phase of our development is now finished. Indeed, we lack practice and
experience nowadays in dealing with primitive conditions. I am sure that, without modern weapons, I would make a very poor show of disputing the ownership
5 of a cave with a bear, and in this I do not think that I stand alone. The last creature
to compete with man was the mosquito. But even the mosquito has been subdued
by attention to drainage and by chemical sprays.

Competition between ourselves, person against person, community against
community, still persists, however; and it is as fierce as it ever was.

10 But the competition of man against man is not the simple process envisioned
in biology. It is not a simple competition for a fixed amount of food determined
by the physical environment, because the environment that determines our evolution is no longer essentially physical. Our environment is chiefly conditioned
by the things we believe. Morocco and California are bits of the Earth in very
15 similar latitudes, both on the west coasts of continents with similar climates, and
probably with rather similar natural resources. Yet their present development is
wholly different, not so much because of different people even, but because of the
different thoughts that exist in the minds of their inhabitants. This is the point
I wish to emphasize. The most important factor in our environment is the state
20 of our own minds.

It is well known that where the white man has invaded a primitive culture the
most destructive effects have come not from physical weapons but from ideas.

An aerial view of Sausalito, California

Ideas are dangerous. The Holy Office knew this full well when it caused heretics
to be burned in days gone by. Indeed, the concept of free speech only exists in
25 our modern society because when you are inside a community you are conditioned by the conventions of the community to such a degree that it is very
difficult to conceive of anything really destructive. It is only someone looking on
from outside that can inject the dangerous thoughts. I do not doubt that it would
be possible to inject ideas into the modern world that would utterly destroy us.
30 I would like to give you an example, but fortunately I cannot do so. Perhaps it
will suffice to mention the nuclear bomb. Imagine the effect on a reasonably advanced technological society, one that still does not possess the bomb, of making
it aware of the possibility, of supplying sufficient details to enable the thing to be
constructed. Twenty or thirty pages of information handed to any of the major
35 world powers around the year 1925 would have been sufficient to change the
course of world history. It is a strange thought, but I believe a correct one, that
twenty or thirty pages of ideas and information would be capable of turning the
present-day world upside down, or even destroying it. I have often tried to conceive of what those pages might contain, but of course I cannot do so because
40 I am a prisoner of the present-day world, just as all of you are. We cannot think
outside the particular patterns that our brains are conditioned to, or, to be more
accurate, we can think only a very little way outside, and then only if we are
very original.

FRED HOYLE *Of Men and Galaxies*

Comprehension

Answer these questions:
a Which idea in the first paragraph is illustrated by the following statement: 'I would
make a very poor show of disputing the ownership of a cave with a bear.' (ll. 4–5)
b How does the author account for the fact that the inhabitants of Morocco differ from
those of California?
c What do you understand by this statement: 'when you are inside a community you
are conditioned by the conventions of the community.'? (ll. 25–26)
d What, in the author's view, could change the course of world history?
e What must a person with original ideas be capable of doing?

Vocabulary

Explain the meaning of the following words and phrases as they are used in the passage:
critical (l. 1); phase (l. 2); I would make a very poor show (l. 4); subdued (l. 6); the
environment that determines our evolution (ll. 12–13); wholly (l. 17); factor (l. 19);
utterly (l. 29); course (l. 36); accurate (l. 42).

Précis

Drawing your information from the last paragraph (lines 21–43) explain why ideas can
be more dangerous than weapons. Do not write more than 110 words. Use your own
words as far as possible. Your answer should be in one paragraph.

Composition

Write a composition of about 600 words on one of the following subjects:
a The evolution of man.
b Brainwashing.

c 'Our environment is chiefly conditioned by the things we believe.' Support or attack this view.

Key Structures

1. Study this sentence:
In man's early days, competition with other creatures *must have been* critical. (l. 1)
Write two sentences illustrating the difference between *must have been* and *had to be*.
2. Rewrite the sentences given below using the opening phrases provided. Do not refer to the passage until you have finished the exercise:
a I am sure that, if I did not have any weapons, I would make a very poor show of disputing the ownership of a cave with a bear.
   I am sure that, without . . . (ll. 3–5)
b It is the things we believe that chiefly condition our environment.
   Our environment . . . (ll. 13–14)
c It is well known that where a primitive culture has been invaded by the white man, the most destructive effects have come not from physical weapons but from ideas.
   It is well known that where the white man . . . (ll. 21–22)
d I do not doubt that we would be utterly destroyed if it were possible to inject ideas into the modern world.
   I do not doubt that it would be . . . (ll. 28–29)
e Imagine how a reasonably advanced technological society would be affected.
   Imagine the effect . . . (ll. 31–32)

Special Difficulties

Note the words in italics in the following sentences. Use these words again in sentences of your own, giving each word a different meaning from the one it has in the example:
a Competition with other creatures must have been *critical*. (l. 1)
b The most important factor in our environment is the *state* of our own minds. (ll. 19–20)
c The concept of *free* speech only exists in our modern society because when you are inside a community you are conditioned by the conventions of the community. (ll. 24–26)

58

A gifted American psychologist has said, 'Worry is a spasm of the emotion; the mind catches hold of something and will not let it go.' It is useless to argue with the mind in this condition. The stronger the will, the more futile the task. One can only gently insinuate something else into its convulsive grasp. And if this
5 something else is rightly chosen, if it is really attended by the illumination of another field of interest, gradually, and often quite swiftly, the old undue grip relaxes and the process of recuperation and repair begins.

The cultivation of a hobby and new forms of interest is therefore a policy of first importance to a public man. But this is not a business that can be under-
10 taken in a day or swiftly improvised by a mere command of the will. The growth of alternative mental interests is a long process. The seeds must be carefully chosen; they must fall on good ground; they must be sedulously tended, if the vivifying fruits are to be at hand when needed.

To be really happy and really safe, one ought to have at least two or three
15 hobbies, and they must all be real. It is no use starting late in life to say: 'I will take an interest in this or that.' Such an attempt only aggravates the strain of mental effort. A man may acquire great knowledge of topics unconnected with his daily work, and yet hardly get any benefit or relief. It is no use doing what you like; you have got to like what you do. Broadly speaking, human beings may
20 be divided into three classes: those who are toiled to death, those who are worried to death, and those who are bored to death. It is no use offering the manual labourer, tired out with a hard week's sweat and effort, the chance of playing a

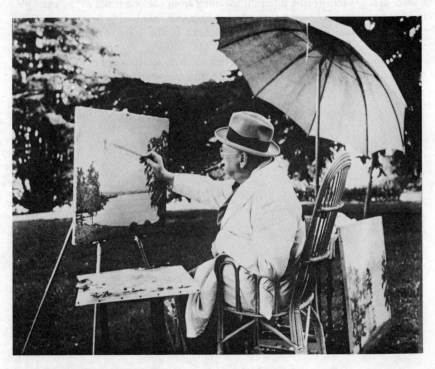

Sir Winston Churchill painting in Switzerland in 1946

game of football or baseball on Saturday afternoon. It is no use inviting the poli-
tician or the professional or business man, who has been working or worrying
25 about serious things for six days, to work or worry about trifling things at the
week-end.

As for the unfortunate people who can command everything they want, who
can gratify every caprice and lay their hands on almost every object of desire—
for them a new pleasure, a new excitement is only an additional satiation. In
30 vain they rush frantically round from place to place, trying to escape from aveng-
ing boredom by mere clatter and motion. For them discipline in one form or
another is the most hopeful path.

It may also be said that rational, industrious, useful human beings are divided
into two classes: first, those whose work is work and whose pleasure is pleasure;
35 and secondly, those whose work and pleasure are one. Of these the former are
the majority. They have their compensations. The long hours in the office or the
factory bring with them as their reward, not only the means of sustenance, but
a keen appetite for pleasure even in its simplest and most modest forms. But
Fortune's favoured children belong to the second class. Their life is a natural
40 harmony. For them the working hours are never long enough. Each day is a
holiday, and ordinary holidays when they come are grudged as enforced interruptions in an absorbing vocation. Yet to both classes the need of an alternative
outlook, of a change of atmosphere, of a diversion of effort, is essential. Indeed,
it may well be that those whose work is their pleasure are those who most need
45 the means of banishing it at intervals from their minds.

WINSTON CHURCHILL *Painting as a Pastime*

Comprehension

Answer these questions:
a In what way is the definition of worry quoted in the first paragraph relevant to the
author's argument?
b Why does the author class as unfortunate those people who can command everything
they want?
c How can people who have everything they want find relief from boredom?
d What is the essential difference between the two classes of human beings defined by
the author? (l. 34)
e Why is it particularly important for people whose work is their pleasure to cultivate
a hobby?

Vocabulary

Explain the meaning of the following words and phrases as they are used in the passage:
spasm (l. 1); futile (l. 3); insinuate (l. 4); recuperation (l. 7); alternative mental interests
(l. 11); vivifying (l. 13); toiled to death (l. 20); trifling (l. 25); caprice (l. 28); satiation
(l. 29); enforced interruptions in an absorbing vocation (ll. 41–42).

Précis

Drawing your information from lines 8–26 ('The cultivation . . . things at the week-
end.') summarize the author's views on cultivating a hobby. Do not write more than
90 words. Use your own words as far as possible. Your answer should be in one
paragraph.

Composition

Write a composition of about 600 words on one of the following subjects:

a Worry.

b Your favourite hobby.

c 'Human beings are divided into two classes: first, those whose work is work and whose pleasure is pleasure; and secondly, those whose work and pleasure are one.' Which class, in your view, would it be preferable to belong to?

Key Structures

1. Complete the following sentences in any way you wish then compare what you have written with the sentences in the passage:

a It is useless to . . . (l. 2)

b It is no use . . . (l. 15)

2. Rewrite the sentences given below using the opening phrases provided. Do not refer to the passage until you have finished the exercise:

a It is of first importance to a public man to cultivate a hobby and new forms of interest.

The cultivation . . . (l. 8)

b If one wishes to be really happy and really safe, one ought to have at least two or three hobbies, and they must all be real.

To be . . . (l. 14)

c Not only do the long hours in the office or the factory bring with them the means of sustenance as their reward, but a keen appetite for pleasure even in its simplest and most modest forms.

The long hours . . . (ll. 36–38)

Special Difficulties

1. Write sentences to bring out the difference between the following pairs of words: late (l. 15), lately; hardly (l. 18), hard (l. 22); alternative (l. 42), alternating.

2. Use each of the following words figuratively in sentences of your own. Do not refer to the passage until you have finished the exercise:

seeds (l. 11); fruits (l. 13); sweat (l. 22).

3. Use the following expressions in sentences of your own. Do not refer to the passage until you have completed the exercise: broadly speaking (l. 19); as for (l. 27); the former (l. 35).

59

Economy is one powerful motive for camping, since after the initial outlay upon equipment, or through hiring it, the total expense can be far less than the cost of hotels. But, contrary to a popular assumption, it is far from being the only one, or even the greatest. The man who manoeuvres carelessly into his five shillings'
5 worth of space at one of Europe's myriad permanent sites may find himself bumping a Bentley. More likely, Ford Consul will be hub to hub with Renault or Mercedes, but rarely with bicycles made for two.

That the equipment of modern camping becomes yearly more sophisticated is an entertaining paradox for the cynic, a brighter promise for the hopeful traveller
10 who has sworn to get away from it all. It also provides—and some student sociologist might care to base his thesis upon the phenomenon—an escape of another kind. The modern traveller is often a man who dislikes the Splendide and the Bellavista, not because he cannot afford, or shuns, their material comforts, but because he is afraid of them. Affluent he may be, but he is by no means sure what
15 to tip the doorman or the chambermaid. Master in his own house, he has little idea of when to say boo to a *maître d'hôtel*.*

From all such fears camping releases him. Granted, a snobbery of camping itself, based upon equipment and techniques, already exists; but it is of a kind that, if he meets it, he can readily understand and deal with. There is no superior
20 'they' in the shape of managements and hotel hierarchies to darken his holiday days.

To such motives, yet another must be added. The contemporary phenomenon

* Cp. the expression 'to say boo to a goose' meaning 'to surprise' or 'to frighten'.

A camping site near Mittelstal in Germany

of motor-car worship is to be explained not least by the sense of independence
and freedom that ownership entails. To this pleasure camping gives an exquisite
25 refinement.

From one's own front door to home or foreign hills or sands and back again,
everything is to hand. Not only are the means of arriving at the holiday paradise
entirely within one's own command and keeping, but the means of escape from
holiday hell (if the beach proves too crowded, the local weather too inclement)
30 are there, outside—or, as likely, part of—the tent.

Idealists have objected to the practice of camping, as to the packaged tour,
that the traveller abroad thereby denies himself the opportunity of getting to
know the people of the country visited. Insularity and self-containment, it is
argued, go hand in hand. The opinion does not survive experience of a popular
35 Continental camping place. Holiday hotels tend to cater for one nationality of
visitors especially, sometimes exclusively. Camping sites, by contrast, are highly
cosmopolitan. Granted, a preponderance of Germans is a characteristic that
seems common to most Mediterranean sites; but as yet there is no overwhelm-
ingly specialized patronage. Notices forbidding the open-air drying of clothes,
40 or the use of water points for car washing, or those inviting 'our camping friends'
to a dance or a boat trip are printed not only in French or Italian or Spanish,
but also in English, German and Dutch. At meal times the odour of sauerkraut
vies with that of garlic. The Frenchman's breakfast coffee competes with the
Englishman's bacon and eggs.

45 Whether the remarkable growth of organized camping means the eventual
death of the more independent kind is hard to say. Municipalities naturally want
to secure the campers' site fees and other custom. Police are wary of itinerants
who cannot be traced to a recognized camp boundary or to four walls. But most
probably it will all depend upon campers themselves: how many heath fires they
50 cause; how much litter they leave; in short, whether or not they wholly alienate
landowners and those who live in the countryside. Only good scouting is likely
to preserve the freedoms so dear to the heart of the eternal Boy Scout.

NIGEL BUXTON *The Great Escape* from *The Weekend Telegraph*

Comprehension

Answer these questions:
a Name three factors which induce people to go camping.
b What do you understand by this statement: 'To this pleasure camping gives an
exquisite refinement.'? (ll. 24–25)
c Why have idealists objected to the practice of camping and how have they been
proved wrong?
d What factors may lead to the death of the more independent kind of camping?

Vocabulary

Explain the meaning of the following words and phrases as they are used in the passage:
motive (l. 1); initial outlay upon equipment (ll. 1–2); hub to hub (l. 6); to say boo to
(l. 16); granted (l. 17); inclement (l. 29); packaged tour (l. 31); insularity (l. 33);
exclusively (l. 36); cosmopolitan (l. 37); preponderance (l. 37); wary of itinerants
(l. 47); litter (l. 50).

Précis

Drawing your information from lines 8–44 ('That the equipment . . . bacon and eggs.') write an account of modern camping. Do not write more than 160 words. Use your own words as far as possible. Your answer should be in one paragraph.

Composition

Write a composition of about 600 words on one of the following subjects:
a Holiday camps.
b Packaged tours.
c What, in your opinion, are the requirements of an ideal holiday?

Key Structures

Rewrite the sentences given below using the opening phrases provided. Do not refer to the passage until you have finished the exercise:
a Though the modern traveller is often a man who can afford and does not shun the material comforts of the Splendide and the Bellavista, he dislikes them because he is afraid of them.
   The modern traveller . . . not because . . . (ll. 12–14)
b The means of arriving at the holiday paradise are not only entirely within one's own command and keeping, but the means of escape from holiday hell . . . are there, outside—or, as likely, part of—the tent.
   Not only . . . (ll. 27–30)
c They argue that insularity and self-containment go hand in hand.
   Insularity and self-containment, it . . . (ll. 33–34)
d The freedoms so dear to the heart of the eternal Boy Scout are only likely to be preserved by good scouting.
   Only good . . . (ll. 51–52)

Special Difficulties

1. Write sentences to bring out the difference between the following pairs of words: initial (l. 1), primary; hire (l. 2), rent; total (l. 2), whole; shun (l. 13), avoid; worship (l. 23), warship; by contrast (l. 36), opposite to.
2. Note the words in italics in the following sentences. Use these words again in sentences of your own, giving each word a different meaning from the one it has in the example:
a The man who manoeuvres carelessly into his five shillings' worth of space . . . may find himself *bumping* a Bentley. (ll. 4–6)
b *Granted*, a snobbery of camping itself . . . already exists. (ll. 17–18)
c Municipalities naturally want to secure the campers' site fees and other *custom*. (ll. 46–47)

60

Although truth and justice may be the most powerful impulses to show moral courage, there are others. Compassion is one of these. Tentatively it can be suggested that this is the main influence upon those who urge the abolition of capital punishment. It is recognition of compassion's part that leads the upholders of
5 capital punishment to accuse the abolitionists of sentimentality in being more sorry for the murderer than for his victim. This is nonsense but with it some organs of the popular Press played upon the emotions of their readers so successfully that many candidates for Parliament were afraid to support abolition for fear of losing votes and the result was the muddle-headed Homicide Act of 1957
10 which made murder with robbery a capital crime and allowed the poisoner to escape the gallows. That illogical qualification shows how flimsy is the argument that capital punishment is a deterrent to murder. The poisoner always works on a calculated plan of action and therefore is able to consider whether or not his taking another's life is worth the risk of his own; the violent thief is usually at
15 the mercy of an instant emotion. The only arguable plea for capital punishment is the right of society to retribution in this world with the prospect of life in another, but since what used to seem to the great majority of civilized humanity the assurance of another life beyond the grave has come to seem to more and more people less certain, a feeling for the value of human life has become deeper
20 and more widespread. This may seem a paradoxical claim to make at a time when mankind is so much preoccupied with weapons of destruction. Nevertheless, it is a claim that can be sustained and if compassion animates those who urge the

The scene outside Holloway Jail as Mrs. Ruth Ellis is executed for the murder of David Blakely. 1955

abolition of the death penalty it is not a sentimental compassion for the mental agony inflicted upon a condemned man but a dread of destroying the miracle of
25 life.

When in the eighteenth century offences against the law that today would not earn a month in prison were punished with the death penalty, the severity of the penal code had no serious effect on the prevalence of crime. When it made no difference to the fate of a highwayman whether he had killed his victim or merely
30 robbed him of a few pieces of silver, there were no more murders then than there were when men like Sir Francis Burdett succeeded in lightening the excessive severity of the penal laws. In those days the sacredness of life on earth was not greatly regarded because a life in the world to come was taken for granted except by a comparatively small minority of philosophers.

35 Nor was the long-drawn ordeal of the condemned cell inflicted either upon the condemned man or his gaolers once upon a time. Those who believe in capital punishment may have arguments for its retention, but surely no reasonable argument can be found for retention of the sickening mumbo-jumbo that accompanies it from the moment that the judge dons the black cap with what looks like
40 a pen-wiper balanced on the top of his wig, to the reading of the burial service over the condemned man before he is dead. Moreover, it was more merciful to launch the condemned man into eternity twenty-four hours after he was sentenced than to keep him shivering on the brink of that dread gulf for nearly three weeks. Hanging is an atrociously archaic way of killing a human being and the
45 self-satisfied modernity of the electric chair is just as atrocious. The administration of a strong sleeping draught to the condemned man every night from which one night he does not awake, seems a more civilized alternative to our present barbarous procedure, if capital punishment through the influence of backward minds be retained.

COMPTON MACKENZIE *On Moral Courage*

Comprehension

Answer these questions:

a How do some organs of the popular Press play upon the emotions of their readers when they argue in favour of the retention of capital punishment?

b Why, according to the author, was the Homicide Act of 1957 'muddle-headed'?

c What distinction does the author draw between the poisoner and the violent thief who commits murder?

d How does the author account for the fact that the value of human life has become deeper and more widespread?

e Why in the eighteenth century did the severity of the penal code fail to have a serious effect on the prevalence of crime?

f How does the author illustrate his argument that a man condemned to death is subjected to a long-drawn ordeal?

Vocabulary

Explain the meaning of the following words and phrases as they are used in the passage: tentatively (l. 2); abolitionists (l. 5); flimsy (l. 11); deterrent (l. 12); retribution (l. 16); paradoxical claim (l. 20); taken for granted (l. 33); long-drawn ordeal (l. 35); retention (l. 38); mumbo-jumbo (l. 38); atrociously (l. 44); barbarous procedure (l. 48).

Précis

Drawing your information from the passage, state the arguments against capital punishment. Do not write more than 200 words. Use your own words as far as possible. Your answer should be in one paragraph.

Composition

Write a composition of about 600 words on one of the following subjects:
a Crime and punishment.
b 'Capital punishment is the only true deterrent to vicious crime.' Argue in favour of this statement.
c To what extent can it be said that society itself fosters an unhealthy interest in crime?

Key Structures

Rewrite the sentences given below using the opening phrases provided. Do not refer to the passage until you have finished the exercise:
a Many candidates for Parliament were afraid to support abolition lest they should lose votes.
  Many candidates for Parliament were afraid to support abolition for fear ...
  (ll. 8–9)
b Because of the fact that the poisoner always works on a calculated plan of action he is able to consider whether or not his taking of another's life is worth the risk of his own.
  The poisoner ... therefore ... (ll. 12–13)
c It made no difference to the fate of a highwayman whether his victim was killed or merely robbed of a few pieces of silver.
  It made no difference to the fate of a highwayman whether he ... (ll. 28–29)
d In those days people did not have a great regard for the sacredness of life on earth.
  In those days the sacredness of life ... (ll. 32–33)

Special Difficulties

1. Write sentences to bring out the difference between the following:
moral (l. 1), morale; recognition (l. 4), acknowledgement; illogical (l. 11), unreasonable; calculated (l. 13), preconceived; prospect (l. 16), perspective; agony (l. 24), struggle; penalty (l. 27), punishment; rob (l. 30), steal; inflicted (l. 35), afflicted; accompany (ll. 38–39), escort; eternity (l. 42), infinity; archaic (l. 44), ancient; draught (l. 46), draft; awake (l. 47), wake up.
2. Write sentences using these words differently from the way in which they have been used in the passage: capital (l. 3); grave (l. 18); sustained (l. 22); granted (l. 33); dons (l. 39); gulf (l. 43); present (l. 47).